THE INTELLIGENT CLIENT

MANAGING YOUR MANAGEMENT CONSULTANT

FIONA CZERNIAWSKA

Hodder & Stoughton

A MEMBER OF THE HODDER HEADLINE GROUP

For Mary and Bob, Richard, Jennifer and John, Susan and Sheila

Orders: please contact Bookpoint Ltd, 130 Milton Park, Abingdon, Oxon OX14 4SB.
Telephone: (44) 01235 827720. Fax: (44) 01235 400454. Lines are open from 9.00–6.00, Monday to Saturday, with a 24 hour message answering service. Email address: orders@bookpoint.co.uk

British Library Cataloguing in Publication Data
A catalogue record for this title is available from the British Library

ISBN 0 340 850531

First Published 2002
Impression number 10 9 8 7 6 5 4 3 2 1
Year 2007 2006 2005 2004 2003 2002

Typeset by Servis Filmsetting Ltd, Manchester
Printed in Great Britain for Hodder & Stoughton Educational, a division of Hodder Headline Plc, 338 Euston Road, London NW1 3BH by J.W. Arrowsmith Ltd, Bristol.

M·C·A
MANAGEMENT
CONSULTANCIES
ASSOCIATION

Series Editor: Fiona Czerniawska, Director of MCA Think Tank.

The MCA was formed in 1956 and represents the leading UK-based consulting firms, which currently employ over 25,000 consultants and generate £4.3bn in annual fee income. The UK consulting industry is worth around £8bn, contributing £1bn to the balance of payments.

As well as setting and maintaining standards in the industry, the MCA supports its member firms with a range of services including events, publications, interest groups and public relations. The Association also works with its members to attract the top talent into the industry. The MCA provides advice on the selection and use of management consultants and is the main source of data on the UK market.

FOR MORE INFORMATION PLEASE CONTACT:
Management Consultancies Association
49 Whitehall
London
SW1A 2BX

Tel: 020 7321 3990
Fax: 020 7321 3991

E-mail: mca@mca.org.uk

www.mca.org.uk

CONTENTS

ACKNOWLEDGEMENTS

This book is based on research on the consulting industry over many years and, as always, I remain profoundly indebted to the innumberable people – clients and consultants – who have generously made time available to talk to me.

I would also particularly like to thank Palgrave for allowing me to reuse some of my thinking about the client–consultant relationship (Chapter 7); and the Management Consultancies Association for granting permission to include an edited version of an article on the implications of Enron for the consulting industry in the same chapter, which was first published in the MCA's journal *Spectra*.

Considerable thanks to Sarah Taylor, the Deputy Director of the MCA, for reading and commenting on my drafts with such care and perspicacity, to Liz Ross at Hodder & Stoughton, for all her help in bringing not just this book but the entire MCA series to market, and to my husband, Stefan, for his unwavering support.

INTRODUCTION

GIVING AND RECEIVING VALUE FOR MONEY

> ‘To many onlookers the work of management consultants is a bit of a mystery. This is understandable because management consultancy is not precise, concrete, predictable or standardized. It is not a tangible product but rather a process of working with someone else's problem that can produce tangible and intangible outcomes . . . Management consultancy is not an exact science.’[1]

Consultancy is one of the biggest, most influential and most pervasive industries in the world today. Almost every major corporation uses consultants on a regular basis; at the same time, consultants are increasingly the butt of jokes, traditionally aimed at ambulance-chasing lawyers and dubious second-hand car salesmen.

How can we square this particular circle? How is it that managers claim to despise people on whom they are apparently dependent? Many niggling sources of dissatisfaction culminate in a single big issue: value for money. Clients are well aware that a few weeks of a consultant's time can be the equivalent of a full-time employee's costs for an entire year; that a consultant's salary may be higher than their own; that the consultant can always walk away from a problem, leaving the manager to pick up the pieces. Moreover, the output of many consulting assignments can be so intangible: how do you measure the value of someone who has facilitated a process? Of the many variables that affect a company's performance, which can you attribute directly and only to the consultants it uses?

Over the last decade, the consulting industry has responded to such criticisms in a variety of ways. Some firms have strived to make their output more concrete, by commoditizing their services, and by moving away from purely process-orientated roles. Others have sought to find alternative payment terms, where fees are tied to measurable outcomes.

[1] Susan Kehoe, *Management Consultancy*, (Brisbane 1988)

TWO SIDES OF THE ARGUMENT

But the hard fact is that, if something has gone wrong, then the probability is that both sides – client and consultant – have contributed to the problem. It is not just a question of consultants being encouraged or forced to *give* value for money: clients need to go and *find* it. Perhaps the consultants have not done what they were asked to do – or the client has not been sufficiently clear in defining what is expected. If knowledge is not transferred from consultant to client, is that because the consultant does not have a process for teaching, or because the client is reluctant to learn?

While there might be considerable benefit in agreeing some high level standards against which the relative performance of consultants could be benchmarked, it would seem foolish to place too great a hope on such mechanistic approaches. Auditing does not appear to have improved financial management (consider the Enron debacle), so why should the codification and regulation of the consulting process result in a better end product?

How do people use consultants? What does and does not work?

The fast-moving consumer goods company

This company makes extensive use of external consultants. There is no single preferred firm: executives pick and choose based on the specialist expertise of the individual or firm involved, but the priority is to be able to work with people who have an enormous depth of knowledge in the areas in which the company is interested. The choice of consultant firms reflects the way in which those firms have positioned themselves to date; strategic consultancies tend to be used for planning and analysis, but for larger scale projects, a Big Four firm[2] would typically be the choice. 'Choosing a consultancy is ultimately a matter of personal preference,' says one executive, 'and we all tend to feel more comfortable dealing with familiar people, rather than with adding another level of uncertainty to an already uncertain environment.' Credibility is crucial.

However, the company's preference for established consulting firms may change: it is already experimenting with newer firms that offer a balance of content to process which is different from that of more established consulting firms. The situation is part of a wider internal debate about whether the company should buy a tried-and-tested consultancy, or a new, more specialized firm.

Of all the types of work undertaken by consultants, the company's executives have been least impressed by process-orientated work, with the consultants doing little more than facilitation, especially in those areas where the knowledge base of clients and consultants is much more equal. 'Consultants need to have an immensely good understanding of the issues facing us in specific industries before they can sound at all credible' is a typical comment. As a result, many of the company's executives prefer to build strong relationships with a few people whom they regard as experts, and to mix and match these people with other individuals as a particular need arises.

The not-for-profit organization

Partnership has become a devalued term so far as the consulting industry is concerned; almost all firms claim to work 'in partnership' with their clients, although there have been few instances of clients and consultants genuinely sharing work, rewards and risks. As a not-for-profit organization, this charity receives a fair amount of *pro bono* work by professionals, but often, it believes, from second-rate staff. When it pays for work, it has to be exceptionally

[2] The 'Big Eight' was a term first coined in the 1980s and referred to the combined audit and consulting firms which had grown so quickly in the previous decade. Subsequent industry restructuring has reduced the number of 'Big' firms, to a point where this term is now used to denote a consulting firm whose origins were as a division of an audit firm.

careful about how it spends its members' money. The act of hiring consultants is therefore a real leap of faith on everybody's part; the consultants have to be trusted, not only to take on tasks for which the charity itself lacks the capacity, but to manage their own resources so that it is not faced with enormous and unexpected bills. With many other activities to oversee and very limited resources, the charity has to rely on its consultants to make many of the day-to-day decisions in a project – to consult with the charity's managers only over the more important issues, but at the same time to keep them regularly updated.

Where consultants are able to add most value is when they take on a problem and solve it – doing whatever it takes, even if they reach beyond the notional parameters of an assignment. Relationships succeed primarily when each side shares the same objectives, when the consulting firm does not regard itself as delivering a specific service or implementing a particular system, but as creating a successful solution.

The government department

This department has used consultants extensively since the first automation of its extensive operational processes, more than 20 years ago. It continues to rely on consultants because, as its IT director puts it, 'consulting firms provide a pool of people whose input we need but whose skill we cannot and do not want to replicate. But consultants do not just provide specialist expertise when the occasion demands it: they also provide an injection of energy and momentum into discussions and projects which might otherwise become bogged down in the inevitable inertia of organizations of our scale and complexity.'

At the same time, this reliance is begrudged, if not at the very top of the organization, then certainly at its middle management levels, by civil servants envious of a very visible differential in remuneration. The problem is exacerbated by a lack of empathy between the consultants and the clients they advise. One manager complains:

> ‘Consultants are arrogant. When I tell them this is the starting point because this is what someone in the government wants to do, they want to change that, and – worse – they think we are stupid because we do not want to change it. That is not the issue: we often think that it would be better not to start from here, but that is what we have to do. Consultants should show more sensitivity about our constraints.’

The airline

Given recent upheavals in the airline industry, the focus of this company has been on shoring up profitability through projects to improve internal efficiency. Latterly, it has been evaluating how it can make the best use of web-based technology to cut its procurement costs. The central worry is uncertainty. According to one executive, 'We still do not know how successful this will be in practice. We all believe that this kind of technology has to be the way forward, but it is an act of faith at the moment.'

Like most large corporations faced with uncertainty, it has looked to consultants for help – initially from software developers – only to find that they could provide little in the way of tangible evidence or practical results. As the company is proposing to spend a very large amount of money on new technology, with uncertain results, it is inevitable that it will encounter a very high level of scepticism internally; this scepticism is likely to be particularly strong if the strategy presented is based solely on in-house work. While the airline may employ may bright people, it does not have the resources or opportunity to look in detail at best practice elsewhere, particularly outside the airline industry. This is therefore an area where the company believes that consultants can genuinely add value, especially in a rapidly changing environment.

Having already embarked on two other related ventures elsewhere in the company, it made sense to hire the same consulting firm again. One of the managers involved in that decision says,

> ‘It is immensely important for us that the consultancy we hire has a well-known name, both in terms of its external reputation and internally, via the quality of the work they have already carried out and the high level contacts within our business they have developed as a result.’

The successful firm, although explicitly hired to assist in developing the procurement strategy and a more detailed business case, is implicitly there to champion the cause of e-procurement internally and to inject an element of pace and urgency into the program. An important factor is the quality of a consultancy's staff at all levels – this ability to expedite a process is as important as, if not more important than, the technical skills of individual consultants.

> ‘In this environment, no one really knows what's going to happen. We all – consultants included – have to make some big assumptions. No amount of technical skill is going to change this: in fact, you can end up with a level of wholly spurious accuracy. What is critical to us is to have access to a couple of very senior consultants who can discuss the issues involved at the highest levels of management and whose input is leveraged by a number of more junior but very dynamic consultants who can help us make things happen. People get excited about the technology and say "we could do this", but that is irrelevant if no one in the organization wants to do it. Web-based technologies are not a revolution: they are a new set of enabling tools. It is persuading people – both senior managers and operational staff – to do something that counts.’

The bank

When it comes to hiring consultants, one of the key changes seen at this bank has been that consultants place a much greater emphasis on practicality than they used to. According to one internal purchaser of consultancy,

> ‘strategy consultancies have spent the last five or ten years making increasingly elaborate excuses as to why they did not deal with technology. These were arguments that were hard to sustain when the business process reengineering market was at its height, and they are impossible to maintain today, when being able to combine strategy with technical skills is crucial. Strategic consultancy has always a tendency to be conceptual and now it is running the risk of sounding platitudinous.’

While the bank finds some of the material produced by consultants extremely good, it has difficulty in distinguishing between firms, and thinks that there is a danger of skirting around the real issues, when what they – like other clients – most often need is clarity, and the ability to focus on the end result which they are trying to achieve, and on how they are going to achieve it.

The bank's executives are willing to pay for specialist consultants, but they are sceptical about the ability of a single firm to provide those people, and increasingly find themselves in a position of pulling together the best firms – and the best individuals within them – in specific areas, and of creating joint client–consultant teams in order to leverage the intellectual capital of each side as effectively as possible.

> 'It's an environment in which the idea of one-stop shopping for consultancy is particularly unattractive. Clients are not going to be satisfied with having second-rate services, just for the convenience of having them come from a single supplier. More than ever before, we want access to highly specialized individuals and firms; we are willing to live with any administrative overhead this may give us.'

Executives here think it essential that they remain in charge. 'It leads to a more productive project', says one, 'because you already understand the internal and know how to get things done.'

The start-up

Like many other new companies, the attitude of executives here is that they do not need consultants. As its Chief Executive says:

> 'When you're leading-edge at what you do – and that is what you have to be if you are going to win and keep financial backing – you do not need anyone to tell you this. Although consulting firms are reluctant to admit it, the majority of their clients simply do not fall into this category. More typically, they are companies that want to follow in the footsteps of the market innovators.'

But that does not mean that this start-up has not used consultants in the past, or that they will not consider using them in the future. Ironically, the company is about to hire a strategy firm to help it with the integration issues which follow from a recently proposed merger. It justifies this apparent contradiction internally by arguing, firstly, that it is looking for a very specific set of skills and in-depth experience in the post-merger integration area and, secondly, that it is a one-off issue – that it does not require these skills on an on-going basis, and that it therefore makes sense to buy them in rather than develop them in-house. Unsurprisingly, the key characteristic it looks for in a consultant is the depth of his or her specialist knowledge.

THE INTELLIGENT CLIENT

An important lesson from the last three decades, which have seen such phenomenal growth in the consulting industry, is that hiring consultants does not, in isolation, solve a problem. Consultants may provide some of the solution, but they are very unlikely to be all of it. Results are achieved because clients and consultants work together.

Yet, for all the wealth of guidelines on how to be a successful consultant, virtually nothing exists on how to be a successful client.

This book is an attempt to redress that imbalance. Its aim is to provide managers who hire consultants, manage and work alongside them, with comprehensive and practical advice for receiving the best value from those consultants at every stage – before, during and after a consulting project (Figure 1).

As the title of Part 1 suggests, its aim is to help you speed up the initial stages. 'Hitting the ground running' is a phrase often used by consultants in relation to their own projects, but it is something that should equally apply to clients. If it takes two sides to ensure a successful project, then it makes just as much sense for the client to be as well-equipped and informed as possible, prior to the start of a consulting project. In particular, this part examines:

Part 1	Part 2	Part 3
Hitting the ground running	**Maximising the value of consultants**	**Outcomes**
• Identifying the need • How to select a consulting firm • Comparing consultancies • Presentations, proposals and pitches • Finding the optimum working arrangements	• Managing consulting projects • The client–consultant relationship • Balancing innovation and structured methodology • The exchange of intellectual capital • Bringing the outside view inside • Change management • Converting theory into practice • Selecting and implementing technology • Outsourcing • Consulting and organizational learning	• Measuring the value of consultancy • Increasing the value added by consultants in the future

FIGURE 1: The overall structure of this book

☐ When and why should you hire consultants? What are the advantages and disadvantages of external over internal consultants? (Chapter 1)

☐ What kind of process should you adopt for selecting consultants? Why does corporate buying behaviour make the process so difficult, and what can you do to manage this? How is the procurement of consulting likely to change in the future? Will, for example, e-procurement ever come to consultancy? (Chapter 2)

☐ Many consultants look the same – so what criteria can you use to choose between them? (Chapter 3)

☐ What should you be looking for from a consultant's sales pitch? (Chapter 4)

☐ What lessons have been learnt about the formal arrangements for consultants, the types of relationship you should have, the relative pros and cons of different fee structures, and so on? (Chapter 5)

Part 2 is designed to help you manage consulting projects in order to maximize their value. No two consulting projects are identical, so this part of the book looks at different aspects of consulting while also being broadly structured around the life-cycle of a project. To illustrate the theory discussed, a wide variety of case studies are used, all of which have been drawn from the Management Consultancies Association awards for Best Practice in Consulting 2002.

☐ What is different about the management of consulting projects? What can you do in terms of the control and administration of a project to increase its chance of success? (Chapter 6)

☐ What are the dynamics of the client–consultant relationship? How can you make such relationships work more effectively? (Chapter 7)

- Consultants are often accused of taking their clients' watch and telling them the time, but, at the same time, one of the most important things that clients look for in a consulting relationship is a structured approach. How can these contradictions be handled? (Chapter 8)
- How can clients make best use of this information by ensuring an effective exchange of knowledge between themselves and their consultants? (Chapter 9)
- One of the most important ways in which consultants can add value is by bringing to any organization a fresh perspective, but sometimes their reports just gather dust on the shelf. What can clients do to minimize the chance of this happening, to ensure that they do not waste their money? (Chapter 10)
- You may have designed the perfect blueprint; you may have implemented a world-class system; but can you persuade anyone to use it? No. The best management ideas in the world count for nothing in an organization unwilling or unable to realize the goals set by its leaders. In such circumstances, bringing in external consultants can make matters worse, further alienating people who already feel marginalized from the decision-making process. Is it possible to use consultants to change your organization? How? (Chapter 11)
- The transition from idea to implementation, from theory to practice, is fraught with difficulty in any project, whether it involves outside consultants or not. So what can you do to ensure that the blueprints which you and your consultants design can be successfully implemented? (Chapter 12)
- Similar, often worse, problems apply when it comes to technology. How can you best manage your IT consultants? (Chapter 13)
- Much of what used to be IT consultancy has now become IT outsourcing, as organizations increasingly seek to focus on their core business by divesting those business processes that offer no potential for competitive advantage. But does outsourcing an issue really mean that it is off your hands? (Chapter 14)
- What about the opposite of outsourcing? What role can consultants play in helping organizations manage their own problems? (Chapter 15)

The third part of the book brings us full circle, back to that thorny issue of giving and receiving value for money:

- Consulting projects vary hugely in intent, scale and complexity: is it possible to measure the value that consultants have added? (Chapter 16)
- How is consulting likely to change, and what are the implications for clients? (Chapter 17)

But although this book is primarily aimed at the people who hire and work with consultants, it is also highly relevant to consultants themselves. One of the characteristics that distinguishes good consultants from mediocre ones is their ability to see things from their clients' perspectives. In an environment where consultants often feel they have to be infallible, insecurity can translate itself into arrogance, into believing that their way of doing things is the only way of doing things. A very substantial number of the problems that occur on consulting projects arise as a result of this failure to recognize that clients have value of their own to add, have concrete goals to achieve and have constraints around which they do not choose, but have to, work around. Indeed, this is one of the most common complaints that clients make about consultants.

If the aim of this book is to help clients manage their management consultants more effectively, then it is equally aimed at showing consultants what clients can do to improve the process, in the hope that consultants themselves will take the initiative and, when faced with a client whose behaviour or attitude falls short of the best practice outlined in this book, will suggest there is a better way of working.

A parallel objective is to show consultants what clients cannot do – just how difficult it can be for the disparate group of people involved in hiring a consulting firm and subsequently working with it to share the same fundamental goals and to have a common expectation of what the consultants will deliver – and to show clients what consultants cannot do – provide panaceas for all possible ills.

In the post-Enron world of consulting, the role of consultants and the contribution they make is understandable under even more intense scrutiny. Overall, the message of this book is a simple one: intelligent clients need intelligent consultants, and intelligent consultants need intelligent clients. Like everything else in business, the consulting process will never be a perfect one, but consultants and clients who have a shared understanding of the value they can each bring will iron out many of its imperfections.

PART 1

HITTING THE GROUND RUNNING

CHAPTER 1

IDENTIFYING THE NEED

It is hard, if not impossible, for a consulting firm to add any value during a project if they have not been hired for the right reasons. As Alfred Martinez, then Chief Executive of Sears, put it: 'If the people at the top of the organization cannot create a clear line of sight to where they want to go, then they are a little bankrupt personally.'[1]

The very first step towards getting value for money from using consultants has therefore comparatively little to with the consultants themselves, and everything to do with the organizations that hire them. Consultancy, like charity, starts at home.

At any one moment, almost every large corporation in the world is using consultants. But the sad fact is that in only a small proportion of these do the managers involved know – let alone agree – why consultants have been hired. Before you decide that this is not a problem in your organization, ask yourself the following questions:

- ☐ Do you have a clear understanding about what you expect them to do?
- ☐ Do you have a clear understanding about the outcome you want to achieve?
- ☐ Do your colleagues agree with your decision?
- ☐ Does your boss agree with your decision?
- ☐ Do your colleagues understand why you have brought in external resources, and what difference you expect them to make?

If you answered 'sometimes' or 'never' to any of the questions, then there is room for improvement. But now look more closely at your responses. What is your Achilles Heel? Are you good at defining the need as you understand it, but less successful at communicating this effectively to your colleagues? Do you tend to think of the role you want consultants to play, rather than the outcome you want to achieve?

This chapter looks at the points you should consider before you bring consultants in – indeed, before you even start to short-list potential suppliers:

[1] James O'Shea and Charles Madigan, *Dangerous Company: The Consulting Powerhouses and Businesses They Save and Ruin*, Nicholas Brearley, 1997.

☐ Accurately pinpoint the issue you want to address.

☐ Understand what kind of client you are.

☐ Choose between internal and external consultancy.

PINPOINTING THE ISSUE

Research in 2001 by the Management Consultancies Association (MCA)[2] into the purchasing of consultancy services shows high levels of satisfaction among users: 88 per cent of those questioned would use their present consultancy firm again, 79 per cent expect to benefit from the consultancy investment within one year, and 54 per cent expect the measurable benefit to be much greater than the cost. The study also indicated that clients are increasingly turning to consultancies for innovative thinking. In a similar study by the MCA in 1995, by far the most important reason for clients to hire consultants was to fill a skills gap. In the 2001 survey, clients also rated a consultant's ability to provide original thinking and an independent view as being very important.

Understanding precisely what you want consultants to do and why can be very hard. It is like going to the doctor's surgery: there may be occasions when the reason for your visit is clear-cut – a prescription to be renewed, a bad back playing up again; but there are also times when you cannot put your finger on the problem, when you go in with a litany of symptoms, rather than a specific cause and solution. A good management consultant will play the role of the doctor, even before a contract is signed (something that is discussed in more detail later in this chapter), but all too often the trust-based relationship that exists between doctor and patient does not apply here. Clients want to – and should – attempt some self-diagnosis before going to an expert.

So, why do you need a consultant?

People tend to respond to this question in terms of wanting to achieve something – a system implemented, a strategy developed, a change process facilitated. But, going below the surface, we can identify eight underlying motivations that can be grouped under three main headings: people, content and process.

People

☐ **Industry-specific skills** – Probably the single most important reason for hiring consultants is to bring in people with a particular set of skills. By and large, the more specialized a consultant is in his or her field, the more valuable they are to clients. Specialist know-how falls into two categories. First are 'industry-specific skills' – you need people who are experts in your sector, perhaps to assess the implications of a move by one of your competitors, or to help decide whether a new management approach (customer relationship management (CRM), for example) would benefit your unique organization.

☐ **Issue-specific skills** – Secondly, there are 'issue-specific skills', which is where you need people who are experts in a particular issue; it may be a problem or an opportunity. You have decided that CRM is for you: now what you need are some CRM experts to apply it.

☐ **Generalist resources** – There are times when you simply need help – bright, energetic people who are well informed, and can help you to produce a new initiative at a time when it is proving difficult to free up your own internal resources. You are quite definitely not looking for specialists here. You need the consultants to be very flexible – rolling up

[2] *Trends in Consultancy Purchasing* (2001), Management Consultancies Association

their sleeves and doing whatever it takes to complete the job. This is something that requires a broad base of knowledge, rather than in-depth expertise in just one or two areas.

Content

☐ **An outside view** – Even in the smallest organizations, managers find it difficult to stand back and analyze what is happening. Opportunities are missed, and threats are ignored. Even where time is allowed for such reflection, how can you ensure that you are seeing what matters most to the organization, not just what matters most to you as an individual? Outsiders, like consultants, can provide you with an invaluable perspective because they are looking at your organization with new eyes. This may be just what you need when, for example, you are wondering whether a difficult decision is in fact the right one.

☐ **Information and analysis** – Sometimes an outside 'opinion' expressed by an expert is enough to jump-start a project. 'Yes,' the consultants effectively say, 'we agree that entering this market with this product is a good idea, now go for it.' And you do. But there are many other occasions when you need hard data to help you decide what to do. Here, you are not so much looking for an opinion which your colleagues will accept, as the underlying information from which such an opinion can be formed by your colleagues themselves. It might be, for example, that a particular initiative which you are proposing is very controversial: in such circumstances, there is no point in introducing an expert to rubber-stamp what you believe in but your peers do not – you only open yourself up to cynicism. It is much better to hire consultants who can lay the facts as they find them in front of your colleagues, enabling each one to take their own decision.

☐ **Innovative thinking** – There are also occasions when you want access, not so much to an outside view, or new data, but to creative thinking, when you want someone to sit down with your organization and create an innovative approach. Perhaps every company in your industry faces a similar threat – for example, the appearance of new, potentially disruptive technology. All your competitors may have adopted the same stance, but you may be looking for a different approach, one that takes the problem and converts it into an opportunity for you to differentiate yourself.

Process

☐ **Momentum** – Sometimes it can be difficult to keep things moving. People who are assigned to projects internally still have day-jobs which they have to think about; not everyone may yet be committed to a particular course of action. A key way in which consultants can help is by providing the energy and determination to make sure a project, once started, is finished. Unlike many internal participants, consultants can dedicate all their time and efforts to this one project, and they are much less likely to be distracted. Consultants can also be helpful in keeping a project going, if your own people start to lose interest or faith in it, as often happens in large projects.

☐ **A road map** – An important part of that momentum will be provided by the extent to which a consulting firm provides a tried-and-tested approach to the issue in hand. Faced with a new problem or opportunity, you may not know which way to turn, what to do next. What you need is a plan that takes you from where you are today, to where you want to be. You may also be looking for confidence that the project that you are about to undertake will meet the expectations of its sponsors. What you are therefore seeking, when you bring in a team of consultants, is a track record in successful implementations of such projects and a structured methodology that captures the accumulated lessons of previous projects.

Think about the last consulting project with which you were involved: what were the underlying reasons why the consultants were hired? The reasons listed above are not mutually exclusive: you may find that several of the reasons apply. You may also find that you have to break the project down into stages, as the motivations might have varied, depending on the work involved. But try and be precise. It is tempting, for example, to say that you hired consultants because you wanted innovative input, but is this really the case? Everyone likes to think that they are being innovative, but there are many consulting projects where having access to specialist skills and a well-proven delivery methodology is far more important.

Recent research suggests the following:

- ☐ Contrary to much of the negative press coverage about consultants, clients who deliberately set out to hire creative thinking are very satisfied with the results, particularly where that thinking is focused on identifying and articulating new business opportunities. However, this remains only a tiny proportion of consulting work.

- ☐ Clients who hire highly specialized consultants for highly specialized work – whether industry- or issue-specific – also tend to be very satisfied. A different skill set is comparatively easy to pinpoint, so there is much less cynicism and resistance from client staff about the decision to bring consultants in. And, because the difference in knowledge between consultant and client is so obvious, there is much more to be gained, in terms of knowledge transfer from the former to the latter.

Not surprisingly therefore, the areas where clients think that consultants add least value are where a generic service is applied to a highly specialized sector – offering 'strategic' consulting advice when the client wants to implement a package, is another good example.

UNDERSTANDING WHAT KIND OF CLIENT YOU ARE

'There is nothing new under the sun' is a statement as applicable to management theory as it is to almost every other walk of life. Every new management idea that hits the book stalls and the business media comes from somewhere: business process re-engineering, the buzz-word of the early 1990s, owed as much to Japanese quality management as it did to the brains of the individuals who made it famous. But in practical terms, ideas and issues that at least *seem* new do emerge from time to time. It may be that you read about some innovation by a competitor or attend a conference on a subject which everyone has just started to talk about. Perhaps your organization simply does not have the skills to solve a new problem – one that it has not encountered before.

None of the reasons for hiring consultants listed above is right or wrong, better or worse; every potential consulting project, every organization is unique. However, certain reasons work less well in certain circumstances – and these circumstances are largely to do with the extent to which the issue you want to address is perceived to be new.

For example, access to specialist knowledge is always very important, but the type of knowledge – industry- or issue-specific – may change. When a new problem or opportunity emerges, you will probably be looking towards experts in your own industry because you will need to be able to interpret that issue in the light of your own organization and those of your immediate competitors. The amount of existing information on the issue is very low, so there are no experts in it. But if the problem or opportunity is much more familiar, perhaps one that you have already seen your competitors dealing with, you will be looking for people with direct experience in that issue. Effectively, a body of knowledge about the issue has evolved, and you need to tap into it.

Equally, when you encounter a new issue, neither you nor a consultancy will have had a chance to develop a formalized approach to it. In these circumstances, it makes sense to hire a group of bright generalists who can work flexibly – and think innovatively – whatever the requirements. But, as the market matures, structured methodologies will emerge that provide a greater guarantee of success.

By and large, when a new management issue emerges, clients tend to buy consultants because they want people who can give an outside perspective and bring fresh thinking to whether this issue is relevant to the client's industry. They are often also seeking information about the new issue, and they are looking for highly flexible, essentially generalist help in developing their response. But, once a management issue has become more accepted – the market for it has matured, in effect – then clients tend to be much more interested in responding quickly and effectively. There is much less debate about what they should do, partly because there is much management literature on the issue with which they have been able to familiarize themselves, and partly because – as more and more of their competitors respond – they will be under pressure from employees and investors to keep up standards. It is therefore possible to divide the 'life' of a management issue into three distinct stages (see Figure 1.1). In Phase 1, a new issue emerges: its unfamiliarity means that both consultants and clients have to spend

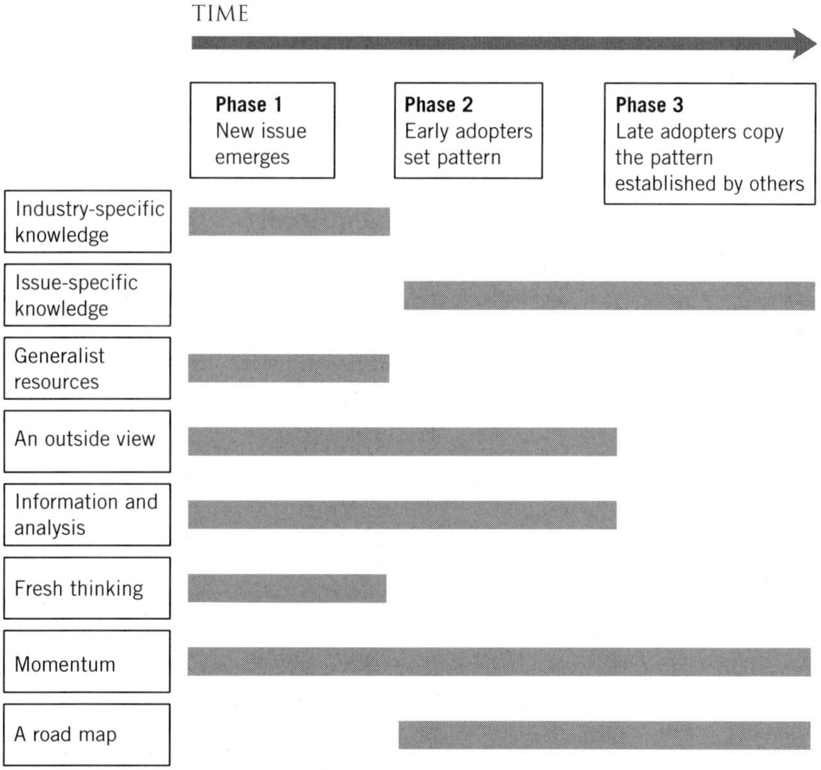

FIGURE 1.1: Clients' needs change as a management issue matures

time working out how (if at all) the issue applies to specific sectors and organizations. By Phase 2, much of this has become clearer, and the clients who adopted the issue in Phase 1 are now starting to reap the rewards of so doing. Their approach begins to create a standard for the other organizations that did not consider the issue when it first emerged, but are now doing so. By Phase 3, the organizations which have been slowest to respond to the issue are now largely copying a set methodology established by others.

It was precisely this development of the market that we saw with e-business consultancy. The emergence of a plethora of dot.coms in the late 1990s, which appeared to change the economic rules of engagement, created an enormous reaction on the part of incumbent organizations, who, afraid of being sidelined, suddenly needed to develop e-business strategies. With a very immature market and little hard information on what was happening, these corporations looked to consultants to provide information and innovative thinking. Not sure what would be required, they were happy to hire consultants who knew little about e-business, simply to help them think through the issues. After all, in such a new field, being an 'expert' was meaningless. But the market rapidly matured: the amount of press coverage which e-business received, as well as the information available via the internet itself, meant that clients quickly went from being novices to sophisticated purchasers, in some cases more quickly than consultants went from being novices to sophisticated sellers. As a result, clients turned away from creative thinking towards finding ways of doing what they knew they wanted to do more quickly and effectively. Among consulting firms, the balance of power shifted, from the e-specialist firms which had positioned themselves as creative thinkers, to more established firms that could demonstrate a structured implementation methodology.

Time, however, is a relative concept: as well as understanding the life-cycle of a management issue, it is crucial to understand how you as a client fit into the three phases described above. It can be difficult, if not dangerous, to generalize about clients: after all, every client is different. What this chapter has looked at so far is the overall picture for all clients – and there are always organizations that will buck a prevailing trend – who will aim to be innovative, even in a mature market, or who will attempt to follow a set pattern even before it has been well-developed.

The model outlined in Figure 1.1 can also be used to categorize types of clients.

- ☐ 'Phase 1' clients are companies which use consultants to explore new ideas; they primarily look to work with people who know a great deal about their sector and can, in conjunction with the client, spot and assess potential opportunities. These are the most innovative clients – the early-adopters, in effect – and are less concerned with copying what their rivals have done than in originating new thinking themselves.

- ☐ 'Phase 2' clients are those who have already identified what it is that they want to do, whether this is the implementation of a software package internally, or the launch of a new business venture. Where they need help is in bringing together the disparate skills and resources required to realize their plans – something which the speed and complexity of e-business has made even more important. 'Phase 2' clients are therefore looking for help in managing their projects. While they want a degree of industry-specific knowledge, they also need program managers who are experienced in the particular opportunity which they are pursuing, and who can perform specific, quite strategic functions (in the case of e-business, help their clients identify and approach potential partners).

- ☐ 'Phase 3' clients are primarily interested in completing the job, in catching up with what their competitors may already have achieved. What they are looking for when they hire consultants is not innovative thinking or a long-term relationship; they need help in quite discrete areas, and they want to know that the consultants they use can almost guarantee success. Of the three types, 'Phase 3' clients are most likely to outsource a project in its entirety.

CHOOSING BETWEEN INTERNAL AND EXTERNAL CONSULTANCY

Once you are clear about exactly what kind of consultancy you need and why, you should consider whether your requirements can be best met using internal or external consultants.

It is a common kneejerk reaction by managers (and something that generates considerable hostility among their staff) to hire external consultants automatically. People within the client organization feel ignored, that they are simply not good enough, that no one ever listens to them. So it is important to go through a process – and be seen to go through a process – of matching the skills and experience of your current organization against your requirements. After all, you may find that you *can* do everything yourself, or most of it, with external consultants plugging specific gaps. Or you may find that this is something that can be done better by an outside team. You also need to think about the demands which you are making on the people you involve internally. Although the roles of line manager and internal consultant are converging, for some organizations and some individuals the shift can be significant.[3]

The image of the 'traditional' manager is of someone who thinks of themselves as being in control: their responsibility is to direct the work of others and, where necessary, to give direct commands. They see the organization in which they work as having clear, largely functional boundaries – one of their key aims is to keep ambiguity and uncertainty at bay. Their office door may be open, but the onus is on 'their' people to come to them, to ask for help or to raise problems. Their status – and the paraphernalia they see as accompanying it (the job title, the bigger desk, the company car) – all breed a degree of dependency in those around them.

However much organizations may think they have reinvented themselves over the last two decades, in the wake of ideas about empowerment, business process re-engineering and so on, some of these attitudes remain, and in some organizations more than others. Indeed, the whole concept of management depends on these facets however much their superficial appearance may have shifted. But the internal consultant works to a very different model: notions of being in control give way to facilitation; internal consultants go to other people, they do not wait for people to come to them; their aim is – or should be – to promote independence not dependency, to help their colleagues learn new skills, not to tell them what to do. And because an internal consultant will have to work with people across an entire organization, functional distinctions are comparatively unimportant. He or she is much more interested in overall processes and is more comfortable with blurred roles.

Re-badging a traditional manager as an internal consultant can therefore be a recipe for disaster. Too accustomed to telling people what to do and potentially lacking in facilitation skills, these people can become *de facto* managers, creating levels of hostility similar to those sometimes encountered by external consultants, although for different reasons. However, find the right person and the right project, and the internal consultant will be able to add considerable value.

Most importantly, therefore, you need to understand the relative pros and cons of internal and external consultancy in relation to your particular circumstances. Of the reasons for hiring

[3] These types of clients are also discussed in Fiona Czerniawska, *Management Consultancy: What Next?*, Palgrave, 2001

consultants listed earlier on in this chapter, some are better suited to one type of consultancy than another. The strengths of internal consultants in one area may translate into weaknesses in another – the same is true of external consultants. Although there is no perfect solution, simply a series of trade-offs to be made in the light of your own unique circumstances, there are some preferred options that combine the strengths of both worlds and minimize their weaknesses. Table 1.1 summarizes the key points.

REASON FOR USING CONSULTANTS	INTERNAL CONSULTANT	EXTERNAL CONSULTANT	PREFERRED OPTION
Industry-specific skills	*Advantages:* familiar with business; knows other specialists; likely to have general knowledge about what other companies in the same industry are doing; accountable for decisions in the long term *Disadvantages:* may not know much in detail about competitor activity	*Advantages:* detailed knowledge of what is going on in a particular industry *Disadvantages:* may have to learn about the client's own organization in more detail; unlikely to be accountable in the long term for decisions made	Use combination of internal and external consultancy
Issue-specific skills	*Advantages:* familiar with business; knows other specialists; likely to have general knowledge about what other companies in the same industry are doing *Disadvantages:* experience beyond the company may be limited; may not know much in detail about competitor activity	*Advantages:* should have extensive experience of working with other companies on the same issue; up-to-date knowledge *Disadvantages:* may not be aware of a client's particular operating circumstances and therefore make inappropriate suggestions	Use combination of internal and external consultancy
Generalist resources	*Advantages:* low cost *Disadvantages:* may be difficult to detach from existing jobs quickly; may be insufficiently flexible	*Advantages:* can be highly flexible and able to adapt to uncertain and changing demands; usually available immediately; can be dedicated to project *Disadvantages:* high cost	Use external consultancy unless costs are prohibitive
An outside view	*Disadvantages:* too much knowledge and vested interest to be able to do this	*Advantages:* able to look at an organization with fresh eyes and question accepted ideas and practices; not afraid to ask questions; senior client executives may be more willing to discuss sensitive issues with outsiders *Disadvantages:* does not know what the organization already knows and therefore runs the danger of telling them this	Use external consultancy
Information and analysis	*Advantages:* familiar with potential internal sources of information *Disadvantages:* may not have access to much external data	*Advantages:* – accustomed to gathering large quantities of data quickly and efficiently; may have proprietary sources of data and analytical tools to which you would not otherwise have access *Disadvantages:* always a danger of stating the obvious – telling you what you already know	Use combination of internal and external consultancy

REASON FOR USING CONSULTANTS	INTERNAL CONSULTANT	EXTERNAL CONSULTANT	PREFERRED OPTION
Innovative thinking	*Advantages:* able to assess the practical application of creative ideas *Disadvantages:* may have narrow experience to tap into	*Advantages:* can be very experienced in applying creative thinking techniques; can draw on a wider base of knowledge from other companies *Disadvantages:* may come up with inappropriate ideas	Use combination of internal and external consultancy
Momentum	*Advantages:* able to tap into the support and enthusiasm of immediate colleagues *Disadvantages:* difficult to sustain when people have many other calls on their time; easy to lose focus and confidence; performance measurements of colleagues may not include delivery	*Advantages:* able to provide dedicated resources who can focus on the task in hand; no distractions from the individuals' day job; future sales depend on making the project a success; fees can be tied to performance *Disadvantages:* can be difficult for a client to retain control	Use external consultancy
A road map	*Advantages:* can create sense of involvement among colleagues; those involved from the client side are less likely to be suspicious of 'scope creep', where consultants continually enlarge a project for their own benefit *Disadvantages:* may end up re-inventing the wheel by developing in-house approaches; higher risk of failure because the approach developed is unlikely to have been extensively tested; may be tempted to create own empire; approach may not be rigorously reviewed	*Advantages:* approach is likely to have been tested with other clients; client does not bear the full cost of development and training associated with the approach proposed; developing structured methodologies is one of the core competencies of a consultant – but it is not necessarily a core competence of a client *Disadvantages:* expensive; lack of ownership in client organization may mean that client staff are less willing to go the extra mile to deliver the project ('it's not my problem')	Use combination of internal and external consultancy

TABLE 1.1: Balancing internal and external consultancy

Clearly, some of the disadvantages listed here could be mitigated by the way you structure the project, for example, ensuring that colleagues being seconded onto the project are being replaced, rather than being expected to do two jobs at once. Equally, the advantages of using an external consultant depend heavily on the person or people you choose: some consultants can think creatively, but not all of them.

SUMMARY

1 The ultimate success of a consulting project is determined long before you have talked to an actual consultant, and depends on the extent to which you have been able to identify and agree the precise reasons for hiring consultants.

2 In most organizations, managers think about these reasons in terms of what they expect the consultants to do, not in relation to the underlying role which they are expecting the consultants to play. There are eight fundamental reasons why organizations hire consultants (Table 1.2).

PEOPLE	CONTENT	PROCESS
Access to industry-specific knowledge	An outside view	Momentum
Access to issue-specific knowledge	Information and analysis	A road map
Generalist resources	Innovative thinking	

TABLE 1.2: The eight reasons why organizations hire consultants

3 With this framework in mind, you need to be clear about:

- ☐ Which reasons apply to which project, or to which stages within a project.
- ☐ How your reasons match the prevailing market conditions – is the issue you face a new one, or are you trying to catch up with your competitors?

4 The extent to which the eight reasons listed in Table 1.2 are important will vary, depending on:

- ☐ the point in its 'lifecycle' the particular consulting service you want to buy has reached
- ☐ the type of client you are.

5 The lifecylce of a consulting service can be divided into three phases:

- ☐ *Phase 1* in which a new issue has emerged and a new consulting service has been developed to meet it. Early adopting clients who look for consultancy help at this stage are typically looking for:
  - ☐ objective and often innovative help around in analyzing whether and how the issue / service is applicable
  - ☐ momentum and resources to carry an embryonic and possible uncertain project forward.
- ☐ *Phase 2* in which the early adopting clients have set a pattern both in terms of the benefits that accrue from a particular consulting service and the process by which these benefits can be achieved. For clients who bring in consultants in this middle phase of the cycle, the most important reasons tend to be:
  - ☐ expertise on the issue and the consulting process
  - ☐ an outside perspective on applying that process within the client's organization
  - ☐ project management and a route map for delivery.
- ☐ *Phase 3* in which clients who have been slow to react largely copy the pattern set by other organizations. The aim here is to implement the consulting service as quickly as possible, in order to catch up with competitors, so the means tend to take precedence over the ends:
  - ☐ expertise on the process is now much more important than an ability to analyze whether or not the process itself is suitable for a given organization
  - ☐ efficiency is more important than effectiveness.

6 Clients (that is organizations or parts of them) that hire consultants regularly tend to do so for the same reasons:

- ☐ *Phase 1 clients* use consultants to explore new ideas, to scan the sectors they, the client, operate in, in order to identify emerging ideas, to assess the relevance of these ideas and to develop a process for implementing them.
- ☐ *Phase 2 clients* already know what it is they want to do, but need help both with specific skills and in terms of managing the process.
- ☐ *Phase 3 clients* want to make up lost ground; they have less time for the strategic nuances of what they are doing and no patience for consulting firms who want to question assumptions they, the client, have already made. For these clients, time and money are of the essence.

7 Having decided that help is needed, the instant reaction of many clients – especially in organizations that hire consultants on a regular basis – is that it is external help that is needed. Internal people may be perceived to lack the skills, time or clout to get the job done. But clients need to question – and increasingly are questioning this assumption: external consultants have distinct disadvantages in some areas (although advantages in others). Every project should be assessed on its own merits: what *precisely* are you trying to achieve? Who is most likely to help you achieve this – internal or external expertise?

CHAPTER 2

HOW TO SELECT A CONSULTING FIRM

The previous chapter looked at why clients hire consulting firms, and argued that most tend to see those reasons in comparatively high-level terms – to implement a particular IT system, or to advise on a restructuring program. The first step in managing your management consultant effectively is to understand the more fundamental reasons – to gain the outside view, to fill gaps in your intellectual capital, and so on.

This chapter looks at the next step – having discussed and agreed the underlying value which you are seeking from consultants, what kind of process should you follow to ensure that the consultants you choose are best suited to the job?

THE PROCESS FOR SELECTING A CONSULTANT

Figure 2.1 highlights the seven key steps in the process, each of which is discussed in greater detail below. At first sight, this might look like a time-consuming framework; however, it is possible to progress through the different stages comparatively quickly, although the exact rate will depend on the scale and complexity of the project, and will vary from organization to organization. A rough guide would be around two weeks per stage, giving an overall timeframe of three months for a medium to large project.

Who, from the client's side, should be involved in the process? Experience suggests that you need to involve:

- ☐ Someone at a senior (i.e. board) level, to ensure that the project has the commitment of the organization behind it.
- ☐ The people (perhaps middle managers) who are most likely to be involved in the project, and who will end up working side-by-side with the consultants.
- ☐ Some of the people who are ultimately going to be affected by the project (the end-users of a new IT system, for example).

FIGURE 2.1: The seven steps in the process of selecting a consulting firm

Create a brief for the consultants

It is unrealistic to expect consultants to guess a client's mind, so the first stage in any purchase process has to be to develop and agree internally an outline of the project for which consulting help is sought. This brief may vary from a few paragraphs to a highly detailed specification stretching over volumes, but, whatever the length and level of detail, good briefs will all include clear statements on the following:

- ☐ The aims of the project.
- ☐ How the consultants are expected to help realize these aims.
- ☐ The reasons for bringing consultants in – the added value they are expected to provide which the client organization cannot itself supply.
- ☐ Expectations about the process which the consultants will undertake.
- ☐ The key deliverables.
- ☐ Who will be involved in the project from the client's side and in what capacity.
- ☐ Anticipated timescales.
- ☐ Expected costs.
- ☐ How the consulting firm will be rewarded – e.g. method of payment, link to results and risks, etc.

Some of these – the objectives and time-scales for example – are obvious and incontestable: some are more contentious. Many clients are wary of spelling out their budget for a project in advance, because they believe that doing so will encourage the consultants who are bidding for the work to increase their price, and it will therefore iron out any price differential across all those firms bidding. While there is some merit in these suspicions, this attitude also has some serious drawbacks. First of all, it often results in clients and consultants wasting time, because the consultants propose a process which does not match the client's expectations – it is either much too expensive (too much as been included) or not expensive enough (too little has been included). It is much better to put the consultants in a position where they compete on their value for money, rather than their absolute cost – in other words, by making them demonstrate just how much of a contribution they can make for a given amount of money.

Send out the brief to a long-list of consultants

Many clients find it tempting to go back to the same firm again and again. Although this is often on a rather grudging basis ('better the devil we know'), there are some real advantages in doing so, especially where:

- ☐ The project is high-risk – where using a new, less familiar consulting firm might raise the overall level of risk involved to a point where the project becomes untenable.
- ☐ The timescales are tight, and the time taken in putting the project out to competitive tender will be prohibitively long.
- ☐ A very high level of internal knowledge about the client is required.

But in all other cases, it makes sense to cast your net widely; a long-list should contain the names of around ten consulting firms. The consulting industry is a rapidly changing one with new firms coming (and going) all the time. By inviting consulting firms which you have not worked with before alongside more familiar competitors, you will receive an up-to-date and broad set of perspectives on your problem. Even the consultants you choose not to put on the subsequent short-list may make helpful suggestions which you can incorporate in your second iteration of the consulting brief. Moreover, it is important here to be clear about just how specialized your problem is. If specialist knowledge is important, then firms which you have worked with in the past (on other issues) may not be the best equipped for this particular work.

Chapter 3 looks at ways of segmenting the consulting industry, and is designed to help you identify, in broad terms, the kind of firm most suited to the work in hand. The internet is the obvious place to start assembling the list of names, if you are trying to track down less well-known, more in-depth specialists, but most associations of consulting firms also provide information on their members (Table 2.1).

Austria	Fachverband Unternehmensberatung und Datenverarbeitung (FUD) www.ubdv.or.at
Belgium	Association Belge des Conseils en Gestion et Organisation (ASCOBEL) www.ascobel.be
Denmark	Dansk Management Råd (DMR) www.danskmanagementraad.dk
Europe	The European Federation of Management Consultancies Associations www.feaco.org

Finland	Liikkeenjohdon Konsultit LJK www.ljk.fi
France	Syntec Conseil en Management (Chambre Syndicale des Sociétés de Conseil) www.syntec-management.com
Germany	Bundesverband Deutscher Unternehmensberater e.V. (BDU) www.bdu.de
Greece	Hellenic Association of Management Consulting Firms (SESMA) www.sesma.gr
Italy	Associazione delle Società di Consulenza Direzionale e Organizzat www.assoconsult.org
The Netherlands	Raad van Organisatie Adviesbureau (ROA) www.roa-advies.nl
Norway	NBF – Norges Bedriftsrådgiverforening www.bedriftsraadgiver.no
Portugal	Associaçao Portuguesa de Projectistas e Consultores (APPC) www.appconsultores.pt
Spain	Asoc. Espanola de Empressa de Consultoria (AEC) www.consultoras.com
Sweden	SAMC, Sveriges Managementkonsulenter www.samc.se
Switzerland	Association of Management Consultants (ASCO) www.asco.ch
United Kingston	Management Consultancies Association (MCA) www.mca.org.uk
US / International	Association of Management Consulting Firms (AMCF) www.amcf.org

TABLE 2.1: Major trade associations providing infomormation on consulting firms

First phase of contact with consultants

Once the brief has gone out, a period of contact follows between the client and the consulting firms bidding for the project. Like the brief itself, this can take many forms. It may consist of one formal meeting (typically a presentation) in which the consultants talk through their proposed approach to a committee. At the other end of the spectrum, the process may be much more iterative, with many, less formal meetings which become a dialogue between clients and consultants. There is no right or wrong approach, but it is important to find one that suits you and your organization (this is discussed in greater detail later in this chapter). That being said, there is considerable value in making use of the consultants' expertise as much as possible. They should have experience of working in the area that you are looking at, and they will almost certainly have a better understanding of which consulting projects succeed or fail, so it makes sense to tap this expertise wherever possible.

However, whatever form it takes, this is a critical period because it helps you to develop an impression of the consulting firms.

Internal consultation on brief and short-list

The initial period of contact with the consulting firms also provides you with an opportunity to validate your and your colleague's views about the project as a whole and the involvement of consultants in it. This is useful, because it can be difficult to develop a consulting brief in abstract, especially if the project is in an area with which you are unfamiliar. As a result, many briefs become the lowest common denominator of internal discussions: they are woolly and bland, and provide little of the precise guidance that consultants require to be effective.

Having refined the brief, a client is now in a position to decide which of the long-list of consultants initially approached should be put on the short-list. Chapter 4 looks in more detail at the points you should consider in evaluating consulting firms.

Second phase of contact with consultants

With a more specific brief, greater internal consensus within the client's organization and a smaller number of previously vetted consulting firms, a client is now in a position to have a far more meaningful dialogue with the short-listed consultants. Once again, this period can be long or short, an informal dialogue or a more formal process. And, once again, it is sensible to bear in mind the comments made earlier about the potential value of having an interactive relationship with the short-list of firms. However, just as your brief has been refined, you should now expect the consulting firms to prepare much more comprehensive statements (in the form of proposals and/or presentations), describing how they plan to approach the project (these are discussed further in Chapter 5). The consulting firms should also be able to supply you with:

- ☐ A number of client referees, whom you can contact directly in order to gauge the extent to which the firm has relevant experience and a track record of success.
- ☐ A list of the people who, subject to your giving the go-ahead for the project within a reasonable amount of time, will be guaranteed to work on the project (you need to ensure that what you see – experienced consultants selling their services – is what you get – the same experienced consultants actually doing the work).

Internal consultation on the decision

Having refined your brief and examined the refined response of the short-list of consulting firms, the moment of truth has arrived, to choose one or two firms who will be the preferred bidders for the project. It can help here to ask everyone involved in the decision to rate their views according to a set of pre-defined evaluation criteria (see also Chapter 4), but such criteria often put a spurious scientific gloss on what is, in fact, a gut reaction. As that is the case, it can be much more productive to discuss those impressions openly – otherwise you run the risk of not taking on board the reservations of individuals, which can have a highly detrimental effect on the subsequent consulting process. The decision as to whether to proceed with one or two preferred bidders, is largely dependent on the kind of project envisaged. For complex, large-scale projects, where many detailed issues have to be finalized during the negotiation of the contact, it makes good commercial sense to involve two firms in the process, in case one has to drop out at a later stage. This is rarely necessary for smaller-scale projects.

Negotiations with one or two preferred consulting firms

The brief prepared for the consultants and the proposals/presentations elicited from them will almost never be sufficient to cover all aspects of the contractual relationship between a client and a consulting firm. For comparatively small-scale projects, most consulting firms have set terms and conditions which cover the most obvious points – confidentiality, duty of care, intellectual property rights and liability. They should also have an outline of the escalation process, describing what happens if, for any reason, you are dissatisfied with the service which you receive. For larger projects, these aspects often form part of a customized contract that will cover issues such as the use of subcontractors.

Many consulting firms belong to trade associations (listed on pp. 24–25) which have Codes of Best Practice to which members must subscribe (that of the Management Consultancies Association is attached as an appendix at the end of this book). Typically, these include statements about the way in which consulting firms are expected to behave during the sales and consulting process, and member firms are liable to disciplinary proceedings if it can be shown that they have not abided by these rules.

DIFFERENT PATTERNS OF BUYING BEHAVIOUR

The process outlined above is a generic one: in practice, there is a broad spectrum of ways in which clients apply it.

In the last 20 years, there have been some dramatic shifts in terms of the process which clients use to buy consultancy. Clients of the 1980s were as unsophisticated in their approach to buying, as consultancies were in their approach to selling. A legacy of the idea that good professionals had no need to sell their services affected both sides; deals were done over lunch, between friends. Two things interrupted this cosy situation. Firstly, consulting firms grew rapidly and, with more mouths to feed, could no longer rely on this largely informal way of doing things; they needed commitments, contracts, fees. Secondly, clients became more sophisticated in their approach, an evolution that was exacerbated by the 1991–92 recession in which, for the first time, clients took control of the client–consultant relationship, bypassing notions of professionalism in order to drive down fee rates. A key way in which clients did this was to introduce much more formality into the selection process: long lunches were superceded by long invitations to tender (ITT), in which consulting firms were expected to demonstrate their compliance with a client's requirements to a very great level of detail. Alongside the ITT came more complex rules governing the interaction between purchasers and bidders.

Since that point, there has been a significant divergence between how the public and private sectors select consultants. By and large, public sector clients stayed with (and indeed, extended) the formal process (principally because of regulations governing purchasing), while private sector companies returned to an informal style combined with a more interactive way of working.

However, a public/private sector distinction is not the only way in which the means by which companies select consultants can be differentiated. A brief survey of how companies' approaches can vary even within Europe illustrates just how true this is.

Although one has to be careful here not to fall into simplistic, national stereotypes, the evidence suggests that, with the exception of the UK (which is closer to the US model), clients in Europe take longer to make decisions about consulting programs. They are perhaps less keen to try something out quickly – a caution which has stood them in good stead, as it meant that they have been less exposed to the dot.com implosion. It is a more considered, iterative approach in which several experts will be quizzed on their ideas before a final decision is taken. This is partly a function of a difference between large-scale consulting projects in the US and Europe. A project setting up an online bank in Europe is much more complicated than an equivalent project in the US would be, because of regulatory issues, differences in the consumer markets, and different standards for compliance. Untangling the pieces of this spaghetti and working out how to build a profitable business that takes it all into account is a very difficult undertaking.

Continental European purchasers also appear to be more conservative and price-sensitive – they want a new idea to be proved before they buy it. Typically, people in Europe take a more intellectual approach than their counterparts in the Anglo-Saxon economies, one that embraces broader management issues, as well as the basic economic ones. They will not take a decision without asking a lot of questions about it first. Is there an alternative approach? How can we do better than we are doing at the moment? But, particularly in southern European countries, the lengthier sales cycle reflects a more bureaucratic approach to the buying process. The further south you go, the more likely you are to encounter administratively-driven projects in which everything is specified in considerable detail. Often it amounts to a more formal, complicated approach to a comparatively simple problem.

There are nuances also in the extent to which clients wish to buy a highly packaged, or a highly customized service. Scandinavian companies appear to fall into the latter category. Perhaps it is because they want to save money, or that they are concerned to extract the maximum value from the consultants with whom they work, but clients want consultants to coach their own people, not walk away with all the good ideas. France is not dissimilar: what French clients often want is *haute coûture* – services that have been designed for their unique circumstances, but delivered with the efficiency and at the cost of an industrial process. German clients tend to combine both an interest in intellectual content with a need to see a clear and rigorous methodology. This means that the presentations consultants give, and the depth they go into, are very different. But it is an attitude that can be contrasted with other parts of Europe. The Netherlands is more like the UK (and the US) in that clients are more interested in clear-cut solutions.

Fundamentally, buying behaviour varies along two dimensions: the level of formality in the process, and the level of interaction between clients and consultants. Organizations tend to buy consultancy in one of two ways. At one end of the spectrum, you have organizations who, by and large:

- ☐ Draw a distinct boundary between formulating a strategy and implementing it, and are therefore pre-disposed to hire different consulting companies for each part.
- ☐ Want to purchase packaged consultancy in all but the most strategic areas.
- ☐ Have a clear brief about what they want the consultants to do.
- ☐ Are buying services where the methodological component is high (not least because standardization across internal and national boundaries is a major issue).
- ☐ Look largely to the brand of the consulting company and its collective track record (either in their country or outside it) to provide them with whatever comfort they require in making their purchase decision.

These clients tend to have formal buying processes in which the interaction of clients and consultants is limited by predetermined rules (such as set meetings, access to only a small number of people on the client's side). Much of the public sector buys consultancy in this way, but so do many large corporations. But, at the other end of the spectrum are clients who:

- ☐ Regard strategy and implementation as part of a continuum, and are therefore predisposed to hire the same consulting firm to help with both aspects.
- ☐ Are more concerned to initiate a consulting process that has been tailored to circumstances which they view as being very specific.
- ☐ Look for older, more experienced consultants who are able to handle the change management and HR issues involved in implementation (but not the technology).
- ☐ Value flexibility and responsiveness above standard approaches.
- ☐ Are more concerned about the qualifications and experience of the individual consultants, than the overall brand of the firm.

These clients tend to have less formalized approaches to selecting consultancies; they also allow more interaction – a dialogue, even – between the two sides before the final choice of consulting firm is made. The clients are more likely to be (but not exclusively) medium and small-sized companies, or individuals within larger corporations who are making the purchase decision comparatively autonomously (i.e. without having to consult a central purchasing team).

Each of these approaches has its own strengths and weaknesses:

☐ **High formality/low interaction** – A formal selection process has the considerable advantage of putting the client fully in control. Much effort is spent in mapping out the brief for the consultants in considerable detail, and evaluating the skills and approach proposed by the consulting firms with great precision. For highly complex or highly regulated projects (e.g. in the public sector), this approach is a necessity. But it also has some major disadvantages: by reducing the level of interaction between clients and consultants, it misses an opportunity to engage the consulting firms in designing a project in order to have the greatest chance of success. After all, consultants are – or should be – the experts in what makes a consulting project work well, not the client. Another key drawback of this approach to purchasing is that there is little room for change – having described the project and expected a detailed response from the consultants, it becomes hard to accommodate suggestions made by the consultants during the sales process, and valuable input may be ignored as a result.

☐ **Low formality/high interaction** – The advantages/disadvantages of this way of approaching purchasing are the mirror image of those described above. Having high levels of informal contact between client and consultants can, in the wrong organizations and for the wrong projects, be a recipe for disaster, with interaction and flexibility rapidly descending into chaos. But for projects in new areas, or for problems of intractable difficulty, where the client (and potentially even the consulting firm) are very much feeling their way towards a solution, the opportunity for both sides to brainstorm a joint resolution is invaluable. Not only does it obtain the input of consultants where it can be most valuable at this stage (developing an effective approach to the project), but it is also a way of building shared commitment and consensus.

There are two important lessons here. The first is that it is important to select a process that suits your organization and the project you have in hand. Keep detailed, pre-defined specifications for the projects where they are most needed, or for the occasions when you have to be in complete control of all the details, but avoid setting up too bureaucratic a process for projects under a certain value. Where possible, be flexible and open about your aims, intentions and expectations. Make good use of the consultants' input – after all, you are not paying for it yet!

The second lesson is one of transparency. Because no selection process (or, indeed, decision) is a perfect one, and because every selection process (and, indeed, decision) is dependent on a unique set of circumstances, both the selection process and the ultimate decision need to be available for scrutiny. Whenever a bad decision of any sort is seen to have been made, we all tend – with the benefit of hindsight – to raise our eyebrows, shrug our shoulders, wring our hands and say 'but how could they do that?'. We can do this because we were not privy to the discussions that took place: we have no appreciation of the constraints that may have accompanied a decision or any of the other potentially mitigating factors. The same point applies to decisions to hire consultants – only those involved in the selection process will understand the thinking process. Already aware of this issue, clients have made significant strides over the last ten years to ensure that senior executives in their organizations are brought into the process of deciding whether to hire external consultants, particularly where the projects are strategic and the fees substantial. Much has been said about the extent to which high-level sponsorship is a critical success factor. However, widening the net of involvement does not necessarily make the process any more transparent to those outside it. Very few organizations subject the decisions they make about consultants to any additional evaluation other than, perhaps, a financial audit.

In the wake of Enron, it seems likely that this will – and should – change. The intelligent client will designate a person (or group of people) whose responsibility it will be to scrutinize the value of large-scale consulting projects:

- ☐ How will this project help our organization achieve its strategic goals?
- ☐ Does it represent the most effective and efficient means of achieving these goals? Could our resources and money be better used elsewhere?

SUMMARY

1 There are seven key steps that take you from an initial decision to hire consultants to making the final choice from a short-list of contenders:

- ☐ Creating a brief for the consultants.
- ☐ Identifying a long-list of consultants to whom you send the brief.
- ☐ A first phase of discussion with the long-list of consulting firms about their overall approach to the brief.
- ☐ Internal consultation to revise the brief and decide on a short-list of firms to focus on.
- ☐ A second phase of discussion with short-list of consulting firms, focusing on their approach to the revised brief in considerable detail.

- ☐ Internal consultation on the decision to narrow the choice of consulting firms down.
- ☐ Negotiations with the preferred bidder(s).

2 How you approach these steps is determined by the level of formality you require, and the level of client–consultant interaction you envisage. Each approach has its particular strengths and weaknesses, and needs to be evaluated on an organization-by-organization, and project-by-project basis. Some organizations – most public sector clients – have no choice in how they approach the purchase of consultancy and have to adopt a formalized approach. Much needs to be spelled out in advance for complex projects, which tends to drive down the level of desirable interaction.

3 However, where possible, it is preferable to have a high level of informal interaction with the consultants on both your long- and short-lists, as they should have valuable input about how the project can be scoped and structured to give it the maximum chance of success. You also need to consider how you will make your decision-making process transparent, even to those not directly involved in it.

CHAPTER 3

COMPARING CONSULTANCIES

There are many ways to skin a cat.

As the nature and scope of consulting services have broadened over the last 20 years, both the number and diversity of consulting firms have proliferated, apparently exponentially, to a point where it is now possible for just about anyone or any organization to describe themselves as a consultancy. For the manager who is considering hiring consultants, this embarrassment of riches brings a multitude of problems. What kind of firm should you choose? Are you buying an individual or a corporate brand? How can you differentiate between consultants who, on paper and in person, may sound and look very similar?

This chapter tries to grapple with these issues: its aim is to help you decide what kind of consulting firm (and what kind of consultant) you need by classifying consultants in four ways, according to whether they:

- ☐ Offer an integrated service – 'soup-to-nuts' – or a specialist service.
- ☐ Take an expert or facilitative role.
- ☐ Have international or local coverage.
- ☐ Are selling themselves as a corporate entity or as individual consultants.

The next stage – choosing between them – will be covered in Chapter 4.

INTEGRATED SERVICE OR SPECIALIST?

Consulting firms have traditionally been categorized by their history into six distinct groups (Table 3.1):

However, this means of categorising firms has become increasingly meaningless in the last ten years:

- ☐ In the late 1990s, a new generation of e-consulting firms sprang up, challenging accepted boundaries within the consulting industry because they combined strategic,

CATEGORY		EXAMPLE FIRMS
Strategic consultancies	Largely continue the traditions of Fredrick Taylor's School of Scientific Management, typified by a highly rational, analytical approach	McKinsey & Co Booz-Allen & Hamilton Boston Consulting Group Bain & Co Mercer Management Consultants
Generalist firms	Originally developed as separate practices within large-scale accounting firms	Accenture Cap Gemini Ernst & Young Braxton KPMG Consulting
Operationally-based firms	Combine strategy with operational improvement	PA Consulting A T Kearney
Computer hardware/software suppliers and systems integrators	Developed as separate practices within technology and IT outsourcing companies	IBM Global Services EDS Computer Sciences Corporation SchlumbergerSema
Niche specialists		Hedra (public sector) BSC Consulting (risk management) Kurt Salmon Associates (retail) Horwath (not-for-profit)
Sole practitioners (independent, self-employed)		

TABLE 3.1: The traditional categories of consultancies

creative and technology consulting. While many such firms have since collapsed with the dot.com market they largely served, their legacy remains, and established firms are looking at ways of combining these types of work within their organizations.

☐ Some firms have merged or been acquired in order to provide more integrated services. Typically, such activity has been designed to move consulting firms up the value chain; thus, systems integration firms have bought implementation and change management firms; Big Four firms have bought strategy practices or high-margin niche firms.

☐ Other firms have diversified organically, by building up practices in new market areas or products, partly to offer a more seamless service, but also to bolster shrinking margins in one area by acquiring credibility in another, higher margin field.

☐ Accounting firms have been under pressure to separate their consulting and auditing functions due to a succession of scandals that have ultimately questioned the probity of any one firm offering both types of service while remaining completely objective.

☐ Hundreds, if not thousands, of alliances have been formed between consulting firms, and between consulting firms and technology companies.

Whatever form it takes, the official reason behind such manoeuvring is to provide an integrated service to clients. One of the classic flaws of consultancy is the gap between consulting projects, between the perfect strategy on paper and its realization in practice, between the blueprint for success and the technology that makes it work. By classifying consulting firms according to their origins, clients have tended to pigeonhole consultants into one activity or another. Integrated services are intended to be the solution to this problem: integration will ensure that the consultants involved in formulating the strategy have a vested interest in making it feasible (because they will have to make it work); it will ensure that those implementing an IT system know what they are trying to achieve (because they were involved in developing the strategy behind it).

It sounds good in theory, but clients are rather more ambivalent about its value. There is certainly no shortage of clients who bemoan the fact that consultants have left them with a report that is gathering dust on the shelf because the recommendations are not practical. But you also encounter people who say, 'We want to ensure we work with a world-class specialist in every field. We do not believe that a single consulting firm can be world-class across the board.' The suspicion about the jack-of-all-trades-but-master-of-none consultancy has some grounding in reality. Specialist knowledge requires investment, and a large, integrated firm, with people working in a myriad of different areas, will not be able to achieve the economies of scale that a small firm which only does one thing will have when it comes to Research and Development.

From a client's point of view, both integration and its opposite – specialization – have different strengths. Integrated services work well when: you have a definite objective that you want to achieve as efficiently and effectively as possible; your project has global/enterprise-wide implications; independence/objectivity are not essential. Specialist services work well when: you are not clear what you are trying to do, and do not want to be locked into a particular process further on; you want to be sure you have an expert opinion; you want independent advice, that the expert whom you approach has no vested interest in selling you a particular solution.

Consulting firms can be categorized according to the level of integration/specialization they can provide. Such a classification assumes that integration and specialization are mutually exclusive, and, by and large, they are.

- **Integrated firms** will have diversified organically, incrementally building up the people and knowledge in areas adjacent to their existing core competencies. They will have diverted resources into skilling-up all areas equally and transferring knowledge between them, rather than focusing on specific areas.

- **Less integrated firms** will have diversified through merger and acquisition. They, too, will have diverted resources to bringing the different groups of people together, although they are never likely to achieve the seamless integration of organic growth.

- **Non-integrated firms** will have groups of consultants specializing in different areas. Any integration or common approach is accidental, as most of the firm's management effort is focused around small business units, and sharing information and resources across these units is antipathetic to the overriding culture.

- **Specialist-orchestrator firms** focus on only a small number of closely connected issues, and they are unwilling to compromise that focus by diversification either organically or through acquisition. At the same time, they recognize the concern of some clients that specialist work in one area should link to specialist work in other areas. To solve this problem, they have formed alliances with other specialist firms in order to help clients create the integrated teams required, but staffed with specialist consultants.

☐ **Specialist firms** are similarly focused on only a small number of issues or industry sectors – and that is all that they do. Even networks with potentially complementary firms are a distraction; all their energies and investment are ploughed into their immediate market.

When you are looking to hire some consultants, a crucial question to ask yourself is, 'how important is integration?' For some work, independent advice may be essential; on other occasions, your main concern may be to ensure that something – a process or a system – works. In practice, integration and specialization are therefore two extreme points on the same continuum: integration may be a critical characteristic of the consulting firm that you are looking to engage, or it may just be something that is nice to have, something that you are willing to trade off if the necessity arises.

EXPERT OR FACILITATOR?

Another way to segment consultants is according to the role they expect to play in a client's organization. Considerable lip-service is given to the concept of working 'in partnership' with clients, although few firms have even attempted defining what this actually means – indeed, it is hard to imagine circumstances in which a client would not want to work 'in partnership'. In fact, different consulting firms have different modes of working, and knowing which mode is suitable in what circumstances is a crucial part of choosing the right consultancy.

Ask yourself: given the nature of the problem that I am trying to solve, which appropriate mode of working with consultants should I adopt?

There are two issues to consider in making this decision:

☐ **What is the nature of the impact you want consultants to have?** Do you want them to act as experts, telling your organization what it should do, and bringing new information or skills to help it do that? Or do you want people who will take a lower-key role, helping your organization to help itself, rather than taking the problem off your hands?

☐ **What is the scope of the impact you want consultants to have?** Is this a project which will be focused on a small number of people – your Board of Directors or a specialist business unit? Or is it something that has implications for large parts, if not all, your organization?

The nature of the impact

As with the integrated/specialist issue, the two ways in which consultants have an impact – the 'imperative' (where the consultant is the expert, telling a client what to do) and the 'facilitative' (where a consultant's help is less direct) – are different points on a continuum. At one extreme, there is 'hard' consulting – where the consultant is an expert, and client is paying the consultant team to devise and implement a set of solutions, using its skills, rather than through consultation with the client's organization. At the other end is 'soft' consulting – where the consultant is expected to interact with the client's organization much more in order to develop a solution with, rather than for, the client. Although, for clarity, it is helpful to look at these models separately, it is important to bear in mind that, in reality, a single project may demand more than one of these styles.

The 'imperative' model of consulting is essentially where a team of consultants is commissioned by a client to examine a particular problem and where, in resolving it, the consultants mainly rely on gathering data on the problem, analyzing that data in relative isolation from the client and on a highly objective basis. To this extent, the imperative model was the original form of consulting – this was the approach adopted by Frederick Taylor and the other proponents of the Scientific School of Management – and it continues to be a very common method of operating today. Some firms, especially the strategy houses, offer this type of consulting and have constructed their differentiated brand around this style of working.

Imperative consulting is used to resolve problems which have one or more of the following characteristics:

- *Factual* – either there is a factual answer, or factual analysis will form the basis of the decision-making process.
- *Discrete* – it is possible to use data to understand the issues involved, something which might not be possible if the problem was particularly complex and open to a variety of ill-defined variables.
- *Finite* – an imperative approach provides a snapshot of a particular situation, it is less effective at addressing on-going issues where the circumstances change almost daily.
- *Technical* – that the resolution of the issue requires technical knowledge, usually of a particular process or system.

However, the strengths of the imperative approach – its objectivity, its focus – are also its weakness. In the first place, the data gathering and subsequent analysis often ignores information which is not easy to assimilate; in other words, there is often a risk in analytical assignments that the data which is gathered to fit an initial hypothesis can only ever prove or disprove that hypothesis, and not suggest more lateral solutions. Secondly, almost all business situations are open and complex; an imperative approach can only handle such complexity by essentially ignoring or simplifying it (thus, even a very well-prepared market valuation may prove wrong in practice). Thirdly – and most importantly – facts may not always be enough to change things in an organization. It is possible for a consultant to write an excellent report, highlighting a clear action plan, based on an objective assessment of the facts involved, but for his or her report never to be implemented because either the facts used were not sufficient to galvanize the client's organization, or because the client's organization was motivated by other factors (the subjective vision of a small number of senior executives, for example), rather than objective data.

By contrast, the emphasis in facilitative consulting falls on the process by which the consulting is done, as much as on its output, the premise being that a client's organization should be consulted with, rather than be presented with a *fait accompli*.

In a facilitative project, consultants work with members of the client's staff to discuss, investigate and design solutions to the problems at hand. This can range from working very closely with a small number of individuals, to having to engage the collective intelligence and enthusiasm of a much larger group. A key component is that the consultant uses the relationships and trust he or she builds, to obtain a more profound understanding of the issues, rather than accepting information at its face value. The facilitative consultant will therefore look for the underlying causes to a problem, rather than the symptoms with which it manifests itself; he or she will listen as much as they talk (by contrast, imperative consulting is very much about talking at clients), and will explore lateral options rather than following through a pre-specified framework.

It is an approach which is clearly suited to confused and complex situations, the nature of which cannot be captured by conventional data sources. During the course of an assignment, the facilitative consultant is able to access more sources of data (many of which will be informal) as well as gauge the views of people within the client organization – both aspects are crucial to the success of difficult assignments.

Facilitative consulting has proved invaluable over the last decade as it has been seen as the industry's response to the frequent criticism that consultants do not engage constructively with client organizations, and tend to impose preconceived ideas on very different situations. It has also allowed consultants to deal with much more complex and lengthy assignments than pure analytical consulting would. There are, however, some significant drawbacks to this approach:

- ☐ Facilitative consulting is highly subjective: it supplements objective data with the personal impressions of consultants, and these may unduly influence the outcome of an assignment. Subjective input is also more difficult to defend to clients, and can mean that the consultants' recommendations are dismissed.

- ☐ Some aspects of facilitative consulting are not dissimilar from counselling. For untrained consultants, there is a danger that they may be asked to tackle problems which are beyond the consultants' power to help resolve (personal problems of the client, for example): by airing such issues but leaving them unresolved, the consultants may be making an already bad situation worse.

- ☐ Clients want to receive value for money from consultants. Often – and this is an unfortunate repercussion – this translates into the consultants providing new information or telling an organization to do something; it neglects the softer side of consulting where the consultant may be working with a client's own staff to help them develop a solution which they can accept. Thus, process consulting may inadvertently expose an assignment team to the charge that they have not contributed anything tangible to the organization.

The scope of the impact

Along with understanding the type of impact you want a consulting firm to have, you need to ask yourself what the scope of that impact should be. There are two extreme answers here, and a whole host of possibilities that lie on the continuum between the two:

- ☐ Do you want the consultants to have an impact at an individual level? In many cases, you may be looking for advice or information, perhaps to help you make a difficult decision. You may be an executive trying to steer a company through a difficult period. You may be a senior manager weighing up various options which, for good reasons, you do not want to discuss with your immediate colleagues. Whatever the cause, you are primarily looking to a consultant to play quite an intimate role, being your personal adviser, perhaps even a mentor or coach. You are expecting the consultant to have an impact, but on you and what you do, or on your immediate team.

- ☐ Do you want the consultants to have an impact at an organizational level? The opposite of the very close, personal way of working described above is to want the consultants you hire to have as wide an impact as possible. You may be hiring them to restructure your organization, or to change its fundamental ways of working.

In reality, of course, every project consists of an element of both: even the biggest corporate restructuring projects have their managers who need one-to-one support. But, when thinking about the kind of consultants you should hire, it is important to understand just what the balance of these two elements is likely to be: a consultant who is good at building relationships at a personal level may not be very effective when it comes to organizational change, and *vice versa*.

Putting these two points together – type and scope of impact – means that you have four essential choices when it comes to selecting the type of firm that is most appropriate for your circumstances (Figure 3.1).

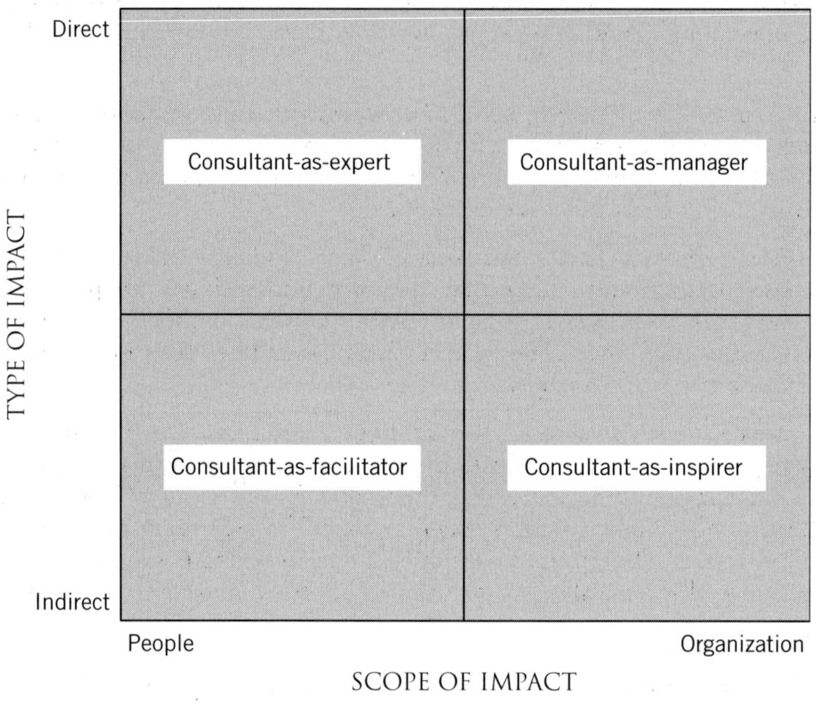

FIGURE 3.1: Segmenting consultants in terms of their intended type and scope of impact

- ☐ The role of the **consultant-as-expert** is to provide a small number of people (a board of directors, for example) with the information they require to make a decision or effect a change. As such, the consultants have a direct, but comparatively limited impact. For some consulting firms, especially in the strategy arena, this is their dominant mode of working: they are excellent at marshalling large volumes of data and identifying the key lessons (move into this new market, withdraw that product, ignore this threat but react to that one), but not necessarily so good at letting clients think for themselves or engaging with a wide audience throughout the client's organization.

- ☐ By contrast, the **consultant-as-facilitator** has a much less direct impact. His or her job is to help clients help themselves, and their attention is largely directed at individual client managers – the role of the executive coach or mentor. This type of consulting is now almost exclusively done by small, specialist firms, often by independent consultants who have themselves held senior positions in industry and can therefore identify with the issues their clients face on a daily basis. Large firms find it much harder to replicate the skills profile required to do this kind of work on the quasi-industrial scale they require.

☐ When it comes to having an impact on the client's organization as a whole, the **consultant-as-manager** effectively takes the law into his or her own hands. Rather than trying to act through an intermediary (a team of senior executives), the consultant-as-manager has a direct impact on an organization by taking over part of its operations – running a particular business process, or a specific business unit. The consultant may be seconded into the client's organization, or the process may be seconded out to the consulting firm (outsourcing), but, either way, the consultant has taken over responsibility for making something happen – a line management role, if you like. Again, there are consulting firms that excel at this type of work: rather than offering to work 'in partnership' with you, they provide you with an opportunity to off-load a particular problem – often a problem where you can see little competitive advantage to be gained from solving it yourself.

☐ Finally, and least commonly, is the **consultant-as-inspirer** – the consultant who uses the indirect mode of working of the consultant-as-facilitator but is able to communicate the ideas on a much grander scale, trying to galvanize an organization to act by presenting it with certain catalytic experiences or ideas. This is essentially a leadership role – providing an organization with a sense of purpose and direction without being overly prescriptive about the means of achieving it. It is rare in consulting: first, because the majority of people capable of playing this role are, not surprisingly, found doing it in industry, not talking about it in consulting firms; and second, because it would be a very high risk activity for a consulting firm to be involved in. That is not to say that consultants do not ever do this: there are specialist, usually small firms experimenting with different communication and change management models, replacing the traditional consulting process with, for example, semi-theatrical productions aimed at creating a cathartic change in an organization, but such techniques are far from gaining widespread acceptance among clients and consultants.

GLOBAL OR LOCAL?

The 1990s saw the globalization of the consulting industry, at least on paper. In response to the increasing internationalization of its biggest and most important clients, large, well-established consulting firms have created global infrastructures capable of moving expertise and resources wherever clients need them. Globalization became a question of credibility: how could a consulting firm advise a global client if it was not global itself?

The feedback from clients is that coverage does matter, but perhaps not in the ways that consulting firms generally expect. 'When we say world-class specialists, we mean world-class specialists,' said one client, 'We do not expect that person to be based round the corner. To be honest, we would probably be worried if they were, because we would not believe it. In our experience, it is better to go to where the experts are, than assume that the local firm will be as good.' But clients are also aware that, when it comes to implementing the ideas of an 'international' expert, there are many national issues to consider. You cannot underestimate the complexity of international markets: different patterns of consumer behaviour, different regulatory issues, different labour markets all mean that you have to develop a distinct approach for each new country you move into. One size definitely does not fit all.

When it comes to considering this issue, clients need three types of help:

1 They need advice in designing their international strategy, ensuring that it has the flexibility and scalability to be applied to one country or several. What matters here is

being able to pull in international experts and to draw on a wide range of analogous situations when the occasion demands it.

2 They need practical assistance in establishing their physical presence in different parts of the world. For smaller clients, this may take the form of people on the ground capable of acting as interim managers. For larger organizations, it is likely to be in the area of change management that such assistance is required. It is all very well for the international hot-shot to dream up a world-beating strategy, but he or she is unlikely to be the person best equipped either to understand the implications of the strategy for the people in the client's organization involved in adapting the strategy to local requirements, or to help with the process of implementation itself.

3 They need access to consistent skills and knowledge across the world. These are typically multinational corporations looking to roll out a common system or set of processes across different countries, where the priority is to ensure compliance, and where a global consulting firm can help to overcome local variations.

It is therefore important to decide exactly what type of global coverage – if any – is necessary for a given project. Going back to the eight reasons for hiring consultants listed in Chapter 2 suggests:

- ☐ The 'content' reasons why clients hire consultants – because they want access to an outside view, to information and analysis, and to innovative thinking – are largely independent of geography. It is rare that intellectual capital and skills of this sort can be distributed across a large network of people: they are much more likely to exist in discrete – 'world-class' – pockets of expertise. Clients looking for this kind of assistance should expect to have to go to such pockets or bring the people involved to them.

- ☐ Increasingly, the 'process' reasons for hiring consultants – to acquire a road map for delivery or to give a project momentum – do require at least an international network. As business itself become internationalized, most substantial consulting assignments will inevitably have some cross-border components. These may range from a minimum of communicating the changes being planned by one subsidiary to others to rolling out a common system and/or process across all the subsidiaries of a corporation worldwide. For consulting firms involved in this kind of work, being able to ensure consistency and coverage in different parts of the world is crucial.

- ☐ The 'people' reasons why clients hire consultants – industry or issue-specific skills, and generalist resources – fall somewhere between these two extremes. Industry and issue-specific skills may well occur in pockets of expertise in different parts of the world, perhaps as a result of a strong local industry or national regulatory imperatives. However, it is also important that such knowledge is related back to a client's unique circumstances – something that requires extensive local knowledge. Similarly, generalist resources may be locally-based or imported from another country, depending on the nature of the work involved. Change management-related work, for example, because it involves a high degree of personal interaction is usually better done by native speakers and by people who understand the cultural nuances of a particular environment.

BRANDED OR INDIVIDUALISTIC?

Large consulting firms have poured millions of dollars over the last ten years into creating brands for themselves: almost all now supplement their expensive brochures with even more expensive press and television advertising campaigns. But at the other end of the scale are all the individual consultants who rely largely on word-of-mouth to recommend them to clients. Each business model adds value, each has its drawbacks, but which should you choose when?

'No one ever got fired for buying IBM' was a common phrase in IT management circles in the 1980s, and safety is still a very important fact in choosing between brands and non-brands. Clients who pick a big firm know both that their decisions are unlikely to be questioned by their colleagues, and that the consultants' reputation will proceed them and may make their job easier – because people are more likely to respect and listen to them. Of course, this can backfire in an organization where people are highly cynical about their managers, a decision to bring in highly visible, 'branded' consultants will be treated with the same derision as other internal pronouncements, and the consultants may find cooperation hard to achieve because they are regarded as being on the managers' side in a them-and-us confrontation.

There are drawbacks to being branded, too, when you look at the internal workings of consulting firms. Like any other brand-owners, branded consultancies have a reputation to protect; this will make them less likely to take on work outside their areas of core competence (a good thing) or to take risks (which may be a bad thing). To protect their brands, consulting firms also have to be consistent. This is no bad thing if you are responsible for, say, a food brand – it means that you will work hard to ensure that quality standards are rigorously adhered to, that storage and distribution are hygienic, and so on; consistency and quality are synonymous. But this is not necessarily the case in consulting. A consulting firm undertaking an identical process again and again has to be consistent, and the quality of its work should rightly be judged in terms of this consistency. But the same way of thinking works less well when applied to a highly variable process, such as formulating strategy. Consistency here does not equal quality: if every strategy was the same, no one would achieve a competitive advantage. In these circumstances a strong brand could be a hindrance, as it could deter the individual consulting firms from making radical suggestions, through fear of damaging their collective brand.

However, it is important to remember that individuals can be branded, and firms can be individualistic. The difference here is not so much between the very large firms and the very small, but between two different approaches. The branded approach offers safety and consistency, but not necessarily inventive thinking or experimentation: it is more likely to mean that you have to fit in with the way in which the consulting firm wants to do something. The individualistic approach offers experimentation and innovation, and is more prepared to rethink what it does to meet your needs, but it is higher risk.

In general, branded firms offer a greater guarantee of consistency; their familiarity is also an advantage. The input of a branded firm is typically useful where the commissioning part of the client organization wants to encourage agreement or enforce compliance – they are telling the rest of the organization what to do, whether at a strategic level ('we will now enter this market') or at a more operational one ('we are going to start using this system'). By contrast, consulting from more individualist firms is more appropriate when a consultative approach is required – the part of the organization hiring consultants is less eager to *tell* people in the rest of the organization what to do, than it wants to develop ideas jointly with them.

SUMMARY

1 Consultants can look very similar. Indeed, there is considerable pressure within the industry to foster homogeneity and make differentiation difficult (if a consulting firm looks too different, it ceases to look like a consulting firm).

2 Many of the conventional ways in which clients have segmented consulting firms are no longer relevant in today's market.

3 There are, however, four fundamental ways in which you should be looking to distinguish between consulting firms that on paper, even in the flesh, look alike:

- ☐ Do they offer an integrated, soup-to-nuts approach, or are they specialists that will work only in very specific areas?
- ☐ In terms of the impact they have, are they experts, facilitators, inspirers or managers?
- ☐ Do they have a global network of offices, or have one or a small number of offices in one country or region?
- ☐ Does the firm has a well-recognized individual brand which provides you with some guarantee of consistency and quality, or are they a group of individuals, each of whom has a strong 'personal brand'?

CHAPTER 4

PRESENTATIONS, PROPOSALS AND PITCHES

Most books on consulting proposals are written from the consultants' perspective. Typically, they focus on how consultants sell work, not how clients buy it; they work on the assumption that consultants have a pre-defined service that they are trying to sell, rather than that clients have a problem which they are trying to fix; such books' ultimate aim is to help the consultant win more work, not to help the client buy better consulting.

Much of what has happened in the consulting industry over the last decade challenges that approach. Clients have become considerably more sophisticated, and less willing to be palmed off with a standard approach that takes little account of their particular circumstances; their attention has shifted from buying a service to buying a solution. The selling of consultancy has changed too. The days of the professional consultant doubling as an amateur salesperson have gone in all but the smallest consulting firms, often to be replaced by dedicated account managers and trained salespeople, backed up by sizeable marketing campaigns. Twenty years ago, a client might have expected a proposal from a consulting firm to focus on the technical issues of a project and the individual qualifications of those involved. Today, proposals have become polarized between hard issues (such as value for money and tangible outcomes) and soft issues (such as cultural fit between the client and consultants, and communications). These issues do not supersede the technical points, but add to them; thus, the factors which differentiated a consulting firm in the 1980s are the 'givens' of the new century (Table 4.1).

The role of the proposal has also changed, from being a dry summary of what a firm can do, to something that provides demonstrable proof of a firm's capabilities; what might have been a simple factual description of the background to a project 20 years ago, has now become an opportunity for a consulting firm to showcase its expert knowledge and analytical skills by providing the client with new insights. 'Look,' the document says, 'if we can give you these ideas simply on the basis of a few conversations with you, think what we will be able to do when we are working with you.' Moreover, proposals are rarely allowed to stand alone these days; to reinforce the message, they are accompanied by presentations, meetings, iterations around the project, its content and scope.

1980s	1990s	2000s
• Technical approach	• Expertise/experience/competences	• Reassurance that the consultants understand the brief
• Project plan	• Understanding of client needs	• Communications
• Project management	• Interaction with the client	• Tangibility of services
• Staffing	• Contractual/administrative compliance	• Cultural fit
• Individual qualifications		• Differentiation
		• Value for money
		• Outcomes

TABLE 4.1: The cumulating content of proposals

At the heart of all of this is the fact that the distinction between the periods before and after a sale have become blurred. Increased competition, certainly where the largest clients and the biggest projects are concerned, means that consulting firms have to make a significant investment in building relationships, researching clients and coordinating global business development plans, if they are to stand any chance of seeing off their rivals. This, in turn, creates a level of expectation from clients which all consulting firms have to meet.

But a greater investment in selling does not necessarily help clients to buy. Indeed, you could argue that it does precisely the opposite. As discussed in the previous chapter, it is notoriously difficult to achieve, let alone sustain, differentiation in the consulting industry, and the more that consultants try to match what their competitors are doing in terms of the sales process, the less easy it is to find areas in which any one firm is truly distinctive.

So how should clients interpret proposals and sales pitches? How should they evaluate them?

A GOOD SELL, NOT A HARD SELL

Good consultants never have to sell themselves: they let you, the client, do that for them by providing you with the information you require to make a decision and the confidence to feel that that decision is the right one. Those closing pages headed 'Why choose us?' inserted in so many proposals, should be useful only in so far as they are a summary of the conclusions you, the client, has already reached. If you learn something new or unexpected in these last moments, then the proposal or presentation which preceded them has failed to do its job properly.

So what should you look for? It is tempting to evaluate proposals as proposals, and presentations as presentations, and to assume that someone who can write a good proposal is necessarily a good consultant. In fact, the skills involved in writing a proposal or making a presentation can be quite distinct from those required in a consulting. What you need is evidence from the sales material that a particular company will be the most capable of resolving your issue. Such evidence falls into three categories (Figure 4.1): first, there are issues related to your particular circumstances and the extent to which the consultancy is both sensitive to, and knowledgeable of, these; the second category of issues relate to the consulting process; and the third to the expected interaction between client and consultant.

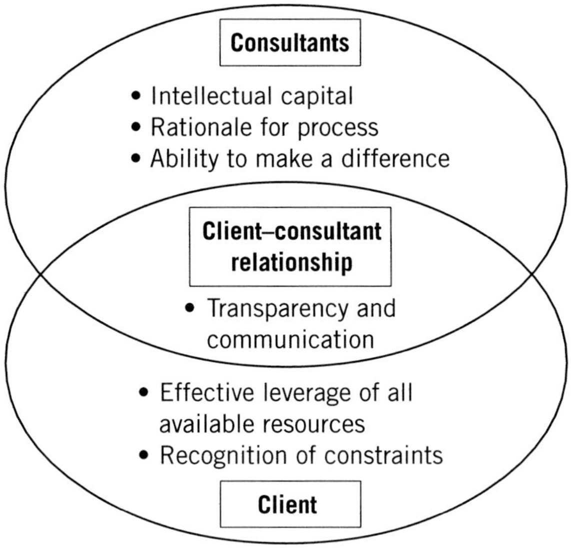

FIGURE 4.1: What should clients look for in a proposal or sales presentation?

Intellectual capital

One of the main problems with the consulting industry is that people – clients and consultants alike – do not tend to think in terms of pure intellectual capital. The traditional unit in which you buy consultancy is people, and it is therefore hard to separate people from ideas.

It is obvious but important: whether you are buying the highest level of strategic consulting, or an in-depth expertise in a specific area, it is crucial that you evaluate the quality of intellectual capital on offer. A good sales pitch will demonstrate the calibre of the consulting firm by showing that they have a body of expertise which they can leverage on a client's behalf, plus – and this is crucial – the ability to demonstrate just how this knowledge can be applied. If nothing else, the boom and bust of the e-business years has rightly taught clients to be very suspicious of management ideas not grounded in practical reality, and the lessons of this should be apparent in any proposal. After all, if a consultant cannot demonstrate this now, in the comparatively controllable circumstances of a sales pitch, what confidence can a client have that he or she will be able to do so during an actual project?

A 'good' sell will demonstrate some or all of the following:

- ☐ External information about how your issue has affected other, similar organizations.
- ☐ Analysis of the factors that either helped or hindered the ability of these analogous organizations to resolve the issue.
- ☐ Interpretation of the extent to which these factors apply to your organization.
- ☐ An ability to communicate the conclusions in a way that will make your organization listen.

Rationale for process

There should be a direct and consistent link between the intellectual context to a consulting project as the consulting firm sees it, and the methodology and resources it requires to complete it. Too many proposals and presentations are compartmentalized: there is no causal link between the nature of the problem faced by a client and the means by which a consulting firm plans to resolve it; brilliant analysis is followed by a humdrum approach and a generic project plan. A sales presentation or proposal should give a clear message: 'This is your issue, and these are the attributes of the issue which are specific to you. In order to resolve this issue, and taking account of its unique characteristics, we will approach the project in a specific way. This specific approach requires, in turn, specific resources.' If you find yourself asking 'why are they suggesting this?' and 'what value does this add?' then that message is not clear enough.

The best proposals/presentations not only make this message very clear, but they also ensure that every aspect of the material, down to the itemization of fees and skills, fits into this single, consistent framework. Every word makes a difference.

Ability to make a difference

Organizations cannot live on intellectual capital alone. Every client and consultant has heard of projects that have failed despite brilliant, insightful analysis, or proven technical skills – failed because they resulted in no lasting change in the client's organization. Behavioural theorists describe consulting as an 'intervention', but in what way have consultants intervened if a client can see no difference between the organization the consultants walked into, and the one they walk out of? Of course, gauging this from written or presented material can be extremely difficult. To supplement this, you should consider asking:

- ☐ Does any of the material provided make you think differently? Perhaps the consulting firm has provided you with new information about the external or internal context to the project; they may have commissioned special research, even on a small scale, to tell you something you did not know. Alternatively, they may be providing you with a structured approach which contains steps that you had not considered, and which will have an impact on your thinking now.

- ☐ In terms of the work carried out by the consulting firm, what have the outcomes been, not just immediately afterwards, but a year or two post-completion? To what extent did the consulting firm contribute directly or indirectly to those outcomes, or is it the client who really deserves the credit?

- ☐ What will happen if you do not hire a particular firm?

Transparency and communication

There is much talk at the moment in some areas of the broader consulting market, such as outsourcing, of open book accounting, in which each side demonstrates to the other the costs which it incurs. Of course, the issue is not so much about finances as about trust and control: trust – each side can feel more confident that it is not being exploited by the other; control – openness reduces the potentially opaque machinations of consultancy, making consultants more accountable to their clients.

People tend to think of project control in terms of steering committees and reporting structures. These are fine in theory, but in practice even the most accountable system will fail if there is insufficient will on the part of the consulting firm or the client to make it work. If accountability is genuinely important to you, then you should be looking for evidence of a consulting firm's willingness to be transparent, even during the sales cycle. Does a firm's proposal/presentation:

- ☐ Provide you with a sufficient level of concrete detail about what the consulting process will involve, so that you feel you know what you are buying?
- ☐ Tell you what the consultants will be doing on the first day, the first week, the first month of the project?
- ☐ Make an effort to render the intangibility of much consulting as tangible as possible?
- ☐ Include some ideas on how the firm's contribution can be measured?
- ☐ Consider how the progress and outputs of the consulting project will be communicated to your organization?

Effective leverage of all available resources

Clients habitually complain that consultants are arrogant and exhibit little recognition that clients themselves may have something to contribute to the consulting process. Consultants seem to regard a consulting project as a black and white, all or nothing affair in which, once the decision has been taken to hire consultants, consultants are what is required. In some cases, this assumption may be entirely appropriate (see Chapter 2): there may be areas where a client organization either lacks the resources to do something or has no long-term interest in building up its own skills, in which case it makes good sense to use a consulting team. But it is much more common for clients to know something about aspects of a problem and to require help from consultants in other areas – specific skills, a structured approach to the issue, additional information not available internally.

What a consulting firm therefore needs to demonstrate is not just that they have the intellectual capital required and can apply it in such a way that will have a positive impact on your organization, but that that impact dovetails precisely with what you can do for yourself (another aspect of demonstrating that they can make a difference).

- ☐ Try dividing up the project into its component elements and working out what intellectual capital will be required for each component. What do you bring to the party? What do you want the consultants to bring?
- ☐ Analyse the extent to which the consultants you are evaluating can provide this intellectual capital. This may mean that you end up 'cherry-picking' as consultants often derisively describe it – but it does mean that you will receive a precise match with your needs.
- ☐ Compare your overall aims (both as you see them and as the consultants replay them to you) with those of the consultants in the project (as they define it). If they achieve their aims, will you achieve yours?

Recognition of constraints

'Scope-creep' is rightly one of clients' biggest concerns. This occurs when a consulting firm, hired to do one piece of work, gradually pushes back the boundaries of their area of focus, increasing the number of consultants on their team and charging fees over and above what had been originally agreed. Although money is frequently the motivation behind this, it is often also a consultant's perception that the root cause of a client's problem lies somewhere else, and needs to be fixed before the consultant can do his or her job properly – that, for example, a product is not selling well, not because the sales force lacks the skills to sell it effectively, but because it is a poorly designed product aimed at the wrong market. Scope-creep works in two directions: either laterally (consultants see that some other function within the client's organization is the source of the problem), or in time (consultants challenge a previous decision (the selection of a particular software package perhaps) and want to wind the clock back to correct it).

Whatever its motivation or form, scope-creep implies an unwillingness to accept the constraints of a particular situation. A client has asked consultants to do one thing, but the consultant, for selfish or unselfish reasons, wants to do something else. From a client's point of view, this is at best frustrating and at worst insulting. If there are constraints, you are probably already aware of them, and they may not be of your making. The remit given to a consulting firm is not so much to solve this problem in sterile laboratory conditions, where the perfect solution can be found, but to solve this problem as far as is practicably possible, given imperfect circumstances. If the consultants do not think they can solve it within these given limitations, then they should say so.

To avoid scope-creep, look through the proposals and presentations from consulting firms in order to identify signs that the consultants intend to respect the boundaries which you have drawn.

- ☐ Does the proposal clearly state your objectives?
- ☐ Have the aims of the project, and the consultants' role within it, been presented in such a way as to dovetail with your own aims?
- ☐ Is the consulting process to be undertaken sufficiently clearly defined and well-focused?
- ☐ Does the proposal contain a clear definition of the outputs from each stage of the project?
- ☐ Have the costs and timescales for the project been clearly defined and detailed?

EVALUATION CRITERIA

Many companies quite rightly use evaluation criteria to allow them to compare the different proposals of consulting firms on a more level playing field, and Table 4.2 gives an idea of how the key attributes of the 'good' sell described above could be analyzed in practice.

In practice, instead of providing a basis for discussion, such evaluation criteria often become the means by which executives justify their choice of firm in retrospect, and serve little purpose other than to legitimize the decision and provide some protection in case it proves to have been the wrong one. The manager fending off subsequent criticism can say, 'We did all the right things, we had a formal process. The fact that things have gone wrong does not mean we did not do our job properly – just that we were unlucky.'

There are problems, also, in taking such evaluation criteria too seriously. They can lead to the false assumption that it is possible to be absolutely scientific in assessing the sales material put together by consulting firms.

- External context
  - ☐ To what extent has external information provided by you been accurately captured?
  - ☐ Has new information been presented?
  - ☐ To what extent has this information been interpreted specifically in relation to your company?
  - ☐ What demonstrable insights into the external context have been made which enable you to think about your immediate environment in a new way?
  - ☐ Is there a clear framework of key points which provides the context into which the consulting project will fit?
- Internal context
  - ☐ To what extent has internal information provided by you been accurately captured?
  - ☐ Has the consulting firm made an effort to gather additional information about the internal context?
  - ☐ What demonstrable insights into the internal context have been made which enable you to think about your own organization in a new way?
- Aims and objectives
  - ☐ Clear framework of key points which provides the context into which the consulting project will fit
  - ☐ Clear statement of client's aims
  - ☐ Clear statement of the aims of the consulting project in the context of the client's aims
  - ☐ Match between client and consulting aims
- Approach proposed
  - ☐ Clearly stated structure
  - ☐ Extent to which there is an over-arching philosophy/rationale to the structure proposed
  - ☐ Extent to which the approach follows on from the context described
  - ☐ Extent to which the approach will achieve the aims of the project as described
  - ☐ Sufficient level of detail to give the client a tangible grasp on what will be involved in practice
  - ☐ Description of resources, and a reasonable guarantee that the people you have met during the buying process will be working on the project
  - ☐ Extent to which resources are related to project requirements
  - ☐ Extent to which benefits for clients are described
  - ☐ Extent to which the proposal differentiates the consulting firm
- Project management
  - ☐ Clear project structure and division of roles and responsibilities
  - ☐ Clear communications structure and reporting lines
  - ☐ Clearly stated outputs/deliverables/milestones
  - ☐ Clearly stated division of responsibility between the client and consulting firm
  - ☐ Project plan and breakdown of fees

TABLE 4.2: Suggested evaluation criteria

Both problems stem from seeing evaluation criteria as an end in their own right, rather than a means to an end. If you analyze both the characteristics and evaluation criteria listed in this chapter, they can all be reduced to one thing – confidence. Fundamentally, what clients need is confidence that the consulting firms they hire are capable of doing the best possible job. That confidence is not something which appears out of thin air, but is developed and reinforced by a thousand small details and nuances. If you like the look of a proposal, or you feel you can trust a consultant based on their manner in the presentation, the most important thing is to ask yourself why – why does one consultancy seem more trust-worthy than another? Why does one proposal make you feel more comfortable than another? If someone (a consultant), or something (a proposal or presentation), has given you confidence that you can make the right decision, where exactly does your confidence come from? Is it from the transparency of the proposal, or the sense the consultants have given you that they will respect your constraints? Is it because they have demonstrated a willingness to make good use of your own resources, or that you can see a logical connection between their perception of the context for the assignment and their approach to it? Finally and perhaps most fundamentally, has the proposal/presentation made a difference? Has it changed your approach or perception of the issue? If the proposal has made a difference, there is a fair chance that the consulting project will do so as well. Conversely, if you have not learnt much from the consultants during the sales cycle, it is unlikely that you will learn anything from them during an actual engagement.

SUMMARY

1 Clients may have become more sophisticated in the way in which they evaluate consultants' sales pitches in the last ten years, but consultants have also become more sophisticated in the way they sell.

2 A good consulting firm does not have to engage in a hard and explicit sell. Rather, the way in which a firm approaches the sales process tells clients a great deal about how the consulting firm will approach the actual project.

3 Good consulting sales pitches do not sell themselves, but make it easier for clients to make a purchase decision. As such, they should provide demonstrable proof of the attributes a client is seeking. A firm that cannot demonstrate its intellectual credentials, before the contract is signed, will probably not do so afterwards.

4 There are six key issues to consider when evaluating a proposal or watching a sales presentation by a consulting firm:

- ☐ The quality of thinking.
- ☐ The extent to which the approach proposed is the logical consequence of the unique set of circumstances which have led the client to decide to use consultancy.
- ☐ The extent to which the consulting firm makes a difference, even during the sales process.
- ☐ The willingness of the consulting firm to be transparent and treat communication between the client's people and the consultants with the seriousness with which it deserves.

☐ The extent to which the consulting firm is prepared to make good use of a client's existing resources.

☐ The clear recognition and acceptance of the client's constraints.

5 Be wary, however, of putting too much emphasis on strict evaluation criteria, as these are rarely as scientific as they appear. It is much better to ask the question: has this proposal or presentation changed anything? If it has not, it is unlikely that the consultants will do so when it comes to the actual project.

CHAPTER 5

FINDING THE OPTIMUM WORKING ARRANGEMENTS

What makes for a good working relationship between a client and a consultant? Many consulting projects have come to grief, not because the brief from the client was not clear, not because the consulting firm did not have the skills required, but simply because the two sides could not work effectively together.

The Management Consultancies Association's Statement of Best Practice (reproduced in the Appendix) highlights four general principles that underpin an effective working relationship between clients and consultants. Although aimed at public sector clients, these principles hold equally true so far as the private sector is concerned (Table 5.1).

CLIENTS	CONSULTANTS
Be truthful and constructive to, and easily contactable by, consultants and other stakeholders	Be truthful and constructive to, and easily contactable by, clients and other stakeholders.
Do not be defensive. The consultants are there to assist your organization.	Respond to the client's initial request and avoid second guessing the problem at an early stage.
Do not be afraid of providing too much information. Consultants would prefer this to lack of detail.	Always listen to the client's opinions first before explaining your own.
In general, ensure that risk lies with the entity with the greatest ability to manage that risk.	In general ensure that risk lies with the entity with the greatest ability to manage that risk.

TABLE 5.1: General principles from the MCA's Statement of Best Practice

Clearly, there are a multitude of factors here that have an impact; this chapter focuses on the four most crucial ones:

- ☐ Trust.
- ☐ Risk.
- ☐ Respect.
- ☐ Value for money.

Why are these so crucial? Because no consulting project can succeed if even one of these variables is missing. Without trust, there can be no frank debate, no challenge to the *status quo*, no willingness to admit that someone else is better qualified to do a specific job. Without respect, neither client nor consultant feels valued or understood; tensions mount, and compromises are made. Without value for money, each side feels resentful and unappreciated, and neither is willing to go the extra mile that so many consulting projects involve.

TRUST

David Maister is one of the world's most respected commentators on the professional services industry. In *The Trusted Advisor*[1] (coauthored with Charles Green and Robert Galford 1996), he argues that:

> ‘The trusted advisor relationship takes place between two individuals and is, therefore, highly personal in nature. It involves emotion as well as intellect. It is dynamic and fluid. Building a trusted advisor relationship involves not only straightforward discussion, rigorous decision-making, and conventional consultation, but also moments of revelation, late-night inspirations, odd actions of connection, and moments of epiphany. At its core, trust is about relationships. I will trust you if I believe that you are in this for the long haul, that you are not just trying to maximize the short-term benefit to you of each of our interactions. Trust is about reciprocity: you help me and I will help you. But I need to know that I can rely on you to do your part, and that our relationship is built upon shared values and principles.’

Maister makes the following important points about the nature of trust:

☐ **Trust grows, rather than just appears.** You may *dis*trust someone when you first meet them, but you are unlikely to trust them, as trust is something that requires time and familiarity to develop.

☐ **Trust presumes a two-way relationship.** It is tempting for a client to think that trust only goes in one direction – the client should trust the consultant. But the reverse is also true (how can a consultant be completely frank with a client who he or she does not trust?). Trust can never be unilateral.

☐ **Trust is not symmetrical.** Trust may be a two process, but the roles of 'trusting' and 'being trusted' are still quite different. At some points in the client relationship the balance may change; from being the person who trusts, the client may become the person who has to be trusted. 'Trust', Maister *et al* comment, 'is more like dancing. One person must lead, one must follow, if it is to work. If there is ambiguity about who is leading and who is following, then the dance collapses into (at best) two parallel exercises in solo movement.'

☐ **Trust is intrinsically about risk.** Risk is inherent in a consulting project (see also Chapter 6), but if there was not any risk, we would not need to trust anyone. As Maister *et al* point out:

> ‘Trust without risk is like cola without fizz; there is not much point to it. We don't "trust" the law of gravity, we assume it. If party A trusts that party B will do something, it means that party B could, in fact, do something different; conceivably might, in fact, do something different; but, because of the relationship, most likely will not do something different.’

[1] Simon and Schuster, 2000

☐ **Trust is both rational and emotional.** Trust is not irrational (it is not the same as having blind faith in something), but, at the same time, it is not wholly rational either (we do not need to 'trust' a traffic light to turn green because we can make a rational judgment that the probability is high that it will do so). In effect, we trust someone because they have given us 'reason' to do so, whether that takes the form of qualifications to do a particular piece of work, or because we have worked with them before.

Taken together, these five points can be translated into precepts which, if observed by both sides, will significantly help to build trust between clients and consultants. There needs to be a conscious process to develop trust. It is tempting to assume that you trust someone (client or consultant) because you had a positive gut feel about them when you first met them – and we all tend to judge people by first impressions. But both clients and consultants need to work hard to resist this temptation, because it is often a source of disappointment. As Maister points out, trust is both a rational and irrational process – making a kneejerk decision about someone is much more about having blind faith in them (because we are not in a position to know what they can and cannot do), than it is about trust. Instead, it is much better to take a cautious, even downbeat view to start with, and then use every opportunity to work together as a much more effective way of building trust. By working together, you build up a reliable picture of people's strengths and weaknesses which you can accommodate in practice (no one is good at everything). It is like the traffic lights – you can build up a picture of their predictability.

Another factor that comes through clearly from Maister's analysis is that trust is a two-way relationship. Trust is often thought of as being something clients have to feel about consultants – but it needs to be equally applied the other way round. Indeed, it is hard for a consultant to be seen to be trustworthy from the client's perspective, if the consultant has not already felt comfortable with the client. Consultants expend considerable time and effort to obtain a client's trust, both during the sales process and the subsequent project, but there is very little onus on clients to reciprocate. In fact, a good case could be made for suggesting that consultants put clients through some sort of vetting process, equivalent to that which they have to go through themselves. As a client, ask yourself why the consultants which you have hired should trust you. If you have asked them to provide references from previous clients, wouldn't it make sense to allow them to talk to consulting firms which you have worked with in the past, who might be able to tell the consulting firm what your strengths and weaknesses are in this respect, so that the new consulting firm can take these into account?

RISK

Trust, as David Maister points out, is indivisible from risk. Indeed, trust is what has to be present because there is a risk. And risk – post-Enron, post-September 11, post the dot.com debacle – is an enormous issue. But we run the risk of forgetting that trust is a virtue we have made from necessity – if we could take all risks away, then we would have no need to trust anyone. Equally, we should not rely on trust being a complete panacea, and forget we should do what we can to mitigate the risk itself.

Risk has always been inherent in a consulting project, just as it is in any other form of business transaction or relationship, but there is a widespread perception that things are becoming riskier. 'If you'd told us 12 months ago that our auditor would go out of business, we'd have laughed at you', said one client. 'If you told us that our telephone company would go out of business, we'd have shown you the door. Both of those things have happened.' Not surprisingly, this organization, like most other large corporations is now carrying out a process of working out which suppliers – whether cleaners or software manufacturers, banks or utility providers – they are most dependent on, and going through some type of due diligence evaluation of them to assess their long-term reliability.

Nor is risk itself the problem. There have always been buyers for high-risk shares, just as there have always been backers for high-risk projects, because of the potential for high return. The problem lies in not being able to put a price on risk. If you can value the up and downsides to a particular risk, then you can take a rational business decision whether or not to accept that risk. If you are risk averse, you may decide this is an opportunity you want to pass on; if you are more risk tolerant, then you may decide to take a punt, but if you cannot gauge either your exposure or the size of the prize, then you probably will not make a decision at all.

From the point of view of a client hiring a consulting firm, you face a multitude of project-specific risks. Will the project be delivered on time and within the agreed budget? Will it yield the anticipated benefits to the business? Risks such as these are not qualitatively different from the risks you would have faced, had you decided to staff the project internally: they are discussed in more detail in Chapter 6. But, by bringing in an external, third party you clearly incur an over-arching risk as a result of the supplier-customer (in this case, consultant-client) relationship. A consulting firm has commercial goals of its own, some of these may coincide with your goals (both sides gain from a successful project), but some may not. You can see what is going on in your organization in a way that you cannot 'see into' a consulting firm, however long you've worked with it or however well you think you know it. Bringing in consultants to help, especially with large-scale, 'mission-critical' projects requires trust because it involves risks – risks that the relationship won't work out, that the consulting firm isn't equipped to do the job, that the consultants don't listen to you or give you what you want, that you will not be able to hold the consultant accountable in the event that something goes wrong or needs to be changed.

Although it is never possible to eliminate these risks entirely, there are three key principles which are worth bearing in mind.

- ☐ **Identify the risks.** Some projects – those that will have a concrete and quantifiable impact (the delivery of a new system, for example), those that take place in a rapidly changing business environment, or which require a very high level of specialist knowledge – are more risky than others. Working out what these risks are from the outset is a fundamental and unavoidable first step in working out how to minimize their impact.

- ☐ **Attribute the risks to their rightful owners.** There is nothing worse that being responsible for getting something done which you lack the capacity to get done – and that applies to clients and consultants alike. Both sides must therefore agree who will have control over what aspects of a project prior to its commencement, so that responsibility for managing the risks associated with those aspects can be assigned to the appropriate party. It is just as unfair for clients to try and make consultants bear all of the risk as it is for consultants to try to carry none of it.

- ☐ **Be transparent.** As we have already seen, risk is much less of a problem than unpriceable risk. What exactly are the financial and non-financial costs of the risks you and your consulting partner face? You will not be able to answer this question (or, indeed, identify the risks and attribute ownership of them) without being open and without asking the consultants you work with to be open as well. 'Open-book' arrangements are rapidly becoming mandatory when it comes to large-scale outsourcing and IT projects, and there is a good argument for extending the same principles

RESPECT

One of the main reasons why clients quite rightly resent the use of consultants is that consultants are often arrogant and treat client staff as if they are at best of little use, and at worst an obstacle to be overcome. A psychologist might attribute this arrogance to insecurity: starting a new job is always a stressful experience and this is what consultants have to do again and again, month after month. Each time they start a new project for a new client, they face what may be an uphill struggle to establish their personal credibility and elicit cooperation.

At the heart of both of these problems lies a perceived lack of respect for each side. The client thinks that consultants are overpaid know-it-alls in sharp suits and flashy cars. The consultant thinks client staff are losers, otherwise they would be consultants too. This lack of respect stems ultimately from ignorance – ignorance of the positive contribution *each* side can make to a project. The working assumption is that such contributions are mutually exclusive: either the client can add value or the consultant, not both together. In other words, clients and consultants (at least, when it comes to working side-by-side on the same project) are in competition with each other. In fact, such ignorance is two-fold: the client and the consultant are not just ignorant of the value that the other might bring, but they are also uncertain about the value which they bring. The client's project manager may not have been clear why he has allocated people to a project; the consultants may not have been fully briefed by those involved in winning the business. The client staff might think, 'the project manager has hired consultants because he does not think we are up to the job'; the consultants think, 'I've got to prove my worth by changing or disagreeing with the people around me.'

VALUE FOR MONEY

The client–consultant relationship is not just about trust, respect and shared risk – it is also about money. Consultants used to be paid according to the amount of time they spent on a project and the direct costs they incurred during it – 'time and materials'. But this method of remuneration has several disadvantages.

- ☐ It can feel like writing a blank cheque. How much will the project actually cost? Can we afford the final bill?
- ☐ This means that the consultant, not the client, is in control. What happens if circumstances change?
- ☐ It puts the consulting firm under little pressure to be efficient. Why incentive is there for the consultants to complete the work more quickly?
- ☐ It provides no positive reward for completing a project. Why should consultants go the extra mile?

These problems are now widely recognized, and the last ten years have seen dramatic changes in the way in which clients remunerate consulting firms. While some approaches have proved more successful (and more sustainable) than others, they all represent attempts by the client to extract a greater and more visible commitment from the consulting firm to the clients' aims and objectives.

Fixed price contracts

The initial response of clients to the problems highlighted above was to demand that the fees which a consulting firm could expect to earn from a given contract should be fixed. Although this is now an accepted way of working, fixed price contracts are problematic because of the frequent difficulties involved in being precise about exactly what work is covered by a specific amount of money. Clients' needs often change during the course of a project through no side's particular fault, and consulting firms have to protect themselves against making an open-ended commitment in which they could stand to lose a considerable amount of money if circumstances change. To mitigate this risk, consulting firms try to be very clear about what is covered by the fixed price – changes then have to be paid for separately. To this extent, fixed price contracts are satisfactory neither from the client's nor the consulting firm's perspective: often changes about the scope and nature of a project deteriorate into arguments about bureaucratic niceties.

Success fees/contingency pricing

A more significant step forward has been to tie consulting firms' payments to the delivery of specific results – for example, the completion of a project by a given date or an improvement in a pre-specified business metric. Success fees have the added advantage of making the goals of a project visible to both sides and encourage collaborative working towards these ends. However, they can also be difficult to implement where those goals are hard to quantify or where there are a number of variables which affect their realization, only some of which are under the control of the consulting firm. Why should a consultancy allow itself to be held to a goal when some of the critical success factors are outside its control? Moreover, unless carefully defined, success fees can lead to short-term thinking: everyone's minds will tend to be focused on the immediate goal, not a long-term business improvement. Thus, the consulting firm may concentrate on delivering a system, not on ensuring that the system is capable of delivering the anticipated business benefits. Chapter 6 makes the point that the control of any project comes down to three issues – time, money and quality – and that project managers often have to make trade-offs between them. To be effective therefore, success criteria in consulting projects need to be defined in all three ways: the time taken to complete the project; the costs incurred in doing so; and the extent to which the final product (whatever form this takes) delivers the business benefits expected. Focusing on the first two (but not the third) leads to short-term thinking, with corners being cut in order to finish on time and on budget. Focusing on the third (at the expense of the first two) can result in a project going significantly over time and budget.

Equity stake

During the height of the 1998–2000 e-business boom, it became comparatively common for consulting firms to accept payment in the form of stock in a client company. For the entrepreneurs involved, what better way could there be to access consulting skills without having to pay cash? And what better way of tying a consulting company into the long term than by rewarding it according to the overall success of the project? In practice, the problems with this approach were legion, for both sides. Clients had to give away large slices of their stock in order to obtain the services they needed, which reduced their ability to manoeuvre in the future. Consulting firms found that their ability to affect a company's share was small compared to, for example, the vagaries of the international stock market. Although taking an equity stake in a venture is still something that many consulting firms say they do in theory, the number of instances where it actually happens has been vastly reduced.

However, there are two practical problems attacked to these approaches. If all projects involved putting in one application in one area of an organization in a short period of time, then it would be easy to attribute success and failure, but this is not the case. The most complex, far-reaching projects are also the ones where it is hardest to quantify success or identify clear milestones; perhaps there are too many variables to be able to say with certainty what effect the consulting firm has had (or not had), or the outputs may remain highly intangible or have to be gauged over a very long term (a business transformation project, for example). But the irony is that these are often the projects that clients are most eager to pay for using some type of incentive-related payment structure – precisely because their outcome is uncertain. They want to reduce the uncertainty of the project, not in absolute terms, but by shifting the uncertainty from themselves to their consultants. This would be workable if it were not for the fact that the risks involved in this shift are rarely recognized. Thus, it is not untypical for a client to make the case for a contingency fee structure in principle, but then baulk when the consulting firm makes a case for increasing their potential reward to match their higher level of risk. Consultants often comment that they have been willing to take, say, a percentage of the operational savings found, only for the client to pull out of the arrangement (and revert to a conventional time and materials or fixed price contract) when the latter realizes how big a fee they could stand to pay in the event that the project is highly successful.

There is a have-your-cake-and-eat-it mentality evident here: clients quite reasonably want consultants to take some of the risks but are unwilling to reward them for doing so. Contingency pricing may work, even in the most difficult circumstances, but there has to be an upside for the consultants who take such projects on, as well as a downside.

As with the other foundations of a good client–consultant relationship already discussed – trust and respect – a genuine sea-change with regard to value for money is required on both sides.

SUMMARY

1 An effective working relationship between a client and a consultant primarily depends on three factors: trust, respect, and value for money.

2 Trust is not something that emerges by accident or gut feel (blind faith), but requires time, effort and – most importantly – an opportunity to work side-by-side. However, clients tend to think of trust as a one-way process – they have to trust the consultant – and do not put much effort into enabling consultants to trust them.

3 Consultants are often rightly accused of arrogance – something that, fundamentally, indicates a lack of respect for the value a client may be able to add. Lack of respect is, in turn, fed by ignorance: in many client–consultant relationships the two sides are in implicit competition with each other because the precise roles to be played by *all* the individuals involved have not been explained sufficiently clearly. Both clients and consultants need to invest more time and effort in doing this, to maximize their mutual effectiveness.

4 Long-term client dissatisfaction, not so much with the overall level of fees paid to consultants, as with the value for money (or lack of it) they represent, has led both clients and consultants to look at alternative payment terms. However, clients are often most keen to ask for such arrangements in the projects least suitable for them and are unwilling to share the potential rewards, along with the risks.

PART 2

MAXIMIZING THE VALUE OF CONSULTANTS

CHAPTER 6

MANAGING CONSULTING PROJECTS

Consulting projects are no different from internal projects: they need to be managed. However, they are different in some of the ways in which they are managed. This chapter looks at the key aspects of project management and highlights the main areas where a consulting project differs from an internal one.

PROJECT INITIATION

Like any other project, a consulting engagement which gets off to a bad start is difficult to turn around. Not only has time and money been lost, but vital credibility too, both among members of the project team (who become demoralized) and in the wider organization (which becomes sceptical).

In a well-managed consulting project, much of the project's terms of reference will have been mapped out during the sales process, particularly in terms of:

- ☐ A statement of the objectives.
- ☐ A definition of the project's scope.
- ☐ An agreed timetable.
- ☐ A description of the overall program of work.
- ☐ A definition of the roles and responsibilities of both the client and consultancy.
- ☐ Deliverables and outputs.

Of these, perhaps the most critical are the objectives. In any project, the objectives provide direction and a focus on results; they are the basis on which work plans and resource schedules are developed, and they are vital in communicating the purpose of the project and thus motivating those involved. Indeed, clear objectives play an especially important role in consulting projects, because they ensure that everyone involved is working on the same set of assumptions and provide a shared sense of purpose, even identity, for people who have not worked together before. For the objectives to achieve all of these things, they need to be:

- ☐ Measurable.
- ☐ Achievable.
- ☐ Consistent and aligned to the client's overall business objectives.
- ☐ Understandable by, and communicated to, all those involved.

But the process of buying and selling consultancy tends to concentrate on the positive attributes of a project – the consultants trying to win the work will inevitably have been upbeat, trying to raise a client's enthusiasm and commitment, rather than depressing them by looking too closely at the potential downsides. The project initiation phase therefore provides an opportunity to explore the possible risks in more depth. For large-scale projects, this will mean drawing up a risk management plan, based on assessing the probability that a given problem will occur and its impact should it occur, and reacting accordingly (Figure 6.1).

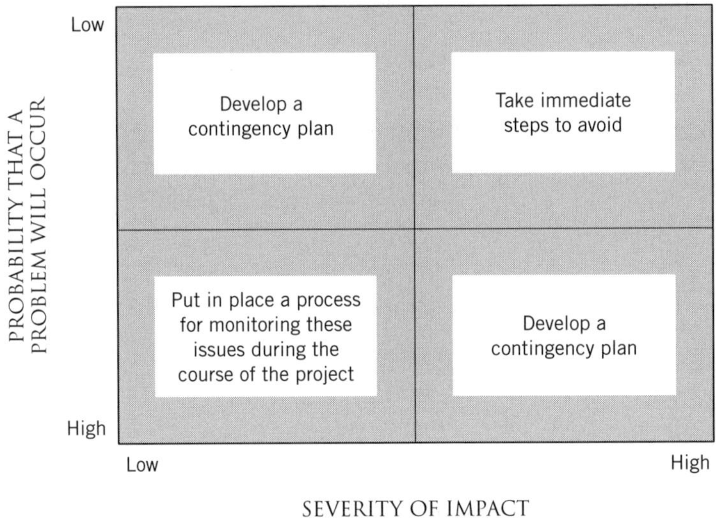

FIGURE 6.1: The key components of a risk management plan

At the same time, you need to recognize that risk is inherent in the consulting process, and that nothing you do will eradicate it altogether. That being said, some projects are undoubtedly riskier than others. One of the key differences between consulting and internal projects is that clients and consultants perceive different risks. From the client's point of view, these risks tend to be as follows:

- ☐ The project, although completed successfully, does not deliver the anticipated benefits, perhaps because those benefits were themselves overstated or misunderstood.
- ☐ The project is delivered to the satisfaction of the client, but one part of its management is unsatisfactory – it is over budget or late.
- ☐ The project is not delivered satisfactorily – although delivered on time, key functionality is missing from a system.

These risks can be mitigated (but not entirely) by ensuring that the contract with the consulting firm ties the firm into some level of payment by results (see Chapter 7). Even the first of the risks listed above, which in theory is outside the scope of the consultants' work, is increasingly becoming a contractual obligation, as the definition of 'results' shifts away from the immediate deliverables of a project to its ultimate business objective (to increase sales or cut costs).

Client dissatisfaction is clearly also a worry from the consulting firm's point of view, but the questions which the consulting firm will ask here are slightly different:

- ☐ How specialized are the skills required? If highly specialized skills are required, how will we find them? Will they be available when we need them?
- ☐ Is the client fully committed to this project at all levels? How realistic are their expectations?
- ☐ What level of change is the client's industry or organization undergoing? To what extent is it likely that the goal posts will move during the course of the project?

For consulting firms, client dissatisfaction does not just raise the risk of not getting paid at the end of project, it may also ruin the firm's reputation within the client's organization and in the market more broadly. Not surprisingly, this concern can make consulting firms very risk-averse, even cautious – perhaps more so than a client's project team would be – and caution can translate into bureaucracy. There is no easy answer to this problem; except to raise issues such as these and understand exactly how each side perceives the risks and will react to them.

The initiation phase of a consulting project is also an opportunity to examine in more detail a whole series of project management-related issues that may not have been covered in depth during the sales process. In this respect, consulting and internal projects are very similar: terms of reference are often drawn up by a project manager or sponsor, and the actual project team, brought together for the first time, will inevitably have a multitude of questions about practical issues. Whether internal or external, these people will need to be clear about who the customer is:

- ☐ Who is the project sponsor?
- ☐ Who will be responsible for monitoring progress and evaluating success?
- ☐ What success criteria will be used?
- ☐ Are there people who will be affected by the project, whose expectations and input also needs to be managed – the end-users of a computer system, for example?

PLANNING AND PROJECT ORGANIZATION

It is unlikely that the proposal submitted by the consulting firm, and accepted by the client prior to the start of the project, will provide sufficient detail about the work to be undertaken. It may provide an overview, but fleshing this out is crucial.

The project needs to be broken down into tasks, as these will be key in maintaining project control. This is the responsibility of the project manager (irrespective of whether he or she works for the client or the consulting firm), but it is also something that can only be done in consultation with all those involved. Always difficult to do (at least in large-scale projects), such decompositions are often even harder when it comes to consulting projects because of the level of specialized work typically involved; if anyone could do the work, why would a client hire a consulting firm? Moreover, it is not just that the work is more specialized, but that it may encompass a range of different specializations, only some of which will be familiar to the project manager. The project manager is therefore immensely reliant on the feedback of expert colleagues in terms of building a workable plan. If the project manager comes from the consulting side, he or she will also need input from the client in terms of internal constraints.

As with the overall objectives of a project, each task should be measurable; they also need clear start and end dates, and to be made the responsibility of one individual.

Allocating tasks and time-scales provides the basis of a milestone plan, designed to measure progress towards a project's ultimate goal, to focus attention on results and to ensure that high-level responsibilities – for groups of tasks – are clearly assigned. But the milestone plan plays an additional role in a consulting project, particularly where the consulting firm is being paid according to the results delivered. In these situations, this plan also indicates when the consulting firm should have discharged a contractual obligation, and when it will get paid.

The task breakdown is then converted into a Gantt chart (a table that lays out the individual tasks and sub-tasks involved in planning a project), so that dependencies on the critical path to the project's completion can be identified, and overall estimates of the work produced. Where internal projects are concerned, this may be the first time that the completion date for the project is calculated. But for a consulting project, this is the point at which the much more detailed plan can be compared back to the consulting firm's initial estimates (and, thus, to the client's expectations, both in terms of time-scales and fees). There is no problem if the two sets of estimates match, but there are occasions when they do not, perhaps because the consulting firm was over-optimistic in submitting its proposal, or perhaps because the client has not been entirely open about their circumstances. Whatever the level of discrepancy, this issue clearly has to be resolved immediately. The case study that follows, of Cap Gemini Ernst & Young's work with General Motors Europe, illustrates both how such controls can come together in practice and the benefits they bring.

Case study – keeping control of a pan-European project

As the world's largest carmaker, General Motors is determined to lead the industry in all aspects of e-business, not least in its dealings with customers, both existing and potential.

As part of this objective, the company wanted its websites to deliver real service to consumers, to add real value to the business – and to do both of these things rapidly, without glitches, ahead of its competitors and in partnership with its dealers. People would be able to review the GM range, select a vehicle matching their lifestyle requirements, configure and cost it, book a test-drive, review finance schemes and costs, review warranty details and arrange credit – all without leaving their homes. Realising this vision would require websites that were live, fully interactive, and kept constantly updated, and supporting systems which could link in real time with a whole spectrum of existing GM IT systems (production, distribution and financing information) as well as third party IT systems (dealers' websites, for example).

GM had already developed the essential technology in the form of a suite of advanced systems known as Global Buy Power: the challenge now was its implementation and deployment – how to make this new IT actually work across 12 different European countries, each with its own language, culture, business partners and GM organization?

GM Europe knew that external help would be vital to get their ambitious programme completed rapidly and chose Cap Gemini Ernst & Young because of the firm's expertise in systems integration and in the management of major IT programmes, its record in working in close and effective partnership with GM, and the credible and cost-effective approach the firm proposed for this work.

Nick Gill, Director of Cap Gemini Ernst & Young UK gives the details:

In order to ensure that work on all fronts could go ahead rapidly and simultaneously, and in a co-ordinated manner, we divided the project into three major work-streams:

- ☐ **Project management and control.** This included refining and applying our tried-and-tested methodology for this kind of deployment, the management and control of third-party vendors, reporting and communications across all areas of the project, and the capture, management and re-use of knowledge – all things which would be fundamental to the success of such a complex and geographically dispersed implementation.
- ☐ **Information systems.** The IT tools and techniques deployed by the joint GM Europe/Cap Gemini Ernst & Young team included a consistent methodology across all 12 countries to enhance speed, reduce costs and avoid duplication of effort, high-level centralized planning and progress tools to support parallel deployment in several countries at once and formal risk/issue/change management processes.
- ☐ **Business processes.** We were responsible for developing the metrics for tracking the business impact and benefits of the program and for communicating the strategy with GM and its dealer community.

A key factor in each of the 12 individual country deployment projects was the application of our 'On Time and Above Customer Expectations' methodology (OTACE), a management tool that aims, at the start of every project, to establish the factors considered by the client to be crucial to success, together with metrics for evaluating performance against those factors. Crucially for a project of this nature, this methodology can give a 'big picture' perspective to senior executives of how well we were performing and the contribution the project, once completed, had made to the success of the client's business. But it can also go all the way down to look at each individual project objective in the finest detail.

Another crucial factor was the multinational 'virtual team' established by GM Europe and Cap Gemini Ernst & Young from the outset. This was genuine partnership working: every member of the team was able to call on the expertise and experience of both companies. Moreover, a strong commitment to formal communications (through regular team briefings, progress reports and a special project website) was supplemented by a wide range of jointly sponsored social activities.

The deployment of Global BuyPower was completed in all 12 countries successfully and ahead of the very tight planned timescale in every case. Indeed, in some cases, the projects were completed a long way ahead of schedule to fit in with the timing of national motor shows. As a result of savings made possible by Cap Gemini Ernst & Young techniques, deployment costs were reduced by 53% below budget. When the project underwent an internal 'Project Health Check' by GM's Information Systems & Services quality organization; it received a 100% quality rating. It also became one of only three 'projects of the year' throughout GM to win an internal award for the projects that meant most to eGM in terms of learning, impact, and establishing General Motors as an e-corporation.

If the project enabled GM to avoid the high costs of individual initiatives in each country, it also reduced ongoing web-hosting costs and delivered rapid results and website consistency across all 12 countries. As a result, GM became the first major motor company to have in place a consistent, full-function internet offering for consumers across Europe.

TRANSPARENCY

Many things conspire to push even the best-planned project off-course, and consulting projects are no exception to this:

- Fundamental assumptions (deadlines, budget) may change.
- Requirements may change or may have been misunderstood.
- Other projects may overtake it in importance, and resources may be diverted to these.
- Unexpected obstacles are encountered.
- Mistakes are made.

Some of these issues are clearly avoidable, others much less so. Project control is therefore concerned with identifying potential dangers before they mature into serious problems (while there is still the opportunity to resolve them), and finding and implementing solutions to them. It cannot happen if you do not have, firstly, an effective baseline against which you can measure progress (the project plan, Gantt chart, budget and milestone plan) and, secondly, a formal control procedure. Someone has to be responsible for implementing the solution once it has been identified.

The control of internal projects typically focuses on three issues:

1 Cost – are we going to exceed the budget?

2 Quality – will the completed project achieve what we wanted?

3 Time – will the project be finished when we expected?

The same three issues are just as fundamental to managing a consulting project, but clients often feel that they are not as fully informed about progress as they would have been if the project had been an internal one. Part of this concern is completely justified; consulting can often seem 'black-boxed' to those not immediately involved in the process. Perhaps the project manager comes from the consulting firm, and the client is never completely convinced that they are made aware of everything that is going on. Equally, some consultants interpret the phrase 'managing the clients' expectations' as a rationale for providing only very limited information. The problem is often one of tight deadlines and complex work – both of which mean that neither side has the opportunity or energy to keep each other fully informed – rather than a conspiracy of silence.

For consulting projects, therefore, the primary issue is one of transparency. Time must be found, reporting channels established, and metrics put in place which will enable both sides – consultants as well as clients – to understand overall progress. But more important than any of these factors is the need to establish an open culture where successes and failures are shared and, crucially, where lessons are learned. This is particularly true where the project team brings together people from both the consulting firm and the client's organization. These people will not have worked together before, and they will not know each other's strengths and weaknesses. Such teams can only function effectively if they can identify problems and learn from them very rapidly. Establishing an open culture depends on:

- ☐ Being rewarded for achieving the same objectives.
- ☐ Locating the consulting and client staff in the same place, rather than having a team of consultants who regularly retreat to their own office.
- ☐ Creating an organizational structure and processes which do not distinguish between clients and consultants – both appear in the charts showing the project hierarchy, everyone has the same email address.
- ☐ Making joint presentations and writing joint documents.
- ☐ Ensuring that both sides report progress.
- ☐ Creating a mechanism in which both sides can see clearly how the other is performing.
- ☐ Taking joint credit and blame.
- ☐ Working together to solve problems that arise, irrespective of whose 'fault' they are.

But is there a tremendous overhead to all of this? Surely, by the time this kind of environment is set up, the tight deadline that consulting projects are typically under will have passed. The following case study, of BT Consulting's work with the UK police, illustrates how this type of collaborative approach can be applied, even in highly complex environment with short time-scales.

Case study: the world's first police portal

The Police Information Technology Organization (PITO) in the UK is responsible for the exploitation of new and emerging technologies to provide better policing services for the public, while optimizing police resources. In November 2000, PITO was asked to bring forward its five-year e-services delivery plan, and to deliver a first working solution within three months.

Police forces deal with a growing number of communications from the public, mostly on the telephone. Callers' demands are wide-ranging, in terms of urgency and the kind of information or response required. A high percentage of calls are of a minor nature, and the pressure on police switchboards has been further increased by the uptake of mobile telephones. A key Government and PITO priority is to reduce the burden of these communications on the police forces, and to make better use of police resources.

The UK Government's policy to 'e-enable' the UK (getting the general public online) was the natural springboard for the development of new media and channels, through which police forces would interface with the general public. The PITO was therefore tasked with providing an internet-based medium for the reporting of non-urgent and minor crime. This would become part of the Government's initiative to provide key e-services, while also establishing a national police online presence for future service provision.

Following discussion with suppliers, the PITO issued a competitive tender for the provision of a solution to meet its requirements in December 2000. BT Consulting (BTC) won the tender in January 2001, to provide and manage an internet-based portal, enabling members of the public to interact with the police online by submitting detailed notifications of non-urgent and minor crimes; this portal was to be running by April 2001, and BTC were to manage the service for 12 months.

This was not a standard web-site hosting contract, so much as a technically advanced managed service:

- ☐ The portal had to be sufficiently resilient and secure to meet the Government's security classification imposed on electronically communicated and stored crime and personal data.
- ☐ There were further security implications in the onward transmission of messages to those police forces tasked to deal with the crime notifications.
- ☐ The portal had to be replicable (to meet the Government's accessibility requirements), while simultaneously maintaining a police 'corporate' feel.
- ☐ Standard police definitions had to be used for reporting purposes so that the portal could be integrated into existing police processes, but the site also had to be comprehensible to the general public.
- ☐ The routing of the crime notification was also important, as notification had to go to the force where the incident occurred (not necessarily the citizen's local force).
- ☐ The differing processes of individual police forces had to be brought together into a single, unified process.

Moreover, the portal had to be delivered in less than three months, so effective project management and establishing a good working relationship with the client were top priorities for BTC.

Matthew Wardle, a Principal Consultant at BTC and Project Manager for the UK Police Portal, takes up the story.

'Because we were working with physically separate police forces, each of which had its own procedures, requirements and resources, we used the consultation period to establish the key requirements of the project as quickly as possible, through a series of discussion papers and workshops. We then used these high-level requirements to propose the technical solution and management strategy we thought most appropriate for the delivery of the portal, and drew up a detailed workplan and description of the tasks involved.

Establishing a collaborative working environment was critically important, and our approach was to provide a small, focused team of e-business consultants and specialists who could take a hands-on approach, working alongside key people from the PITO. We also provided the PITO with a working online demonstration of a possible solution, allowing PITO to present a realistic and tangible model of the service to the Government Minister responsible for the reduction of crime in the UK, as well as to elicit feedback and sponsorship of the idea.

The keys to a successful project delivery were communication, flexible management, and the partnership approach. The "hot team" approach had been proven in previous assignments to optimize project management and streamline project delivery, enabling shared communications through the team to an extended group within the client's organization and elsewhere. Team-working was strengthened by the fact that the BTC delivery team worked largely in PITO premises. Rapid communication between remote key parties was effected by establishing an online information interchange bulletin board. Each team member had defined responsibilities and a clear remit to investigate and collect the information required for effective project delivery, one that would meet all Government requirements and, importantly, be acceptable to each individual police force. Flexible working practices ensured that all team members worked efficiently and were in close communication. Working on-site enabled the team to keep tight control on project development and to keep the consultation process rolling throughout delivery.

We also encouraged collaborative working by taking an integrated approach to project management. For example, establishing a project office at the client's premises maximized consultants' availability and provided a real hands-on resource. This joint method of delivery built a high level of trust and mutual confidence. Providing a system that met all the police and Government's standards and processes meant an intense initial consultation period, with a program of feedback and input from all forces throughout the process of building the portal. Once again, collaborative working played a hugely important role in allowing us to have this kind of dialogue, while also ensuring that we hit the delivery deadlines.

All this enabled us to deliver a world first: the Police Portal links the 53 UK police forces, and:

- Enables UK citizens to notify any force of a crime online.
- Provides a new method for the police to interface with the public.
- Enhances the profile of the UK police as a world-class service.
- Improves management statistics and control.
- Helps free up resources for more higher visibility policing.

We met all the client's expectations in terms of time-scales, costs and technology, and we now have a continuing relationship with them in managing the portal.'

CONTINUOUS LEARNING

Good project management doesn't stop with the end of a project, but ensures, not only that any long-term benefits are delivered, but also that the people involved in the project learn from the experience. Without some type of feedback loop, the same mistakes will be made in the future and instances of best practice will be lost – it is very much a case of those who do not understand history are condemned to repeat it.

Consulting firms have been aware of this issue for some time and most will now hold a post-engagement review which brings together people involved in all aspects of the project to discuss what went well and what went badly. Team conflicts can be aired, and more serious procedural issues can be escalated to those responsible elsewhere in the firm. Increasingly, too, these reviews have been extended to include clients. In some cases, this may done by canvassing a client's view of a completed project in both qualitative and quantitative terms (a satisfaction rating that can be benchmarked against other projects and feed into the performance appraisals of the individual consultants involved in the project). In other cases, clients will be invited to take part in the post-engagement review. However, such joint meetings are not always the best vehicle for a productive discussion of the issues raised. When a project has gone well, there is a tendency to indulge in a bit of mutual back-slapping over a dinner rather than an attempt to pinpoint *why* the project has been a success. When a project has gone badly, everyone is on the defensive: for all the claims that organizations make about being willing to learn from failure, it remains very hard, especially where two different organizations are involved, to have a measured and sensible discussion about the problems encountered. These situations are made worse by a desire – again on both sides – to cut and run. The consulting firm suspects it will not get any more business from this client; the client thinks they probably won't hire this consulting firm again. Neither side has an incentive to solve the problem for the longer-term.

This is ironic because most businesses recognize that they have a lot to learn from customers who complain. Indeed, there is a growing body of research that suggests that customers who complain – and see their complaint being appropriately dealt with – become the loyalist of loyal customers. Clearly, clients need to complain more and consulting firms need to have a better process by which those complaints are not only resolved, but are seen to be resolved. Fundamentally, both sides have to take a longer-term view. The consulting firm has to recognize that the lessons it learns from working with a client will improve its performance for all clients, even if it still loses the opportunity for repeat business from that particular client. A client has to see that the lessons of one consulting project are not confined to that specific project or that specific consulting firm, but are almost certainly applicable to all the projects it does and all the consulting firms with which it deals.

For this reason, it is not enough that the consulting firm holds its own post-engagement review, or even that it tries to involve its clients in that process – clients need to have their own reviews tackling the mirror image of the points that the consultants themselves will discuss:

- ☐ Have we achieved what we set out to do?
- ☐ If we have, how has success been achieved? Between us and the consultants we have been working with, who contributed what towards this success?
- ☐ If we haven't, what went wrong? Could we have done something to rectify the situation? Could the consulting firm?
- ☐ How effective were we (the client) as a team? Were we clear about our shared objectives and the contribution we each made individually?
- ☐ How did the consulting firm rate us as a client? To what extent did we meet their needs?
- ☐ What lessons should our organization as a whole take from this particular project? Who needs to understand these lessons, and how can we communicate them to these people most effectively?

SUMMARY

1. Consulting projects are no different to internal projects in that they require careful and sustained management. They do however have some special requirements, about which clients should be fully aware.
2. The initiation of a consulting project is important because it may be the first opportunity to compare both clients' and consultants' expectations, in terms of deliverables, time-scales and costs. Although much may have been covered prior to the consulting project being signed, more details will inevitably have to be ironed out, and the downside or risks of the project more closely examined.
3. Similarly, the project must be broken down into its key tasks, and responsibility for achieving them must be clearly defined. This process is fundamental to being able to control the project effectively, and is particularly important in a consulting environment because of the specialized, complex nature of the work often involved.
4. The key to successful project control is transparency, as this allows both client and consulting staff to work together in a genuinely collaborative working arrangement.

CHAPTER 7

THE CLIENT–CONSULTANT RELATIONSHIP

The consulting industry is at a watershed in its development. Chronic pressures (for example, the inability of clients to be able to measure the value for money that consultants deliver) have combined with more immediate problems (massive layoffs to correct the over-capacity built up in the consulting sector during the dot.com boom, and the Enron scandal – to name but two) have combined to precipitate a debate about the future direction of the industry. Much of this debate focuses on internal issues for consulting firms, but it also has direct bearing on the client–consultant relationship.

This chapter looks at these changes, and the implications which they have for clients.

THE CLIENT–CONSULTANT RELATIONSHIP

Chapter 1 introduced a framework for categorizing client needs into three distinct phases in the life-cycle of any management idea (Figure 7.1):

☐ **Phase 1:** the need for additional resources, new ideas and industry know-how predominates – this is the point at which clients are exploring and testing new ideas, but have not yet settled on the way in which they will apply an idea in practice.

☐ **Phase 2:** this is marked by a shift in which clients want to extract specific services from their consultants – in which, essentially, they know what gaps there are in their intellectual capital, and they want to fill them. In particular, they are looking to combine industry-specific knowledge with knowledge about the opportunity they are pursuing, and they want consultants to carry out key roles in helping develop the opportunity (which, for the e-business market took the form of helping to build a network of contacts).

☐ **Phase 3:** the need for industry-specific knowledge has been almost wholly superseded by opportunity-specific knowledge. Clients are looking for a tried-and-tested way of implementing their opportunity; their focus is now on reaching the end-game as quickly and successfully as possible.

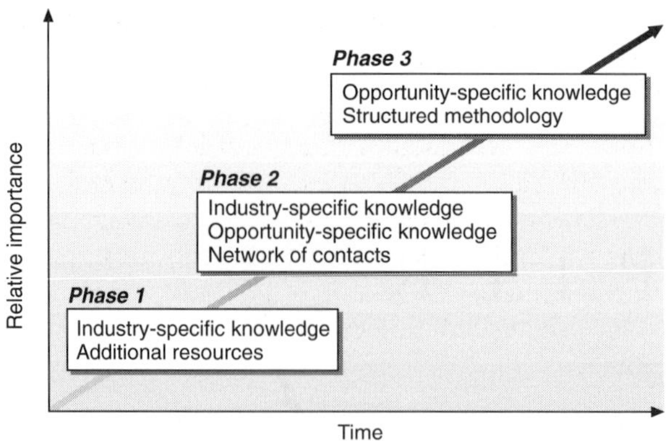

FIGURE 7.1: The three-phase evolution of client needs

This analysis focused on developing an overall picture of what happens in a consulting market – a pattern which is repeated with every new consulting service or management idea to emerge. But it can be difficult, if not dangerous, to generalize about clients in this way; after all, every client is different. What we see at the overall market level is just the summation of how individual clients are behaving: most, but not all, clients will fit the pattern outlined. While some clients evolve through the process, others may have a preferred mode of working; thus, some clients will always be looking for industry-specific knowledge and additional resources, but others will only look for opportunity-specific knowledge and structured methodologies.

It is therefore possible to use the model outlined in Figure 7.1, not only as a means of describing the level of maturity of a market for a given consulting service, but also as a way of categorizing types of clients.

MENTORING, MANAGEMENT, SPECIALIST RELATIONSHIPS

Three types of relationship emerge (Figure 7.2): mentoring, management and specialist. Mentoring relationships are initially built, in which the consulting firm acts as a catalyst, bringing new ideas and information, but also facilitating a client's own abilities to identify and

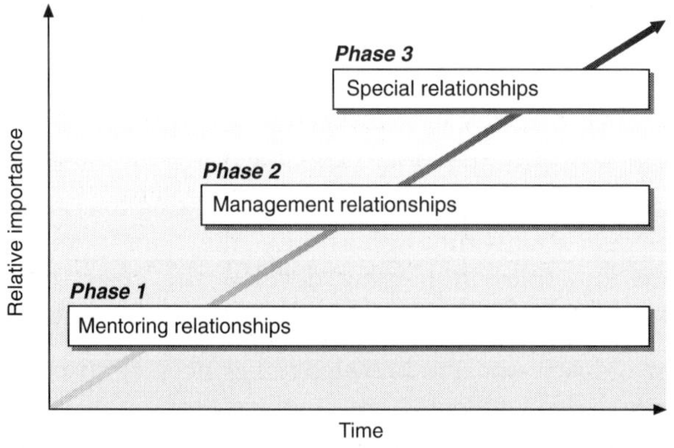

FIGURE 7.2: The three-phase evolution of client relationships

evaluate new opportunities. Such relationships are characterized by their informality and longevity. To be successful, they require a very high level of industry-specific knowledge. However, they also offer some additional, variable resources.

While mentoring relationships are based on trust (not least because the outputs will usually be intangible and unmeasurable), specialist relationships are based on effectiveness (precisely because it is possible to measure whether a package has been implemented or a process completed). Management relationships are based on a combination of both effectiveness and trust – a consulting firm is being hired because of its track record (effectiveness) and because the project manager has convinced the client that he or she is capable of delivering a successful outcome (trust).

Successful mentoring relationships are more likely to occur at an individual-to-individual level, whereas successful specialist relationships are more likely to take place at an organization-to-organization level; for example, a client will hire a consulting firm accredited in the software they wish to implement. Successful management relationships will be forged at both the individual-to-individual level (clients need to be able to trust the individual program manager appointed because of the stakes involved and the visibility of the project) and the organization-to-organization level (clients also need to be reassured that the individual in charge, however experienced and competent, is supported by a structured and proven methodology for delivery).

Although all three types of relationship currently coexist, many firms are already finding that they only have one type of relationship with one client. If they work with Client A in a specialist capacity, they are highly unlikely to form a mentoring relationship with them, even though they have a mentoring relationship with Client B. Clients, far more than consulting firms, are segmenting the firms that serve them. As this effect snowballs, firms may end up in a position from which they find it difficult to extricate themselves; for example, only working with clients in specialist relationships. Consultants have always tried to be all things to all people, but this attitude will be harder to sustain in the face of growing barriers which, in clients' eyes, prevent one firm from having more than one relationship 'style'. In this environment, the key challenge, as a consultant or as a client, will be to know where you fit.

RESTRUCTURING IN THE AFTERMATH OF ENRON

The collapse of US-based energy company, Enron, has alerted people to the potential dangers of buying different types of professional services from a single supplier. While the focus here has been on the relationship between audit and consulting firms, it is clearly an issue which is equally applicable where consulting firms are selling a multitude of services under a single umbrella. Wherever a client is buying a combination of one very substantial service and a host of smaller-scale services from one firm, there is a risk that the independent nature of any advice given as part of the smaller projects is compromized through fear of losing the larger one. This is an issue that has already been mentioned in Chapter 4, which makes the point that, while independence is a virtue in some consulting projects, it may be a limitation in others, and that two quite distinct models of consulting are emerging as a result. However, the potential 'unbundling' of individual consulting services has further implications.

The pitfalls of integration

For the last 20 years, consultants have encouraged clients to believe that they need a one-stop-shop for professional services. The best example of this is the continuing erosion of the distinction between strategy and implementation: clients, dissatisfied with consultants recommending options which proved unworkable in reality, demanded greater accountability in the crucial transition from theory to practice; consulting firms responded by offering a 'soup-to-nuts' approach – something that found particular favour during the heights of the enterprise resource planning and e-business eras, when technology became recognized as a driving force in business, not simply an operational enabler.

But there was always a division between what clients said they needed, and what consulting firms told them they needed. With the demise of the dot.coms and the genie of technology at least temporarily back in the bottle, clients have increasingly questioned the value of 'bundled' services. Enron has added to this backlash, but it did not initiate it. Clients have become distrustful of professional services firms which claim to do everything equally well. Consulting firms now acknowledge that the pressure to offer bundled services was driven by internal, as much as external, priorities – keeping pace with competitors, the desire to secure long-term sources of revenue, keeping costs low.

With all the merger and acquisition activity in the consulting sector over recent years, conventional wisdom decrees that size matters. But is the 'mega-firm' really the only option?

In order to answer this, we first have to understand the two primary motivations driving this consolidation: money and technology.

- **Money:** at the current time, money is the obvious rationale. Almost all smaller firms are coping with shrinking client demand. Most of them are finding it hard, if not impossible, to fall back on institutional funding to see them through a difficult period. Being bought out by a bigger firm sometimes guarantees the jobs of individual consultants, even if it obliterates their brand in the process. But cash is largely a temporary issue. At present, we are still in the backlash to the e-business hype – it has become fashionable to denigrate e-business, just as it was previously fashionable to extol its virtues. But at some point in the future, there will be a backlash to the backlash, when, no doubt, many of the firms currently in financial difficulties will rise, phoenix-like, from the ashes.

- **Technology:** this is a far more important matter – the relationship of a consulting firm to the technology its clients choose to implement has an impact on its long-term survival. Part of the reason for this lies in the increasing 'technocratization' of consultancy: you cannot draw up a supply chain strategy without thinking of the systems required to support it, but you also need complex computer modelling tools to optimize it. Similarly, can you prepare a credible marketing strategy which is not based on exhaustive analysis of data on consumer behaviour? Even in the highest echelons of strategy formulation, the software now exists to evaluate scenarios and to calibrate systems' thinking diagrams. Mergers between technology and consulting firms have benefits for clients, reflecting a long-standing desire for more concrete outputs and for theorization to be linked more closely to implementation. There are advantages, too, from the supply side, from being able to bundle consultancy and technology together in the same package for a single fee.

But how do you integrate the skills of a very large firm? One of the key changes wrought by e-business on the consulting industry has been the recognition that the whole is greater than the sum of the parts. Clients obtain more value from a consulting project in which the disparate skills involved are genuinely integrated, than from a series of projects in which each skill is quite distinct. Before e-business burst upon the scene, a typical consulting project was sequential; the effect of e-business – because companies believed that the time-to-market was critical – was to compress this structure so that each stream overlapped. The attraction to clients remains immense:

- ☐ Integrated teams mean shorter (although not necessarily less expensive) projects.
- ☐ Such teams also mean that that perennial weak link in the consulting chain – the transition from strategy (theory) to implementation (practice) – is much less likely to be a problem, as the same team that designed the strategy would be involved in executing it.
- ☐ Another benefit has been the resulting quality of thinking – just as companies were discovering that making links between different industry sectors could allow them to create whole new business models, so clients have discovered that bringing different people and perspectives together, in an environment in which they could enhance and challenge each other's ideas, resulted in a better end product.

The problem for the consulting industry is that integration does not always sit comfortably with large-scale acquisition. Logically, it should do so: what better way is there, on paper, of ensuring that clients can have access to the full range of skills they require than by bringing all those skills together under one umbrella? But, in reality, many consulting firms have proved themselves just as divided into hierarchical departments of expertise as the clients they advise.

Being able to field integrated teams was one of the key differentiators of the new entrants into the consulting market. Even established firms, quick to deride the contribution of the e-consultants in other areas, acknowledge the significance of this trend. So far, consulting firms have responded by absorbing potential rivals; most acquisitions have been driven by competition, not by generating value for clients.

Collaboration

A different, and perhaps a better, model for the industry is emerging: collaboration.

Other sectors already do this. When a film studio has an option on a particular idea, it discusses it with a small number of executive producers with whom the studio has worked in the past; at some point it takes the decision to make the film. A producer is hired, who, in conjunction with the studio and the executive producer, appoints a director. While the director takes charge of hiring the cast and filming, the producer pulls together the highly complex logistics of film-making – hiring the crew, finding the locations, building the sets, etc. – as well as keeping control of the overall timetable and budget. The key feature about the way in which the film industry works is that a multitude of independent specialists come together for a short period of time, with a specific goal (making a film). Some of these specialists play a very specific role and are only involved for a very short period; others, like the director and producers, are involved from start to finish. Once the film is completed, the crew disbands.

Consulting is not so different. A client has an idea; they brainstorm the idea with a small number of consultants with whom they have a long-term relationship, and then hire a consulting firm to manage the development of the venture; this firm, in turn, orchestrates a whole host of specialist firms, each with a specific role. But, for the consulting industry to work in a structure not dissimilar to that of the film industry, consultancies must know where they fit into a more complex value chain, and consulting projects must be more visible.

One of the recurring irritations of the consulting industry is that the vast majority of firms who have expanded beyond the niche on which they were originally focused, remain unclear about the precise nature of their intellectual capital. People, clients and consultants alike, do not tend to think in terms of pure intellectual capital. The traditional unit in which you buy consultancy is people, and it is therefore hard to separate people from ideas. In fact, consultants make this even harder by being bad at articulating their knowledge proposition. Clients need to define precisely the intellectual capital they require, and to match this against the intellectual capital on offer from a given set of firms.

But the consulting-project-as-film analogy also only works if consultants can feel confident that they will be given credit – that, when a project is success, potential clients can be made aware of the firm's contribution. Where consultants remain anonymous, they are dependent on their input to the process (their brand), rather than their output (the results of the project). And a key difference between the film and consulting industries clearly lies in the profile of their respective output. A film is publicized and highly visible, and every contributor is mentioned in the final credits. By contrast, a consulting project typically happens behind the scenes, cloaked in the mystique that the industry has gathered around it. Most importantly, consultants have played the part of facilitators, not prime movers: the credit (and the blame) is all the clients'.

Two factors are changing this:

1 Consultants have, for the first time, been coming out from the wings to take a bow. Having found that taking public credit for successful projects represents a fast track to gaining credibility in this instance, consulting firms are likely to repeat the strategy when it comes to the next management bandwagon.

2 Persuading consultants to ally themselves publicly to specific ventures also has advantages for clients. Clients have always been frustrated in their attempts to make consulting firms accountable for their actions; consultants have claimed many factors – for example, the number of variables that affect an outcome, changing market conditions, the client's role in implementation, but, ultimately, the confidentiality of the client–consultant relationship – to avoid being held responsible for what happens. An environment in which consultants accept credit (and therefore can be attributed with blame) may resolve this issue.

The way forward

The future consulting industry may therefore look far more fragmented than it does now, with consulting firms playing different roles:

- **'Splendid isolation' firms** will have no formal links with any other company; the value they bring to clients is their guaranteed objectivity.

- **'Broker' firms** will also have no level of integration links with other companies, but will have an extensive network of contacts which they are capable of marshalling for a particular client project. Their role, however, will be one of coordination – putting the client in touch with expert firms rather than managing the process of integrating the latter's input.

- **'Single issue' firms** will have highly integrated working relationships with just one or two other companies, extending to joint product development and planning, as well as sales, marketing and delivery.

- **'Orchestrator' firms** will be less integrated with their partners than 'single issue' firms (typically, collaboration will be limited to sales, marketing and delivery), but they will maintain these relationships with far more partners; effectively the prime contractor in client relationships, the role of 'orchestrator' firms will be to integrate the work of different partners, so that the project delivery appears seamless from the client's point of view.

Each strategy will have its own advantages and disadvantages. Absolute objectivity may mean that a firm is well-positioned to help clients in the earliest stages of their decision-making processes, but is much less likely to be involved in the detailed implementation – a position that most strategy consulting firms have already adopted. The strength of 'broker' firms will lie in their ability to know which specialist firm to deploy in which area, whereas that of the 'orchestrators' will be in integration.

THE IMPLICATIONS FOR CLIENTS

From a client perspective, these changes have important repercussions. Consulting firms will increasingly work in just one way, and will tend to have one kind of relationship with a client. They might be a mentoring firm, a management firm or a specialist firm, but they are unlikely to be all three. This means that clients will have to work with a larger number of consulting firms: some will be specialists, but others will be firms that 'specialize' in helping clients coordinate the work of other specialists; some will have a focused, comparatively formal relationship with their clients, but others will have more informal relationships, based around exploring new ideas rather than concentrating on a single, given deliverable.

This more complex environment has many opportunities, not least the chance to source world-class expertise from a variety of different consulting firms. But, at the same time, it also brings some potential problems. One of the fundamental reasons why people come together to form organizations is that it is easier and cheaper to do something collectively than individually. Thus, organizations have traditionally had lower transaction costs for internal than external processes; a parent company which ships products to subsidiaries around the world can save the costs of employing agents and may even find tax-efficient ways of attributing the revenue. Similarly, clients who hire just one consulting firm might expect to pay less overall than if they hired several specialist consulting firms. However, the trade-off between the level of specialist expertise and cost is far less clear-cut than might be assumed. The larger a consulting firm becomes, the more difficulty it often has in keeping track of exactly who does what and whether they are available. The largest firms can afford to solve this problem by using technology, but resource databases, however sophisticated, can never hold the full wealth of information which an HR manager might need to make the optimum decision about who to put where.

The critical question, therefore, is how can a client best exploit the potential opportunities of this more pluralistic consulting market, without costs escalating out of control? Clients essentially have two options. They can hire a consulting firm to manage the other consultancies involved in a project (the prime contractor role), or they can take over the coordination role themselves. Either way, achieving a precise match between what clients want and what consultants can provide will only be achieved by taking a more proactive approach to managing the overall relationship.

SUMMARY

1 Client needs can be categorized into three phases, depending on the stage in the evolution of a particular management idea. These phases can also be used to describe the three different types of client–consultant relationships:

- ☐ Phase 1 clients like to explore new ideas and want to work with consultants who are similarly innovative.
- ☐ Phase 2 clients typically know *what* they want to do but not *how* to do it, and they primarily want to work with consultants who understand what is involved in a project.
- ☐ Phase 3 clients simply want to complete the task; their overriding objective is efficiency, and they use consultants for precise tasks, nothing more.

2 Although a single client organization may have different relationships at a given moment (every organization is the sum of many individual clients), consulting firms are finding it increasingly difficult to sustain more than one type of relationship – a trend that has been exacerbated by the debate about the role of Enron's auditors. In particular, it is becoming harder for consulting firms to justify 'bundling' their services.

3 Moving away from the idea of a one-stop-shop for professional services provides clients with an opportunity (to bring in world-class expertise, irrespective of the firm in which it is located), but also a threat (the escalating costs of managing the client–consultant relationship).

CHAPTER 8

BALANCING INNOVATION AND STRUCTURED METHODOLOGY

One of the most commonly told jokes about consultants is that a consultant is someone who takes a client's watch to tell them the time. Worse still, the way that some clients tell it, the consultant takes the watch away and charges for it.

The joke does make a serious point (in fact, it makes several – see also the following chapter). Nothing makes a client feel more cheated than when their expectations are not met – and the expectations of clients are often very high (however sceptical clients may purport to be). 'A tale of mystery and imagination' is how *The Economist* has described consultancy: 'nobody seems to know quite what it is, let alone whether it delivers value for money' (Adrian Wooldridge, 'The Advice Business', *The Economist*, 1997). A crucial part of those expectations is that consultants do something a client cannot – to extrapolate from the joke, either that they have a new watch that tells a different (more accurate?) time, or that they have a different (faster?) way of telling the time.

This chapter argues that the reasons that consultants are often perceived to be lacking in innovation stems partly from the nature of the industry itself, and partly from client pressure. Both of these factors encourage consulting firms to back away from being too innovative, and instead to offer a structured methodology for delivering the results clients want. But this chapter also suggests that a small amount of structured methodology goes a long way; many of the problems which clients encounter with consultancy come from the application of too much structure to the consulting process. Clients looking to maximize the value they obtain from consultants should be seeking to find a balance between innovation and structured methodologies.

THE PRESSURE TO STANDARDIZE AND THE VALUE OF CUSTOMIZATION

The consulting industry functions as it does because consultants take ideas from client to client; consultants are in the business of codifying new ideas, taking them to organizations that might find them useful, and implementing them. Indeed, the process of identifying the winners from among the myriad of new business ideas, and then converting this into something relevant to more than one company, has fuelled the growth of the consulting industry since the Second World War. As David Maister points out in *Managing the Professional Services Firm*:

‹Management consultants like to portray themselves as anonymous aides-de-camp devising winning strategies for the generals of free enterprise in the war of the bottom line. They wrap their products in elegant brochures, erudite book jackets, or the colourful pages of the *Harvard Business Review*. But strip away the pontificating prose and ubiquitous graphics and a simple formula for the successful consultant remains. Devise an idea, repackage it, give it a catchy name, then sell the something in a new wrapper to another client. Few would like to admit it, but that is what the consultancy business is all about.[1]›

But this has not happened without some impetus from clients. Under pressure to produce good results, clients have demanded more controllable costs and lower risks, neither of which are characteristics of innovation. At the same time, we should also recognize that this situation is not vastly different from that in other industries. We do not expect a manufacturer only to turn out a constant stream of new products, but to have a portfolio of new and established products, products at the end of their life-cycle as well as those at the start. Similarly, all but the very smallest of consulting firms have portfolios of services – question marks, cash cows and dogs. Some firms will feel comfortable with a higher proportion of question marks; some will be resigned to their dependency on dogs; all of them have to have some cash cows. Indeed, one of the lessons from the e-business consulting boom has been that consulting firms cannot survive on innovation alone. One of the key barriers to achieving sustainable levels of profit faced by the e-consulting specialists founded in the mid-1990s was their unwillingness to sacrifice their reputation for creativity by standardizing the way they worked.

Bain & Company has been publishing an annual survey on the use of management tools since the early 1990s. Focusing on the 25 most popular management tools – such as activity-based costing, the balanced scorecard, one-to-one marketing and scenario planning – the 2001 survey concluded that the most widely-used tools were strategic planning, mission and vision statements and benchmarking (all of which were used by more than two-thirds of the respondents to Bain's survey, irrespective of the industry in which they worked). However, it also revealed that 'new economy' tools – such as corporate venturing and customer relationship management (CRM) – have the lowest rates of satisfaction. Respondents were sceptical of those tools they see as over-promising and under-delivering, and 77 per cent of them thought that most management tools fell into this category. Despite this fact, almost three-quarters of those responding thought it is important to stay on the cutting edge of tools and techniques.

Darrell Rigby is the Vice President at Bain responsible for the survey:

‹I think the fundamentals of how you succeed in business have not really changed – companies are trying to create superior results, and you only find superior results at the intersection of a customer opportunity, a competitive vulnerability and a distinctive

[1] David Maister, *Managing the Professional Services Firm*, (Free Press, 1993)

capability. Seizing any one of those opportunities is hard enough; doing all three together is enormously difficult. And doing that repeatedly, over years, is an absolutely Herculean task. Executives have trouble keeping their organizations sufficiently motivated on each of those tasks. I also think that there is a tendency in organizations to take a concept and push it a little too far in order to test the boundaries of its effectiveness . . . One of my greatest hopes is that the value of our research will demonstrate that there are no silver bullets out there, and that things most often go wrong, not because the tool itself was bad, but because it was naively misapplied. Almost every tool we have ever surveyed has created highly satisfying results for some companies. But, as soon as other companies believe that – because it worked for others – it will also work for them, and do not recognize that management tools never eliminate problems, all they really do is exchange one set of problems for a new set of problems. Unless you go in understanding what those new set of problems are that you are going to be forced to live with, and preparing to deal with those problems from the very beginning, you are likely to be blind-sided and not get nearly as much value out of the tool as you had hoped.[2]❞

Rigby's comments are born out in research by Eric Abrahamson[3], an academic who has carried out an extensive analysis into the questionable value yielded by the succession of management fads, which seem to emerge ever more frequently. Although comparatively unknown in business circles, his conclusions have substantial implications for the effective use of consultants. These conclusions can be summarized as follows:

- Management theory works best when it is still at its most embryonic – the value that early adopters obtain comes as much from the process of customizing the theory to fit their organizations' unique circumstances as it does from the idea in isolation.
- Once an idea has evolved into a full-blown band-wagon, it acquires a set of 'rules' – in effect, it becomes a process that has to be adopted for its own sake, not a result that is to be achieved.
- This evolution is reinforced when the early adopters – who have to customize the theory to their individual practice – obtain substantial benefits. These benefits encourage companies (who had previously dismissed the idea) to adopt it against their better judgement. These organizations spend much less effort trying to customize the idea to fit their sets of circumstances, partly because they are following rules and partly because they are trying to catch up with their competitors.
- As the level of customization goes down, so do the benefits achieved – but people's reaction is to demand greater structure because they see it as a means of increasing the likelihood that the idea will be made to deliver the anticipated benefits. Another irony of this situation is that it is quite the reverse: it is lack of structure that produces the most benefits.

This model can be applied directly to the consulting industry. The early adopters create a standard that drives the consulting industry, and, because it is likely that the early adopters (assuming they are large-scale organizations) will have hired consultants to help in the process of customizing the management idea. Although the consultants involved will not necessarily have any experience of this idea (because it is new), they can provide input in terms of how the management idea may change a client's industry. They can also provide a group of bright energetic people who can help assess this in greater detail at a time when the client itself is unwilling to dedicate many resources to it (because the idea is untested). Once these first

[2] Quoted in Fiona Czerniawska, *Value-Based Consulting*, (Macmillan, 2002)

[3] Abrahamson and Rosenkopf 'Institutional and Competitive Bandwagons: Using Mathematical Modelling as a Tool to Explore Innovation Diffusion', *Academy of Management Review*, (1993)

projects have been completed, the consultants involved will want to replicate the results, rather than re-invent the idea on behalf of each new client; as we saw earlier in this chapter, constant reinvention cannot deliver guaranteed results and can be very costly. Rules breed rules, not least because rules provide a tangible basis on which consulting firms can compete ('our rules are better than our competitors'). Moreover, as clients want to emulate the results of their rivals, they increasingly look for consultancies that have a track record, and a structured methodology is, again, a very effective way of doing this. One irony here is that the consultancies that do not have too codified an approach may well be those able to add the greatest value, but they are also the firms least likely to find themselves on a short-list for work.

Costs also play a part here. When a new management idea first emerges, both the benefits and costs are high (see Figure 8.1). As a way of applying the idea starts to be established, the costs fall dramatically, and the difference between the benefits and costs is at its highest. Finally, as the application methodology becomes more rigid, there comes a point at which the costs actually exceed the benefits. We have seen this pattern many times: business process re-engineering, enterprise resource planning, and so on. Current bandwagons – customer relationship management, for example – may face the same fate.

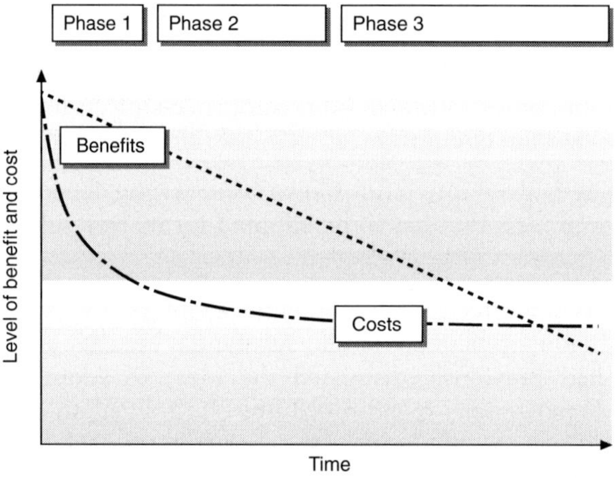

FIGURE 8.1: The changing cost–benefit balance during the life of a management issue

Knowing how your expectations match market conditions is hugely important. There are advantages and disadvantages to each phase in an issue's 'life'. For the companies that pick up on issues almost as they emerge, there are considerable benefits in working out exactly how an idea will apply to their own, unique set of circumstances. With no prescribed rules about what they should and should not do, they are free to make up rules that suit themselves. But the costs of doing this may be high: it takes time and money to think creatively, and not all organizations are willing to accept the uncertainty involved in this kind of work. Although there may be some benefits to your organization, they are as yet unclear and need to be found, rather than assumed. Even where you are confident of the benefits, the means of delivering them – the processes and technology required – may be untested. Coming second to market (in Phase 2) has the advantage that someone else has prepared the ground for you; the risks and costs of responding will be lower. But, at the same time, the benefits may also be lower:

the early adopting companies may have established a pattern based on their own situation which works less well when applied to your own. And it is becoming increasingly difficult to go back to the starting point and work out what it means for you, because there will already be a fair amount of thinking about what the issue 'is'; no one wants to be accused of reinventing the wheel unnecessarily.

Phase 3 plays these trends out to their logical extremes. By now, the issue has become such an established way of doing something that organizations have little choice but to respond in the accepted way. The benefits are usually much lower as a result. The costs will be lower, too, because much effort will have gone into making the process of responding as efficient as possible. However, as more companies go for what appear to be quick wins, without considering the extent to which the issue is relevant to their own organization, the costs of implementation may fall more slowly than the benefits. At some point, the two lines cross: the costs of implementation exceed the expected benefits – and the market for the management issue implodes.

Let us look at three high-profile management issues of recent years:

- ☐ Business process re-engineering (BPR) – streamlining your internal processes by cutting across internal boundaries – is an idea that has existed since the late 1980s. The initial promise of its earliest adopters was difficult to replicate in those that picked up on the idea later. The costs of implementation may now exceed the benefits.
- ☐ Customer relationship management (CRM) – the idea that you can improve customer acquisition and retention by gathering individual data on customers and communicating with these on a one-to-one basis – has existed since the mid-1990s. Already many methodologies for implementation exist and organizations are starting to become more concerned with the means, rather than the end which they are trying to achieve.
- ☐ E-procurement – where organizations use web-based technology to streamline and control their collective purchasing – is still in Phase 1 of its life. A minority of organizations have achieved very significant benefits, but there is as yet no accepted practice for implementation.

So why expect everything consultants do to be innovative? Why apply the 'watch test' across the board? Part of the answer probably lies in confusion about the reason for hiring consultants: were they really being hired to be innovative or, to add some extra people to an understaffed client project? Another part of the problem undoubtedly lies in the way in which almost all consulting firms market themselves as 'thought-leaders', rather than followers. But, if we strip out these excuses, and confine ourselves to those projects where clients genuinely want to gain access to innovative thinking and where the consultants they hire are equally genuinely committed to delivering this innovative thinking, what are the key factors that determine the success of these projects and how can clients best manage them?

ACHIEVING A BALANCE

Structured methodologies are therefore something that clients want, especially as an idea becomes more familiar; they are also something that consulting firms are happy to develop, as they make their costs more controllable and their role more measurable. The trouble is that they can become too 'successful' for their own good, actually destroying the value which they are intended to create. What is needed is a balance – some methodology, but not too much. Of course, some companies are the exception to this; there will always be 'Phase 1' clients who are prepared to take risks in order to ensure they remain on the cutting edge, and there are other organizations that find it hard to move unless an idea has been extensively tried and tested.

In practice, it is hard to withstand the internal and external pressure to 'methodologize'. Consultants accurately point out that clients are less likely to trust them (or, indeed, buy their services) unless they are equipped with a manual the size of a telephone directory; they do not want to hear that the consultants are not sure. Clients and consultants therefore find themselves playing an invidious version of the prisoner's dilemma.

This philosophical conundrum shows how people are unwilling to cooperate if there is more to gain from acting independently. Two people are arrested on suspicion of robbing a bank, but the police, who put the men in separate cells, have only circumstantial evidence – not enough to convict them unless at least one of them confesses. If one of the prisoners confesses and the other does not, then the confessor is released (for helping the prosecution case) while the other will be sent to jail for a long period. If both confess, then they are both sent to jail for a short period, but if neither one confesses, then neither goes to jail. Neither prisoner knows what the other prisoner has done: has his friend remained silent or spilt the beans? The nub of the problem lies in the fact that, if each prisoner acts selfishly, they will each confess to the crime, leaving their friend to carry the can for not cooperating. Collectively, they would gain more by both remaining silent, but the higher incentive to act selfishly encourages them to act otherwise.

This model can be applied directly to the dilemma facing clients and consultants when thinking about the balance of innovation to structured methodology in a consulting project. A consulting firm which offers clients a structured methodology is more likely to win the business, because the project is made to look more controllable and less uncertain. If two competing consulting firms offer structured methodologies, then clients – and, ultimately, the consultants – lose out, because the value delivered by the project will be less (following Abrahamson's analysis). To achieve the maximum value for a client, neither firm has to offer too structured an approach – something they are not incentivized to do, because if they do not offer a structured approach and their rival does, then they stand to lose the project.

Is there a way of meeting the demand for efficiency and certainty without giving in to standardization and rigidity?

Clients need to understand that efficiency does not necessarily guarantee certainty. Efficiency can be a barrier to delivering value, but it is still tempting for a client who looks at an efficiently run process to believe that it will yield more benefits than an inefficiently run one. This is partly what we want to believe – 'if I hire these consultants who have a ten-step plan for doing what I want, I am more likely to get what I want'. It is partly what we are trained to believe – 'if I run my business more efficiently, it will be more successful'. Consultants therefore pander to this assumption, by packing their presentations and proposals with structured methods.

The key has to be to balance structure and innovation, as the following case study illustrates.

Case study: Amey Asset Services

Amey Asset Services is part of Amey plc, providing design, construction, whole-life maintenance and associated support services to a range of public and private sector clients in the UK. In March 2000 the former Amey Construction Division was incurring significant losses on contracts based around traditional construction activities, and needed to be completely restructured to survive as a viable business. Oakland Consulting was commissioned to help the senior management team define a new business direction for the renamed company, establish a platform to turn around its poor financial performance and plan the implementation of required changes.

Keith Thompson was Oakland's project manager.

'It was immediately clear that a major change in the mix of work was required. Our task was to assist the new managing director and his team to achieve a transition from engaging in a large number of small, short-term, low margin construction projects, to providing fewer but larger, higher margin, infrastructure services for the life-cycle of the asset. Some rival companies were already doing this, but most were not. Under the leadership of Chief Executive Brian Staples, Amey had recognized an opportunity in a niche market to provide comprehensive services to clients who wanted to outsource their activities. This was part of an overall repositioning of Amey from the construction sector to the support services sector. For Amey Asset Services, however, the immediate business priority in 2000 was to reach the end of the year with a small profit or minimum losses. This meant terminating low-margin or loss-making projects that often carried high risks, and developing some capability in projects with higher margins and longer-term growth potential.

We therefore designed and facilitated a series of senior management workshops to establish a vision, mission and a set of values for the new business, and to prioritize short- and medium-term actions for the business which would achieve a realistic recovery position. We also identified its critical success factors, core processes and key performance indicators (all of which would be key components for development and ongoing management), and provided one-to-one coaching for senior managers to transfer knowledge and plan for implementation. This stage of the process was comparatively structured, as it was important to have a framework – in this instance, the European Business Excellence model – around which complex discussions could take place.

The vision for Amey Asset Services was to become the leading provider of infrastructure and lifetime asset support services. This meant developing the right set of new skills for managing risk, design, work-space engineering and life-cycle maintenance – all of which represented a major change from the organization's traditional skills of construction engineering. Other critical success factors included building a strong and compelling brand identity and choosing effective, value-adding partnerships with other organizations of the right culture.

But the framework itself only took us so far. One of the greatest challenges which we faced in implementing the programme was to create room for the workshop and individual coaching interventions in the running of the day-to-day business. Initially, these were often perceived as additional time-consuming tasks on top of running a deteriorating business, where the financial situation and other problems were understandably consuming a large amount of senior management attention. The key players needed to leave the day-to-day issues aside for a while to concentrate on the very important task of defining the future of the business and how they, as the senior management team, were going to make it happen.

They had to ask themselves: "are we all up for the challenge?" After all, what was the point of developing a brave new strategy, if people were not willing or equipped to implement it? The management team had to respond both from an intellectual point of view (was the challenge the right one?) and also from a personal point of view (am I personally ready to go through all the heartache that this will inevitably entail?). Real engagement required emotional buy-in to the changes envisaged, and the team's positive response was a key breakthrough at this time.

With the overall framework agreed, the next phase was to communicate the vision and values throughout the business in order to start driving the right behaviours at all levels. Our initial phase of activity included formal presentations and interactive sessions involving all staff. Working groups were also established to focus on specific areas of business change and development, engaging people below the executive group level. All of the CSFs and core processes were allocated to these working groups – and part of our role was in the key areas of communication and organizational development, to achieve the required changes and maintain momentum.

In the early stages, it was vital to set the right direction for the business to function properly. It was important to ensure agreement within the team about the business direction, and this small caucus group of senior executives had to make the transition. The priority in the early work was to ensure total clarity and agreement about the business imperatives, focus the team's efforts and energies in one direction, from a common base.

Subsequently, Amey Asset Services has had to rationalize its organization to suit the new requirements. The new business model can operate with less than 50 per cent of the original workforce, reflecting requirements for different competencies. Some of the original people had skills that were not transferable within the new business; they were redeployed elsewhere in Amey or left the company.

As a result of Oakland's work, Amey Asset Services refocused its business direction and agreed a framework for action to help senior managers and their teams through the change process. It established a new vision and values, and agreed high-level measures to direct future performance management. While this work was continuing, Amey Asset Services had to win new business, of the type most needed to provide concrete evidence of the transition to the new mix of work. Two key projects were won during this formative period. According to the managing director of Amey Asset Services, "Oakland added value in setting up a new business, and providing a skeleton of processes around which the business structuring activity has been done – all of which was vital. The work has taken up a lot of people's time, but it has been good value for money; much was accomplished, particularly during and as a result of the Oakland workshops." ❜

SUMMARY

1 One of the most frequent criticisms made of consultants is that they're insufficiently innovative, but the irony is that most clients prefer to work with consulting firms that offer them a structured approach (both because the latter is more efficient and because it goes some way to guaranteeing the outcomes of the project).

2 In fact, research suggests that the value of a new management idea to an organization declines as the idea becomes more standardized. Value is maximized by tailoring an idea to suit the unique needs of organizations, not by following an approach already used by others.

3 Applying this research to consulting suggests that innovation and structure should be balanced within a consulting project. Too much innovation and the costs of implementation may be prohibitively high; too little, and the value delivered by the consulting firm will be much lower than anticipated.

CHAPTER 9

THE EXCHANGE OF INTELLECTUAL CAPITAL

Let us return to that joke about the watch.

Another question which it raises is, who gains most value from a consulting project? Is it clients, who hire consultants, often at considerable expense, to acquire a skills or to access information they would not otherwise have? Or is it the consultants, who not only pocket the client's fee but can take the lessons which they have learned from the project and promptly charge another client for them? As clients become increasingly concerned about the value for money they receive from consultants, knowledge transfer becomes an important, if not contentious, issue.

The first thing to recognize is that clients and consultants have a symbiotic relationship.

As discussed in Chapter 1, one of the principal reasons why clients hire consultants is to acquire new intellectual capital, either about an industry or about a specific business issue. Essentially, clients have a gap in their intellectual capital which they want consultants to fill. This gap may take many forms – it may be hard data on a new market, or softer skills, perhaps on how a particular process can be best managed. Uncertainty and complexity in the wider business environment both increase clients' tendencies to identify gaps – 'a new problem has arisen that we do not know how to fix' – and, thus, the demand for consultancy remains. Moreover, as uncertainty and complexity increase, so does the demand for consultancy. But the process is not linear. When a consulting company fills a gap in the intellectual capital of Company A, it often creates a need for the same solution among Companies B to Z, all of whom now realize that Company A has something which they do not (and did not until recently even know they needed). And because no solution is ever quite the same, in filling the intellectual capital gaps of Companies B to Z, the consulting company creates intellectual capital for itself and further demand in Company A – 'our competitors have learnt from our experience and are now overtaking us'. Clients are therefore dependent on consultants' help in resolving issues – and consultants are dependent on clients to create a sustainable market.

But the problem from the client perspective is that, while intellectual capital moves in both directions – from consultant to client, and from client to consultant – money moves in only one – from client to consultant. Having had their watch taken by the consultants, many clients end up wondering why they are the ones who have to pay.

This imbalance poses two questions, both of which are considered in this chapter:

- ☐ How can clients ensure that they acquire intellectual capital from the consultants they hire as efficiently and effectively as possible?
- ☐ How should clients react to, and potentially manage, the fact that consultants take intellectual capital from them?

TRANSFERRING INTELLECTUAL CAPITAL FROM CONSULTANT TO CLIENT

The ease and effectiveness with which intellectual capital can be transferred from consultant to client varies, according to the precise nature of the intellectual capital involved. Intellectual capital typically takes one of three forms:

- ☐ Raw **data**, collected from customers or from a corporation's IT systems.
- ☐ Once aggregated, stripped of irrelevancies and analyzed, this data becomes **information** – facts that mean something to someone.
- ☐ But information is not enough – **knowledge** (the skills gained from experience) has to be applied in order to make the information meaningful and useable.

Similar stratifications can be applied to different areas of consulting. A client who wants to implement a new IT system may buy an off-the-shelf package (data), or they may choose to hire people to develop or customize a system on their behalf (information). Alternatively, clients may choose to bring in consultants who will train their own staff to develop or customize the system for themselves (knowledge).

Although most consulting projects involve an element of each of these forms of intellectual capital, the balance of the different elements will differ substantially. There has also been a shift: in its earliest days, much of consulting involved gathering data (because this was something which clients found hard to do, prior to the widespread use of IT in business). As the process of gathering data has become easier, consultants have migrated, from collating data to analyzing it. And once technology provided the analytical tools, they migrated again, to the knowledge required to make the resulting analysis actionable in an organization.

But the irony in this development is that data and information are much easier to transfer to a client than knowledge. There are two reasons for this:

1 Because this kind of intellectual capital is written down, it can be physically (or electronically) handed over and disseminated. A client who has received a thick document from a consultant, has something tangible to show from the consulting project. The track record of knowledge transfer seems dismal by comparison. When you ask clients about what they have gained from a consulting assignment in which knowledge was supposed to be transferred, their response varies depending on how involved they were in the project. Perhaps not surprisingly, people who were very involved, who worked side-by-side with the consultants, think that they have gained the most, but the level of gain declines, the

further away from the project a person was. Thus, while data can be disseminated to an organization as a whole, knowledge is usually something that only a small number of individuals acquire (Figure 9.1). Nor is this an easy problem to solve. Because data and information are easier to disseminate than knowledge, the knowledge transferred by the consultants is typically converted back into information and data when it is communicated to other people in an organization.

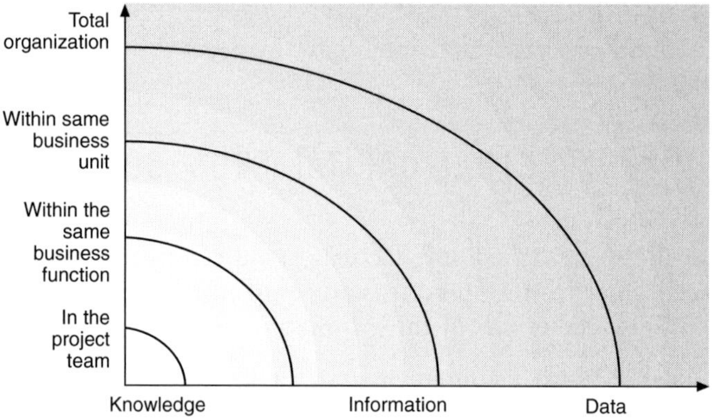

FIGURE 9.1: The varying impact of data, information and knowledge

2 Unlike data and information, knowledge is hard to measure. Once we have acquired a new skill – whether that is reading a book, or driving a car – it is hard to remember a time when we did not have it. Fundamental to the idea of knowledge transfer is assimilation; it is about integrating new ways of thinking, new insights, with our existing knowledge and skills. We do not always know when we have a skill, but equally we cannot imagine life without it.

The transfer of knowledge is hard to see, let alone measure in concrete terms; at the end of the project, there is little for the client to put their finger on and say 'this is what we have bought'. It is not surprising therefore that, for the last decade, clients have been increasingly tempted to buy data and/or information. After decades of 'process' consulting in which consultants have sought to help clients help themselves, clients' impatience with the inherent wooliness and unpredictability of this way of working is running out. Exacerbated by a more difficult economic environment, clients are demanding concrete output, delivered in increasingly short time-scales.

Seen from this perspective, consultants are trapped between a rock and a hard place. Increasingly under pressure to make the intellectual capital component of their work as tangible as possible, many consulting firms now steer clear of process consulting, choosing instead to market themselves either as the purveyors of data and information (essentially returning to the Taylorist origins of the industry) or as outsourcers (people who will run a process for you, rather than trying to effect a transfer of skills to your staff so that they can run it for themselves). And it is not just consultants who suffer as a result of this; one of the clearest lessons to have emerged as a result of the e-business boom of 1998–2000 is that even the best business ideas need people and processes if they are to succeed in the long-run – knowledge and skills are still important.

So what can be done to improve the effectiveness with which consultants transfer all types of intellectual capital to clients – knowledge, as well as information and data? It all comes down to three issues: clarity of definition, access and follow through.

Clarity of definition

Not all intellectual capital is equal, but it is tempting to treat it as such. In Chapter 1, we discussed the difference between industry-specific and issue-specific intellectual capital, but both of these types can be broken down in terms of data, information and knowledge. Just as it is important for clients to be clear about whether they are buying industry-specific or issue-specific intellectual capital, they also need to understand which category of intellectual capital they require. Fundamentally, the decision which a client makes should be based on how important the intellectual capital is likely to be in the long term, and the extent to which the intellectual capital itself is highly specialized.

If you are taking a one-off decision about a specialist topic (for example, which financial systems package to implement, or whether you should move into a particular new market), then taking the time to acquire the knowledge of your consultants is likely to be a waste of time and effort. You will not need the knowledge again, so why bother to obtain it? Conversely, if you think that the intellectual capital involved may be useful to you, either because the particular issue is unlikely to go away (such as running your chosen financial systems package), or because the knowledge involved in resolving it may be useful on future occasions, albeit in different circumstances (such as analyzing new markets in general), then it makes sense to widen the scope of your consulting project to include acquiring the knowledge of your consultants.

This understanding has to be matched against the skills and market positioning of the consultants which you use:

- ☐ Some firms see themselves as primarily undertaking a process on a client's behalf which the client has no interest in doing for itself. Market research is a good illustration of this; few companies (other than market research companies) regard market research as a core competence which they either have or need in-house. They therefore choose to buy it in when required, rather than undertake the time-consuming and expensive process of developing market research skills among their own staff.
- ☐ Other firms, particularly consulting firms involved in large scale systems implementation and organizational change projects, are more likely to stress their willingness to transfer their skills to their clients. Some even regard it as a core competence.

Access

You cannot always separate the message from the medium in which it is expressed. If you want to obtain information from consultants, you need to ask yourself, who would find the information valuable, and how can you facilitate their access to it? Is the intellectual capital:

- ☐ A discrete, focused subject (information on best practice in a particular area, for example)? Or is it much less clear cut? Does the channel by which you access this intellectual capital have to be broad-ranging and flexible?
- ☐ Required for a one-off reason, or will it be needed on an on-going basis (in which case it will need to be updated, but how, and when?)?

- ☐ Something that people will read, or is it something (or somebody) with which the recipient needs to interact? Should it take the form of a document, computer-based training, an interactive workshop?

These three questions point to the three key characteristics of access: the certainty/uncertainty of the *scope* of what you require, the type of **communication** involved, and the length of **time** for which it is required (Figure 9.2). Each of these characteristics represents a choice – and that choice will determine the way in which you obtain the intellectual capital from your consultant.

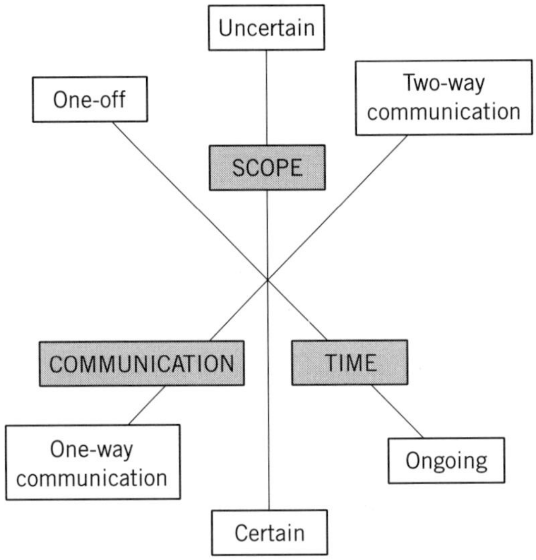

FIGURE 9.2: The three dimensions of access to intellectual capital

This choice is important because consulting firms increasingly work in one of two ways: they tend to be good either at providing intellectual capital, where the scope is well-defined and certain, communicated from the consultant to client on a one-off occasion, or at providing less structured intellectual capital in a way that creates an ongoing dialogue between client and consultant. This point is made by Thomas Tierney, then worldwide managing director at the strategic consultancy Bain & Company, in an article by him and various colleagues in the *Harvard Business Review*. Tierney argues that there is no single, 'correct' way in which consultants should manage intellectual capital; different consulting firms have different needs. The focus of Bain's strategy is to ensure that its consultants have access to experts as well as documents: rather than try to capture every single piece of written work which the firm has produced, the aim is to put consultants in touch with other consultants – a highly sophisticated telephone directory. This enables Bain to be very flexible, and develops a continuous dialogue with clients (there is no end to the intellectual capital). Tierney *et al* contrast this with the strategy of Cap Gemini Ernst & Young, in which formal documentation plays a much more important role, driven by the different nature of the latter's market:

[1] Morten T. Hansen, Nitin Nohria and Thomas Tierney, 'What's Your Strategy for Managing Knowledge?', *Harvard Business Review* (1999).

'Consultants . . . do not take a uniform approach to managing knowledge. The consulting business employs two very different knowledge management strategies. In some companies, the strategy centres on the computer. Knowledge is carefully codified and stored in databases, where it can be accessed and used easily by anyone in the company. We call this the *codification strategy*. In other companies, knowledge is closely tied to the person who developed it and is shared mainly through direct person-to-person contacts. The chief purpose of computers at such companies is to help people communicate knowledge, not store it. We call this the *personalization strategy*. A company's choice of strategy is far from arbitrary – it depends on the way the company serves its clients, the economics of its business, and the people it hires. Emphasizing the wrong strategy or trying to pursue both at the same time can, as some consulting firms have found, quickly undermine a business.'

Follow-through

It is not just the consultants who determine the extent to which knowledge can be transferred to clients; clients themselves have a crucial role to play.

When companies evaluate their use of consultancy, they usually focus on the mechanics of the consulting process (selection, integrated project teams, etc.) and its financial benefits. This approach has two drawbacks: firstly, it assumes that the consulting process – not its content – generates value; secondly, it has always been very difficult, if not impossible, to assign a financial value to a process. As a result, most conclusions do little more than stress the need for good project management skills. Instead, the focus should be on analyzing:

- ☐ What 'new' intellectual capital has been gained during the course of the project, and how it has been communicated to the relevant parts of the organization.
- ☐ The extent to which this intellectual capital is used effectively, once the consultants have left.
- ☐ The potential and actual benefits (financial and non-financial) of the new intellectual capital, and the factors that will facilitate or obstruct their realization.

This kind of survey can be done by speaking to a small number of people in a sample of projects, in order to understand the perspective of those involved in realizing the benefits of the project, including:

- ☐ Their understanding of the potential and actual benefits of the project, and the extent to which their work has changed as a result.
- ☐ The 'new' intellectual capital that has been communicated to them, and the means by which they have captured and will be able to retrieve it in the future.
- ☐ The potential value which such intellectual capital could have to other parts of the organization.

It also makes sense to speak to a small number of people to whom the knowledge gained from these projects should, in theory, be of use in the future, in order to understand:

- ☐ The ways in which this knowledge may be of use and the probability that it will be of use in practice.
- ☐ The factors likely to help or hinder its use.
- ☐ The implications of all of the above for the way the knowledge should be captured, stored and communicated.

From this, it is possible to identify practical recommendations to ensure that:

- ☐ You obtain intellectual capital from consultants as effectively as possible.
- ☐ The short- and long-term value of this intellectual capital – and the way in which this value will be realized – is understood.
- ☐ The amount of value that 'leaks' following the completion of the consulting engagement is minimized.

TRANSFERRING INTELLECTUAL CAPITAL FROM CLIENT TO CONSULTANT

The points listed above should help to make the transfer of intellectual capital from consultant to client more effective, but what about when intellectual capital goes in the other direction – from client to consultant?

This is a serious issue. People writing about consultancy (indeed, about professional services in total) in the 1970s and 1980s constantly referred to the need for so-called 'Chinese walls' which were intended to stop engagement teams (who were in the same consulting firm but working for competing clients) from exchanging confidential information. Similarly, clients talked of having exclusive agreements – clauses in the contracts with consulting firms which ensured that either the individual consultants who worked with them, or sometimes even the whole firm, was prohibited from working with direct competitors on comparable issues for a specified amount of time.

But in this age of rapid information circulation, the focus of concern has shifted and, to some extent, receded. This is partly because it is much harder to keep anything secret these days, whether inside or outside an organization. There are too many companies – publishers, research companies, information providers – whose business it is to identify and comment on new trends. Not surprisingly, considerably more attention is being paid to protecting the ownership of intellectual capital; establishing patents, for example – if you cannot hide your advantage, then the best you can hope to do is prevent other people from replicating it. Indeed, what is the average shelf-life of a competitive advantage in today's economy? Fifty years ago, an innovative market positioning might have given your business several years' lead on your rivals: today, you might get six months.

The transparency dilemma

Consultants are one of the channels through which new business ideas are disseminated. Alongside an exponential increase in business publishing, business schools and the internet, they are one of the reasons why that shelf-life of competitive advantage is shrinking. It is not because consultants are industrial spies, but simply that the business of consultancy is to take *some* of the intellectual capital gained during the course of an engagement for a client to other clients. Confidential data and information gathered by the consultants *must* be treated absolutely confidentially. Often, it has been gathered for a one-off reason to meet the need of a client's unique circumstance. As such, it is often what clients want to defend most vigorously (and can, because it is on paper or in an electronic format). By contrast, the knowledge (the generic skills and insight) which a consultant accumulates during client work becomes a part of that consultant's overall knowledge base, and it would be both impractical and unreasonable to try and prevent consultants from taking the generic lessons which they have learned to their next assignment.

Indeed, all clients benefits from this process. A report by a consulting firm on the financial systems package to be selected by Client A is unlikely to be of interest to Client B, because the two companies' circumstances and decision criteria will be different. But the process of deciding which financial systems package is best is something that is relevant to both clients. A consulting firm which has completed this work for Client A will then have learned something about the generic package selection process that it can usefully apply to Client B. Should Client A be irritated by this? Surely Client B has the better deal? The answer in practice is a little more complicated. Client B (and Clients C to Z even more so) will certainly have benefited in terms of the efficiency of the process – the experience curve (itself the product of a consulting company) tells us that the more you do something, the better you become at doing it. But will the outcome be any better? There is no reason to think so; assuming that the consultants looked at all the factors relevant to both Client A and Client B, the decision should have been equally good. If anything, Client B (and certainly Clients C to Z) may have a less relevant decision, because the decision-making process, as it becomes more generic, may lose sight of a client's particular circumstances. What Client B gains on the one hand, it may lose on the other.

Segmentation and polarization

As with the transference of intellectual capital from consultant to client, the key here is segmentation. Suppose that you are the Chief Executive of a beleaguered company. Once dominant in your industry, you have watched your major competitors catch up and overtake you. What do you do? Do you hire a consulting firm to develop a radically new strategy designed to put space between yourselves and your rivals? Or do you go for some quick wins which stem the tide of shareholder discontent, by rapidly replicating some of the steps taken by competitors? In reality, you would probably do both – but you probably should not hire the same consulting firm in each instance. For the first of these projects, independence and confidentiality are hugely important. If you are investing in an innovative strategy, you clearly need to be confident of a return over as long a time as possible. But, if you are trying to match what someone else has done, confidentiality is much less important than speed.

Not surprisingly, the consulting industry is starting to polarize between these two positions. In one corner of the ring are the (primarily) strategic consulting firms, which make a virtue of their independence and are prepared to enter into an exclusive agreement with a client, limiting their ability to work with the latter's direct competitors for a given period. In the other, are firms who stress their track record – the fact that they have implemented the same process with other companies, including competitors. These firms offer no guarantee that they will not re-use the knowledge (but never the data or information) which they have acquired in working for a client; it would be hard for clients to insist otherwise, given that they are beneficiaries of the knowledge which the consulting firm has already accumulated elsewhere.

Where this issue – the transfer of intellectual capital from clients to consultants – is concerned, clients cannot have their cake and eat it. If you are buying a well-honed process from a consulting firm, it is unreasonable to expect that firm to agree to not honing that process further. Similarly, if you want to have access to leading-edge knowledge about what is going on in your industry, it is naive to assume that your competitors will not want that too. There are choices to be made here. What is most valuable – innovative thinking and the absolute confidentiality of all the intellectual capital generated during the course of a project, or knowing what your competitors know? You cannot expect to have both from a single team of consultants.

Should consultants pay you for your watch?

For clients experienced at working with consultancies, the issue here is less about confidentiality (concerns about which can be dealt with in the contract between client and the consulting firm), and more a sense of moral outrage – the feeling that the consultant who has taken their watch should pay for it. Indeed, the client-consultant relationship seems inequitable: consultants get paid to increase the intellectual capital (whatever form that takes) of their clients, but clients do not get remunerated for increasing the intellectual capital of their consultants.

There are, in fact, instances where clients have tried to change this: clients who have hired consulting firms to develop a bespoke IT applications have, for example, tried to re-coup some of their investment by allowing the consulting firm to sell the idea to other companies in return for some type of licence fee. Although, on paper, such opportunities look to be a means of cementing a client-consultant relationship (revenue-related goals are the easiest to share), the practice is fraught with difficulty:

- ☐ You need to have been very clear from the outset who will own the intellectual property rights (IPR) for any of the outputs from the consulting process. If you, as a client, came up with the idea, but asked a consulting firm to implement it for you, then you may feel as though you are the rightful owner – but the consulting firm, having put so much effort in, may think otherwise. And what happens in instances where a consulting firm has approached you with an idea, but needs your help in testing it in practice. Legal waters such as these are inevitably muddy and the simplest way to forestall any conflict is to assign the IPR as part of the contract you sign, irrespective of whether you think that anything of commercial value will emerge from the project.

- ☐ Even if you and the consulting firm agree that there may be a wider market for a specific intellectual 'asset' – whatever form this takes – you may not agree on exactly what that market is. The consulting firm will, quite logically, see your competitors as the best source of revenue in the short-term, whereas you may want these players to be the last to be approached, thus preserving your competitive advantage for longer.

- ☐ Such points of conflict can turn into more significant problems when it comes to control and management of the project. A large corporate client that launches a joint venture with a small, specialist consulting firm to sell on particular service or system may reasonably feel that it is in charge – it is comparatively easy to see what the consulting firm is up to and the size differential means that the client can – for want of a better term – throw its weight around. But put a large client together with a substantial consulting firm that has offices throughout the world and a fast-paced and efficient knowledge management system, and it becomes hard for the consulting firm, let alone its client partner, to control the route to market. Not realizing that there may be particular sensitivities involved, eager consultants may take the initiative and, quite innocently, over-step whatever mark the client thinks is in place.

- ☐ But by far the most fundamental argument against such arrangements is that selling consulting services is not (or not usually) a client's core business. In a world in which companies are already struggling to work out what areas they should focus on and what parts of their business are peripheral, embarking on an initiative that may take money as well as management time does not seem like a rational use of resources. This may be a bitter pill for the more entrepreneurial manager, but it is one that has to be swallowed nonetheless.

SUMMARY

1 In the client–consultant relationship, intellectual capital is transferred both from the consultant to the client, and from the client to the consultant.

2 The ease and effectiveness with which consultants transfer intellectual capital to clients is dependent on the type of intellectual capital involved; data and information can both be transferred comparatively easily, but it is much harder to inculcate knowledge.

3 Improving the effectiveness with which knowledge can be transferred to clients involves:

- ☐ Being clear about the type of intellectual capital involved.
- ☐ Streamlining the way in which people are going to access and use this intellectual capital.
- ☐ Making a positive effort to evaluate how successful a consulting project has been at transferring the intellectual capital required.

4 It is an inevitable part of the consulting process that consultants gain knowledge from the work they do, but this is quite different to a client's data and information (which must be treated confidentially). While clients may resent this, they also benefit from it – one of the reasons for hiring a consulting firm is to access the knowledge that it has been able to accumulate in a particular field.

CHAPTER 10

BRINGING THE OUTSIDE VIEW INSIDE

No one finds it easy to see the wood; whether you are running the largest of corporations or the smallest of small businesses, almost all of your time will be spent on seeing the trees. They might take the form of products, people, processes, customers, markets – but they are trees, nonetheless. Being an outsider is therefore one of the most valuable functions of a consultant – someone who sees your problems with fresh eyes, who challenges established assumptions, who helps you refocus on the wood at least for a period of time. But making good, effective use of consultants in this role also involves understanding exactly what the consultant's role is in this respect. Developing that understanding, and analyzing its practical implications for clients, is the focus of this chapter.

THE TRUTH IS PROBABLY NOT OUT THERE

When clients ask consultants to come into an organization and assess a particular issue, they are, implicitly or explicitly, asking the consultants to uncover the truth.

In a process not unlike the plot of a detective novel, consultants are presented with the facts and suspects, and asked to say who (or what) is responsible. A company which suspects that its supply chain is operating less efficiently than its competitors', may hire a team of consultants who collect and analyze the operational data, interview a sample of people involved in the process, identify the cause of the problem and recommend corrective action.

But this is something which an organization could do for itself, so why hire outside consultants? Like detectives in the crime stories, consultants should: have additional resources not at the client's disposal; have experience in, even specific tools for, analyzing such problems; be disinterested outsiders with no personal stake in the resulting decision; have a tried-and-tested process for carrying out such work.

The key difference between a detective novel and a consulting project lies in the nature of their outcome. The objective of the country house mystery is to reveal the truth – to identify and punish the villains. The ultimate outcome of a consulting process is to persuade a client's organization to do something, usually to take a decision, which it could not do before. What is needed in the latter case is not so much the 'simple' truth, as the truth which will precipitate that organization into acting and/or deciding.

A good illustration of this distinction is the report that is often left on the client's desk at the end of a consulting engagement. What is the purpose of this report? If it just tells the client the truth, then the way in which the truth is presented does not matter, nor does it matter if the client never picks it up and reads it, let alone acts on it. But given that a constant criticism made by clients of consultants is that such reports 'gather dust', it is reasonable to infer that stating the truth is not the only function of a report. Clients instead expect the report to galvanize their organization, perhaps because it marshals the available facts to create a compelling case for taking a specific decision, or because it shows a clear and unequivocal process by which a decision already taken can be implemented. Indeed, if this argument was taken a step further, and clients were asked to say whether they would want a report that was 95 per cent accurate but able to effect this kind of change, over one that was 100 percent accurate but never likely to motivate them into acting, the vast majority would prefer the former. What, after all, is the point of perfect information, if you never do anything with it?

This partly explains why clients hire consultants to go through a process that they could probably do for themselves. Consultants may have more efficient ways of doing this work and no vested interest in its outcome, but their key advantage from a client's point of view is that they can present a version of the truth which is designed to help an organization make a choice – something which it was transparently failing to do by itself (or it would not have needed consultants in the first place).

Uncovering the truths

Without becoming too philosophical about it, it is important to understand that, when it comes to consulting, there is not a single, perfect version of the truth that consultants have to uncover, but multiple versions, each of which is believed by different people and through which the consultant has to navigate. How many times have you been at meetings where people have disputed what happened at a previous meeting, and where the minutes only muddy the situation further? Have you ever agreed something with a colleague, only to find that his or her memory of the conversation is very different to your own? Such things happen to us all of the time, and are much more likely to happen if the disputed discussion was on a complex issue and took place some weeks previously. For consultants, problems such as these pose a very significant challenge: a consultant, trying to work out what happened when a particular decision was taken, will look through reports of the meeting and talk to the people involved, but may receive several different views of the facts.

Consulting is the opposite of empirical science, in that the more information is gathered, the more complex the picture becomes. At the end of the process, your conclusions are based on consensus and compromise – they are not based on yes/no tests.

This subtly, but significantly, changes the role that consultants play. If the detective's job is to identify the guilty suspect, the consultant's is to focus on building sufficient evidence to convince its audience. If consultants present the truth but do not persuade their audience to 'convict', they have failed; consultancy is as much an exercise in creating shared belief, as it is about revealing the truth. The consultant has to encourage organizations to act (why be there otherwise?), and only shared belief in the need to act in a particular way can do this.

This does not mean that consultants can be inaccurate. If you are presented with material which contradicts known facts or your experience, then you will rightly reject it. Consultants therefore have to make sure that the 'truth' they present fits as many of the facts as possible. One visibly incorrect fact, however tangential to the main argument, will tarnish the reputation of the rest. This, in turn, means that a key part of the consulting process is – or should be – to understand what people think of as true. Consultants need to be able to gauge the extent to which the 'truth' they present will either confirm existing views of the 'truth' or challenge them. If the consultants' 'truth' simply confirms what people already believe, there may be a danger that a client will claim that the consultants have not added anything (see Chapters 7 and 8 for a more detailed discussion of this issue), but little extra effort is needed to convince people. Conversely, where the 'truth' as presented by the consultants is substantially different from the view that most people within the client's organization hold, then considerable time and thought has to be invested into changing and managing expectations.

THE IMPLICATIONS FOR CLIENTS

It may sound manipulative, even unethical, but the consultant's situation is not so very different from the parent who cajoles their reluctant toddler through the library door by saying that the library's about to close and they have to be quick. Galvanising an organization of tens of thousands of people is considerably harder than persuading a toddler to move, but the technique is not dissimilar: present information which puts an end to prevarication.

Parents can legitimately claim that they have a right to act in this way, because it is in the long-term best interest of their toddler to read books. But can consultants claim the same moral authority? A consultant who is genuinely acting with a client's long-term best interest in mind can (this was discussed at the outset of this book, in Chapter 1). If a consultant believes that an organization should follow a particular course of action, his or her responsibility is to help the organization do this by presenting a version of the truth which, while being sufficiently close to the truth to ensure that people within the organization believe it, also provides such an unambiguous case for this course of action that further debate becomes irrelevant. Indeed, the consultant who prefers a particular course, but does not believe in it sufficiently strongly to push an organization to pursue it, may be being far more unethical.

That being said, clients do not have to be passive, but quite the opposite: the more they are aware of the process and take an active part in making it happen, the greater the value which they will obtain from using consultants. So what should clients do?

The key is to make a virtue of a necessity. One reason why so many clients continue to think that they are hiring consultants to uncover the truth, is that this reason is easier to defend internally. You cannot argue with a colleague who wants to find the truth: you can with someone who claims that your organization is failing to take an important decision. Asking a consultant to uncover the truth can also be seen as something that an organization could do for itself, but perhaps lacks the available resources to do – it is not an implicit criticism of the organization. It could do this, but it does not have the time. Saying that you need to hire consultants because your organization is procrastinating is very different. This may be a hard discussion to have internally, but it is a hugely important one. It does not help a consultant to be hired to do one job at face value, when they are really being asked to do something else.

Clients therefore need to think seriously about how they take decisions, and the factors that help or hinder their decision-making process. What is the point of hiring consultants to help your organization decide something, if you don't know *how* your organization makes decisions? Some organizational decision-making is highly rational ('the facts say we should do this'), some is much more emotional ('I do not want to expose myself by disagreeing with my boss'). More often, it is a combination of the two. And, of course, any organizational decision is the aggregate of many individual decisions taken independently or in consultation with others.

Without becoming either too complex or simplistic about this, it is worth considering four fundamental characteristics of decision-making, all of which have an impact on how effectively you use consultants.

- ☐ The first of these is the extent to which **reason/emotion** play a part. Consider meetings which you have recently attended: are issues decided because people review the facts, or because they have a gut feel about something? If you think that decisions in your organization are taken largely after due consideration of the available data, then you need to ensure that the consultants you work with do, indeed, present you with facts. Nothing is more likely to deter a 'fact-based' organization than to present them with high-level conclusions based on expert opinion but little data. But expert opinions might be just what you need if your colleagues tend to debate summaries of key issues which make a succinct, but compelling, case for a particular course of action. In this context, allowing consultants to produce reams of statistics wastes their time and your money.
- ☐ Closely related, but not identical to this, is the issue of **ownership**. Some organizations are more open-minded than others – they are prepared to accept someone's word, and listen to advisers (internal or external). But in many other organizations (probably the majority), people want to feel that they have contributed in some way – opinions ventured by advisers have to be assimilated and reworked before they are accepted. Again, this is a characteristic of the business which the consultants need to understand. In these latter types of organization, time and opportunity needs to be allowed for people to consider what consultants say – and claim it for themselves. There also has to be the recognition that the consultants' reputation may suffer as a result. The process of assimilation can be so effective that it leads to a degree of historical revisionism – clients take ownership of ideas so effectively they forget that the idea may have originated with a consultant.
- ☐ Another important consideration is the level of **consensus** required within an organization. Some businesses afford individual managers a high degree of autonomy and make them personally accountable for the decisions they make. In this environment, the consulting process has not only to help the individual client make the right decision, but support, even potentially defend, him or her. Conversely, in a consensus-driven organization, consultants have to understand that convincing one manager is not enough, and the process of decision-making has to be as inclusive as possible.
- ☐ Finally, whether people react to data or emotional impulse, internalize decisions or credit their advisers, take decisions separately or collectively, it is important to recognize that they will work over different **timescales**. Some people and organizations reach decisions more quickly than others. What is the benefit of using consultants to deliver a short, sharp shock, if your decision-making is a very considered process?

Case study – SAS International

A successful family business built from scratch by the current owner may not be the obvious place for management consultants, but this case study demonstrates that the good can always do better . . .

SAS International is the market leader in the ceiling systems sector, manufacturing and exporting a range of products, from off-the-shelf standards for next-day delivery, right through to bespoke contracts for highly customized, prestigious building projects such as Hong Kong airport. Employing 450 people in four factories spread across the UK, the company thrives on challenge – like realizing architects' ground-breaking design concepts – and they have excelled in clever automation of pressed product, folding-in sequence to make complex shapes and apertures that are well ahead of the competition.

Group Director Mark McElhinney is passionate about improving his factories, but in 2001 he faced a very specific challenge: to cope with a 30 per cent increase in volume, with a corresponding increase in revenue of only 9 per cent (a testimony to the downward pressure of prices in this sector). To help him respond to this, McElhinney hired Bourton, a medium sized UK-based consultancy specializing in operational improvement.

Keith Bisset, Bourton's managing director takes up the story.

“Our specialist, Simon Carr, led five one-week *kaizen* events in the Bridgend factory following the manufacturing process: perforating, auto bending and turret punching, press shop, assembly, and paint. The success of these prompted further commissions in the grid and insulating factories.

For each event, we created a multi-functional team of up to 12 people, including staff from all levels and including support functions (we always involve the people who actually work in the target area and those who are impacted by what goes on there). The same team was actively involved for the whole week – doing the analysis, identifying “do-able” improvements and then making the agreed changes.

For many, this was the first time they had been exposed to the type of rigorous analysis techniques that we use. In some cases, hard data was not as readily available as was first thought. We overcame this by applying a range of tools, first gauging how far the team already understood these, and then holding “teach points” to fill knowledge gaps. Our inclusive approach ensured that the findings were accepted as indisputable, eliminating time-consuming debate.

All outputs were displayed in a project room that became the reference point for the before-and-after comparison at the end of the event. Some of the improvements made are astonishing – and yet they had all been achieved using simple solutions, in the space of a week. The actions taken were all within the capabilities of the combined team members themselves, and required very little in the way of expenditure.

Having solved some of the most pressing problems in the manufacturing process, we moved on to tackle the next constraint – the split-site sales order processing activity which had become unnecessarily complex and labour-intensive. Lead times were too long, with poor visibility and right-first-time levels, but there was little hard information to rely on.

We customized our approach to suit this environment. A team of nine people handled four different order categories: off-the-shelf, made-to-order, designed-to-order and export. The timescales were also different – instead of a five-day “blitz”, we held three two-day sessions, allowing time for follow-up actions in between.

As always, the starting point was to analyze the situation and produce meaningful measures so that remedies could be identified and prioritized. We plotted, on large wall displays, all activities from postbag to acknowledgement. These included both formal rule-book procedures and “work-arounds”, plus all logs, paperwork etc. raised, making it easier to see where duplications and nonsensical things were happening. It prompted suggestions and generated enthusiasm for sorting the problems. We established, for example, that only 5 per cent of lead time was spent actually working on an order.

During the mapping process, potential improvements were captured and then prioritized for action, according to ease of implementation and benefit anticipated. Within 12 weeks, overall process time went from six days to half a day, quality performance more than doubled, and headcount was cut by a quarter.

Our involvement was by this stage sufficiently advanced to enable SAS International's own people to take our ideas and hold similar workshops in the other factories – there had been a genuine transfer of skills from us to them. As one manager commented to us, "There has been a ripple effect, with others taking ownership – it is not just managers 'getting' at workers". We think that this transfer of skills is a reflection of ability to establish credibility quickly, motivate all involved (and deal with a range of attitudes, including scepticism) and still produce results. Engaging people's interest and helping to release their discretionary effort is a benefit of our work with SAS, that has the potential to out-perform all the other savings made so far.

Comments made by the people on the factory floor both before and after Bourton's work reflect this. The initial reaction was cynicism: typical comments were "we do not expect to be able to make any major changes to the factory" and "this is just another thing that will last for a week then be forgotten about". But this quickly gave way to surprise and enthusiasm as it became apparent that the consultants had not come to tell them what to do. "I have been very impressed," said one client employee, "by the way all members of the team got stuck in and managed through the facilitator to agree on some radical change." "It has been very constructive and interesting," said another, "if we keep it up, we will see a vast improvement. I've been surprised by the number of issues uncovered". ❜

Bourton's work is a testimony to the valuable role that consultants can play in enabling clients to see their own organization with new eyes. By providing a combination of analytical techniques, compelling internal facts and an environment where employees were actively encouraged to identify, implement and – ultimately – own performance improvements, the firm facilitated significant change. One thing particularly stands out: the extent to which Bourton's process took into account the way in which this client was likely to react to the external impetus of a consulting firm.

This is the crux of the issue. Bringing in consultants to give an outside view is often thought of as a one-way process – the consultants gather information and tell the client their conclusions. In reality, however, it is not possible to divorce what the consultants say from the way in which they say it and the way in which clients react to it. Even in this type of consulting assignment, there should be a two-way process – a dialogue between clients and consultants.

SUMMARY

1 Bringing an objective perspective is one of the most valuable roles that consultants perform.

2 While it is important that this perspective is as accurate as possible, clients also need to recognize that part of this value comes from the consultants' ability to present a version of the truth which helps the client organization move forward. There is little point in hiring a consulting firm that does not present the information it has gathered in a way that an organization can assimilate.

3 To maximize the effectiveness of a consulting firm, clients need to understand how people in their organizations take decisions. Using consultants who appeal to people's reason in a highly political organization, where most decisions are made by gut feel, is only likely to reinforce the status quo. For consultants to make a difference, there has to be a match between the way they present their analysis, and the way in which people in the client's organization assimilate data and make decisions.

CHAPTER 11

CHANGE MANAGEMENT: CONSULTANTS AS 'BELIEF AGENTS'

The previous chapter examined the role that consultants play in helping organizations to make decisions. Making the decision, however, is only one part of the picture. Decisions taken are not always acted upon, and, for clients to maximize the value they receive from consultants, this 'conversion rate' needs to be as high as possible. Once again, what is the point of hiring consultants to help do something, if you do not follow the process through to its conclusion?

RESISTING RESISTANCE

What is it that stops an organization which has taken a decision from taking the next step? Primarily, it is because other people (and sometimes even the people who took the decision) do not believe that it is the right decision. Senior management decides to axe an established but poorly performing brand, but the marketing manager still believes it has untapped potential, so he delays the execution and tries to identify an alternative; a manager's attempts to establish employee discussion groups fall on deaf ears because her colleagues believe the meetings will serve little useful purpose; a consulting firm implements a new IT system to streamline a process, but the end-users do not believe the changes will work and continue to work in the way in which they are accustomed. Resistance to change is a key hurdle.

From the point of view of a client hiring consultants, resistance to change is a serious issue because people only start to resist change when they believe that it is being forced on them by other people, a feeling that is exaggerated when external consultants are involved. You cannot force someone who is ill to go to the doctor – and nagging them often makes them dig their heels in further: they have to decide for themselves to go. Similarly, it is far better for a group of people to persuade themselves they have to change, than to send someone in to persuade them. This not-invented-here syndrome creates enormous problems for consultants. In the 1980s, after two decades of consulting firms implementing IT systems for clients, both sides realized that only a fraction of the potential benefits of automation was being achieved because people were not adapting to the new systems as quickly or effectively as expected. This recognition essentially resulted in two parallel initiatives. On the one hand, it gave rise to business process reengineering (BPR). Initially pioneered by James Champney and Michael Hammer in the early 1990s, this approach relied on empowering employees to streamline processes end-to-end, prior to that process being automated. And on the other hand, it gave birth to a new discipline – change management – designed to minimize and mitigate the inevitable reluctance to adopt new ideas by people not involved in their development.

Both approaches generated considerable income for consulting firms during the 1990s; while BPR has now largely fallen from favour, change management has enjoyed something of a renaissance, as managers who are constrained by recessionary pressures have sought to leverage the latent value in their people, processes and systems. At the same time, hiring external consultants to manage change seems contradictory. If resistance to change is a reflection of the extent to which individuals perceive the change to come from pressure outside them, then how can consultants, coming in from the outside, hope to overcome that resistance? It is the equivalent, surely, of *telling* someone that they are empowered: by telling them this, you are automatically disempowering them. Consultants have, indeed, learnt that a direct approach in these circumstances makes little sense; successful change management has to rely on a facilitative approach, helping people to help themselves, building trust and keeping open channels for communication.

Case study: changing purchasing behaviour at Boots The Chemists

In 2001, Boots The Chemists, the UK's largest pharmacy/health/beauty chain, embarked on an ambitious program to reduce costs by $150 million. The savings would be used, in part, to invest in the business and revitalize its customer offer. Part of this program focused on embracing best practice in procurement. A fragmented approach to procurement had developed across the company's business units, with very little central control or understanding of groupwide spending patterns. A key part of Boots' new initiative focused on the procurement of 'indirect' goods and services (e.g. IS/IT, marketing, logistics).

To achieve these savings, Boots would have to make radical changes to the way it purchased and sourced goods. These changes included not only developing and implementing a strategic vision for groupwide 'indirect' procurement, but establishing common processes consistently across its business units, and sustainable change by establishing a culture of continuous improvement and by building cost-reduction targets into performance contracts. The company hired KPMG Consulting to help it realize this aim and, in particular, to achieve world-class procurement practice through the design and implementation of a procurement services unit (PSU). The PSU would drive procurement at both the strategic and tactical levels, with business units retaining responsibility for individual requisition to payment transactions. Senior management would be able to track and measure against targets by means of performance contracts with the business units' executive directors, and through service level agreements between the PSU and the business units themselves.

KMPG Consulting's assignment manager, Adeeb Dhallai, gives the story:

‘We had two primary objectives during the first four months of the project: to agree in outline the vision, structure and organizational design of the PSU and communicate this to the business units, and to deliver a series of quick wins (which, by themselves, amounted to over $4.5 million) which would demonstrate the benefits of the project from the outset. The focus of the subsequent five months was implementation. Working as a joint KPMG Consulting–Boots team, we recruited PSU employees and trained them to use tactical category management techniques, implemented the agreed policies, processes and practices, and delivered a further $14 million of savings towards the target identified in the first phase.

Most indirect purchasing at Boots had been done by non-specialists, and creating a central resource with first class procurement skills was a key challenge. Success relied on building and transferring knowledge to a unit of high-calibre people who would develop a mix of strategic and tactical procurement skills, and who would accept increasing amounts of responsibility as the project progressed. We conducted a programme of learning sessions to kickstart the development of high-calibre procurement skills.

But this situation was complicated by low-awareness of the PSU programme and its value at middle management levels, where there would be most resistance to change. Furthermore, the previous decentralized approach to procurement made it extremely difficult to identify and communicate with all the people who would be affected by the program's changes. We devoted a great deal of time to managing change and especially to communications. We developed a structured, comprehensive communications program involving presentations, roadshows, newsletters, and the launch of a PSU website to communicate the message. The website was used to update the business on projected savings, and on people, events and general progress. We also focused on communicating facts and figures in a meaningful way. For example, we created a "Did you know?" sheet, which demonstrated that:

- ☐ Groupwide, Boots had more than 18,000 suppliers.
- ☐ The Group had over 10,000 suppliers with whom it spent less than $1,500 pa.
- ☐ 50 per cent of total spend was with only 75 suppliers.
- ☐ The Group spent $175 million with only seven suppliers.

We were able to use these facts during presentations and roadshows to bring home the need for change and increase understanding of how the PSU could help.

A similar challenge arose with business unit management teams, who did not understand the full impact of savings well enough to be good advocates for the PSU. To resolve this, we implemented a transparent benefits-tracking process, which translated savings into impact on business unit profit and loss, and capital accounts.

We also communicated cost reductions both in year and annualized savings rates. To enhance their credibility, all savings opportunities were qualified by business unit managers. Armed with a greater understanding of where the savings were coming from and what they meant, the business unit management teams were able to adopt an advocate role with confidence. ❜

As a result, $26 million in annualized cost savings were realized in the first nine months and the project has continued to deliver savings of $60 million within 18 months. Where there were previously 30 ways to purchase an item, the new system offers just five methods. Where business units previously worked autonomously, the new structure has engendered a high level of collaboration. Julian Coles, Director of the PSU, summarizes the impact:

❛ Big change programs such as this require trust, not only from the board but also from other employees. Obviously, change takes time, but we have already witnessed a transformation of attitudes on the part of some team members who were initially sceptical. As a result, the reputation of the PSU has been greatly enhanced. Throughout this project, the emphasis has been on knowledge transfer, and on the development of ongoing support tools and techniques which ensure that our people are equipped to carry out their new roles. ’

Case study: Heineken – brewing a culture of efficiency

Heineken has a fine tradition of brewing, and a dominant position in today's global markets. Its origins date from 1864, when Gerard Adriaan Heineken acquired the Hooiberg brewery in Amsterdam. Today, Heineken beer is available in 170 countries worldwide, and the company has a portfolio of over 80 brands. In 2000, the Heineken Group brewed almost 10 billion litres of beer, making it the second largest brewer in the world.

While the beer market in Heineken's home territory of the Netherlands is relatively stagnant, demand is escalating rapidly in the group's export markets. The Zoeterwoude plant in the Netherlands packages beer for both domestic sales and export. In 2001, the plant's management faced a double challenge: additional capacity was needed to deliver to the highly seasonal export markets, but, at the same time, cost-competition at home meant that there was tremendous pressure to take out unnecessary costs.

Celerant Consulting was commissioned to help identify and implement a solution. Frank Rohmer managed the project:

‘ Our specific target was to increase operational equipment efficiency (OEE) at Zoeterwoude by 20 per cent. With 20 per cent additional OEE, Zoeterwoude would be able to meet demand up to 2003 without additional capital investment on the scale required for a new bottling line. Both management and shopfloor workers at Zoeterwoude recognized that this level of improvement would require a step-change in performance and in the culture at the brewery. When we came in, a program was already under way at Zoeterwoude to move the culture from a traditional command-and-control environment to one that was more team-orientated. This program had started in 1996, by increasing the skill levels of individual operators; it had then moved on to improve the capabilities of people working together as teams. We needed to help the organization to move to the next stage – using these teams to achieve results.

The key was to improve the availability of critical machines at all times. At peak times, the additional capacity would be used to meet demand; off-peak, it could be used for other essential activities such as training. A two-pronged strategy emerged, focused on turning operating data into business information for shaping decisions, and creating a culture that would make and act on decisions quickly and effectively. The premise was that, if we could give people at all levels in the Zoeterwoude plant access to reliable, accurate and up-to-date management information, and if we could ensure that they were focused on achieving results rather than simply doing their jobs, then they would have both the means and the motivation to compare their performance with the targets set, and take immediate steps to close any gaps. This philosophy was in stark contrast to the existing situation in the plant, where problems had tended to be chronic (unresolved over a long period of time) rather than acute. Temporary fixes were rife, and people were constantly fire-fighting, because they had neither the time nor the incentive to develop structural solutions.

We examined each bottling line in the plant, and used problem-solving techniques to help the teams identify why equipment availability was falling below optimum levels. In the past, lack of communication between different functions and departments in the plant had meant that there was little agreement about the real causes of problems; for example, maintenance people might think that operator mistakes were causing breakdowns, when operators believed that poor quality maintenance was the root of the problem. By classifying problems in the bottling lines according to whether their causes were (mechanical, man-made, technical, process-based etc.) the teams were able to identify appropriate solutions quickly (such as maintenance, training, etc.). Out of this analysis came a complete package of measures to achieve the desired objectives, including a new management control and reporting system, a new approach to problem-solving and a new process for setting and agreeing targets.

At the same time, we faced three distinct challenges. The first was the seasonality of demand for beer. While we found it was easy to motivate people to make improvements when there was a shortage of capacity to meet demand, keeping the pressure on when demand slackened (in winter) was much harder. We solved this by ensuring that there was better information on when demand would peak and trough, so that production, training and maintenance could be better balanced and scheduled. Regular team meetings and team-building activities also helped to keep people focused on maximum performance. Secondly, it is always difficult to persuade people to do something different when they do not see the need for change. In some groups within the Zoeterwoude plant, there was a much bigger gap between what was happening and what was needed than elsewhere, and there was much resistance from people accustomed to "the way we do things around here". By bringing people of different departments together, we were able to encourage a better shared understanding of what the problems were and what the different departments could contribute to solve problems together.

Finally, there was the issue of leadership. Some of the team leaders were better suited to leading the type of change needed in their area of responsibility than others were. Different leaders were found to be at different stages of development; not all were able to support their team to the same extent. We therefore coached some of the managers extensively, until every team had a leader who took accountability for, and was focused on, achieving results. As a result, they had the motivation, the orientation and the authority to demand the same of their team members, and empower their team members to deliver.

Throughout the project, we worked side-by-side with employees at every level: attending their meetings, encouraging their ideas and initiatives, helping them to stay focused on achieving the desired results. We made it clear from the outset that we could not achieve the targets set by ourselves; ownership of the problems and the solutions had to rest firmly with people in the Zoeterwoude plant, if the improvements achieved were to be sustainable. Previous encounters with consultants at Zoeterwoude had left memories of intelligent people with bright ideas but ultimately little impact. We were thought of as different because we did not spend weeks refining the strategic plan to the nth degree. Instead, once the basic plan had been developed, we put our energy into making the changes happen – guiding, supporting and coaching the plant employees as they took the actions planned, assessed their impact, adjusted the plan, and moved on to the next stage.

In less than a year, the teams at Zoeterwoude rose to the challenge set by the business. They achieved the 20 per cent OEE improvement across nine packaging lines. Zoeterwoude's increased efficiency had positive knock-on effects, too. In the past, the recurring problems at the plant had meant that it could not be relied on to deliver what it promised, when it promised, to partners further down the supply chain. As a result, costs were incurred to make up delays and deficits. Such costs became history when the project made Zoeterwoude a more stable, reliable partner in the supply chain. ’

CHANGING BELIEFS

The work of KPMG Consulting with Boots The Chemist shows how effective a comparatively low-key approach, focused on transferring skills, can be when applied to an environment where people might easily have resisted the proposed change. Business unit managers could have resisted their loss of autonomy; purchasers might have resented having their choice of supplier limited; almost everyone might have seen the intervention of the procurement services unit as a bureaucratic intrusion, designed to make their lives more difficult.

But the key to the success of this project lay in one thing: **credibility**. What KPMG Consulting managed to do – through effective communication, by marshalling compelling facts about Boots' existing purchasing behaviour, by finding immediate savings – was to make employees *believe* that the creation of the PSU was the right strategy. In effect, they took a decision by the company's senior management and made the people affected by it *believe* that it was the right decision.

The same is true of Celerant's work with Heineken. Again, the consultants did not act like stereotypical consultants: they rolled up their sleeves in order to deliver some quick wins, and helped to ensure that Heineken's employees had the data and freedom they required to take decisions for themselves. They made them believe that it was possible to work differently.

Building credibility and creating belief is therefore central to making effective use of consultants. If people are resistant to changes suggested by their senior managers because they are cynical, then they are doubly cynical about consultants. Consultants are people who earn more than they do, drive flashier cars and jet around the world. Crucially, consultants are people who can walk away from the day-to-day problems for which a client is accountable. Consultants may help your organization move forward by taking a critical, but difficult, decision (see the previous chapter), but if you cannot persuade those involved in the implementation of the decision to believe that it is the right decision, their input will be entirely wasted.

Business offers few frameworks for generating belief. But belief is out there – in organizations with long heritages of which their employees are rightly proud, in small entrepreneurial companies driven by a vision of doing something different, in large corporations that have faced down significant challenges by reinventing themselves. So what is common to these examples? How can it be harnessed to improve the way in which clients use consultants? In fact, these organizations share four fundamental characteristics (Figure 11.1).

Overcoming resistance to change starts with someone at the top taking an inspirational lead, setting out clear but comparatively high level objectives about what could be different. This is followed up by quick wins which demonstrate that this vision is achievable, and by organizational stories which disseminate these wins and their significance. Finally, it involves identifying advocates within the organization who will not only spread the word but also become responsible for making the initially high level ideas work in reality (and thereby take over from the visionary leader as the owners of the strategy).

Table 11.1 summarizes the key ways in which consultants can help in this process, and draws parallels with the Boots/KPMG Consulting and Heineken/Celerant cases described above.

Consultants can do little to supply visionary leadership, nor is it their role to do so. Occasionally, a consultant makes it to 'guru-status', and his or her ideas may provide the starting point for corporate transformations. But, even in these instances, there is usually someone within the adopting organization who is laying out how this new idea could be successfully applied. Indeed, without such commitment, it is probable that the change,

Organizations with strong beliefs …

… have (or had) a visionary leader who has not only established the organization's guiding principles, but also embodies those principles in his or her behaviour.	Leadership
… have, under the influence of their visionary leaders, managed to do things they didn't think they could do – launch a new product in a fraction of the time taken previously, for example. Such 'miracles' challenge organizational inertia and scepticism: they prove that the visionary leader is not all talk.	Making the impossible possible
… tell stories about their leaders and the successes which the organization have achieved. The 'parables' build a shared understanding of the meaning of these achievements; they establish the key values of the organization.	Creating common values
… have a group of people who adopt the ideas of the visionary leader and work at all levels and in all areas of the organization to persuade their colleagues to buy-in to them. They are 'evangelists' seeking to 'convert' the people around them.	Champions

FIGURE 11.1: The four characteristics of belief-driven organizations

KEY CHANGE CHARACTERISTIC	ROLE OF CONSULTANTS	BOOTS / KPMG CONSULTING	HEINEKEN / CELERANT
Visionary leader	None	N/A	N/A
Making the impossible possible	• Identify and deliver quick wins • Cut down bureaucracy and other barriers	• Initial cost savings of US$26 million • Total savings of US$60 million	• Initial improvements in OEE • Not insisting on a detailed plan before rolling up their sleeves and starting work
Creating common values	• Set up formal and informal communications processes which make people aware of quick wins and overall objectives	• Multi-strand communications process • Focused on key statistics to gain people's attention and raise awareness of the potential impact overall	• Providing immediate accessible information
Champions	• Help develop the detail of the vision • Set up support infrastructure (e.g. systems) • Training	• Developed operational vision for PSU alongside client's own staff • Transfer of specialist procurement skills to PSU staff	• Encouraging individual ownership of problems and resolutions • Creating results-focused teams • Coaching of key team leaders

TABLE 11.1: The role of consultants in generating belief

whatever it involves, will fail. This means that one of the first questions that clients should ask, if they are thinking of hiring consultants to help effect some sort of change, is, what level of commitment is there within their own organization? The one thing consultants absolutely cannot do is create visionary leaders: if you do not have one when you start a project, you cannot expect to have one at the end. Nor can consultants supply the evangelists whose job it is to build commitment to an idea across an organization as a whole. Consultants may be able to help indirectly, by ensuring that the potential evangelists have the skills and information they require, but, as external agents, they cannot be evangelists themselves.

Consultants cannot, therefore, change organizational beliefs by themselves. The value that consultants can bring (primarily in terms of making the impossible possible and creating common values) has to be matched with the role that must be played by internal people. Organizations have to provide their own visionary leaders and evangelists; they cannot rely on consultants alone to effect change.

SUMMARY

1 The main reason why decisions taken are not implemented by organizations is that people that make up the organization are not fully committed to that course of action; they do not believe that it is the right thing to do.

2 When this happens to a decision taken with the help of consultants, it quite rightly breeds resentment about the apparent waste of money in hiring consultants – their report is simply gathering dust on the shelf, or the process they have implemented is circumvented and the application they have developed goes unused.

3 In order to maximize the value consultants can add, clients and consultants need to recognize that the latter should not just be involved in gathering data for a report or implementing a new system or process, but also have a role to play in communicating the information and changes, and in gaining commitment to them. If consultants are going to make a difference, they have to help convince the organization that a decision or change is the right one.

4 There are four steps to changing organizational beliefs:

- ☐ A visionary leader needs to establish the guiding principles and inspire people, by being a role-model for them.
- ☐ Some significant changes are delivered, contrary to the expectations of people within the organization.
- ☐ Common values are created by communicating and embellishing the importance of these changes.
- ☐ Champions are found who are willing to motivate and galvanize their colleagues with their more detailed blueprint for how the overall vision can be achieved.

5 Of these four steps, consultants are most effective in helping organizations do something they thought they could not do, and in facilitating the communication of these 'miracles'. Change management is not something that can therefore be wholly 'outsourced' to a consulting firm – clients and consultants have to work together if fundamental change (a change in organizational beliefs) is to be achieved.

CHAPTER 12

CONVERTING THEORY INTO PRACTICE

Going from design to reality has always been the weakest link in the consulting value chain. How many consultants' reports have ended up as office door-stops or hidden away in filing cabinets? How many strategies, which looked compelling on paper, have proved unworkable in practice? How many new systems or processes, once implemented have not been used?

Of course, it is not just consultants who are at fault here. Indeed, they are often scapegoats for a much more fundamental problem, endemic in business, of failing to execute strategy. Some organizations produce brilliant strategies, but have difficulty in implementing them; others are good at implementation, but poor at planning; very few are good at both. Problems occur along one or both of two dimensions:

☐ **Separation of process** – to what extent do you see planning and doing as separate activities? Do you have a planning process that occurs at a set time of the year (whereas implementation goes on all the time)? Is planning closer to budgeting than implementing? Are you expected to finish a plan and then implement it, or can you iterate between the two?

☐ **Separation of people** – do you use different people to plan and implement? If so, why? Is it because different skill sets are involved, or because these are separate functions in your organizational chart?

Having a high degree of separation in terms both of people and process (see Figure 12.1) is a recipe for disaster. It can result in strategies that have little grounding in reality, generated by people who have neither the power nor responsibility to ensure that anyone else in the organization takes notice, let alone follows them. If a process exists in which strategy formulation and execution are closely linked (prototyping is a good example), there will be workable ideas but no sense of ownership among those responsible for realizing them. Conversely, if those responsible for planning and execution are combined together in a single team, while also forced to treat the two activities completely separately, and there will be much frustration and disillusionment.

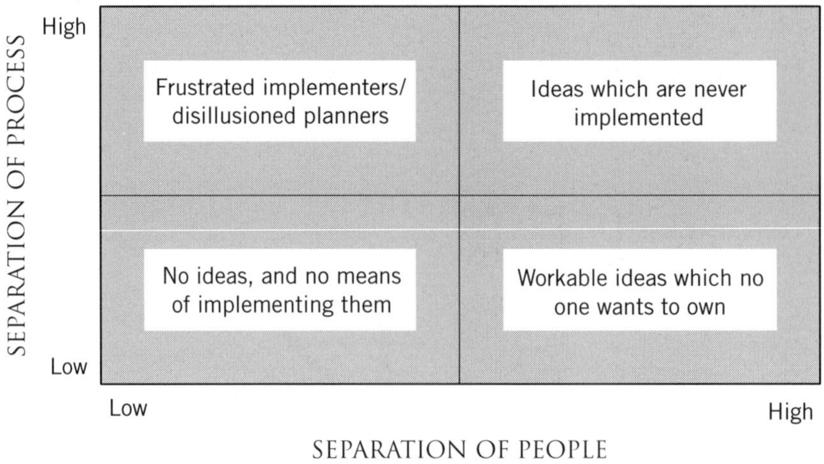

FIGURE 12.1: Degrees of separation in implementing strategy

This same model can be applied just as well to the use of consultants. Bring in a consulting team, leave them to work in isolation on discrete parts of any project (formulating strategy or implementation), and the output will almost inevitably end up in a rarely-used filing cabinet. Bring consultants in to develop an integrated approach to strategy development and execution, and your own organization will feel disempowered. Bring consultants into a joint client/consulting team, and then tell them that they have to complete each stage of a process before moving on to the next, and some of them (client people and consultants) will become demotivated, and their disillusionment will infect the rest of the project team.

The solution clearly lies in the bottom left-hand corner of the above matrix, in minimizing the level of separation across both dimensions simultaneously. But what does this solution actually look like in practice?

MINIMIZING SEPARATION

The e-business boom of 1998–2000 taught clients and consultants an important lesson in this respect. E-business projects were unusual because they typically combined complexity with speed; clients were looking to develop and implement technology-dependent multi-channel strategies, in an environment in which the competitive landscape had become unprecedentedly fluid and fast-moving. In this context, a linear consulting process that could take months to investigate fully every possible avenue, was not appropriate.

The comments of one client at the time illustrate this.

‘With so many systems that have to be linked together faultlessly behind the scenes, ours was a hugely complex project. One of the most important lessons we learned was the need to have a dedicated organization for projects such as these. If you do not have this, you will become endlessly bogged down in that complexity. Moreover, you will be in danger of replicating the technology and processes of the parent company. We could have gone down the traditional enterprise resource planning route – we had plenty of options to choose from – but, by standing back and looking at what we were trying to achieve, we were able to find a solution that was roughly one-fifth of the cost. Similarly, we learned that we had to simplify our processes if the venture was going to succeed: it was the only way to limit the technical complexity. We have concluded that e-business projects are not things that you can – or should – do alongside your day job. ❜

Under pressure from clients, consulting firms compressed their conventional ways of working in order to bring together people with different skill sets and make them work in tandem, rather than in isolation. A consultant recalls:

❛ We had a US client who had been in the affinity market for 25 years, who wanted to extend their franchise to the internet by creating a branded portal. Our involvement started with the strategy and, almost imperceptibly, continued into the detailed planning and then implementation phases. But this was not because we were facilitating the process: we were not orchestrating formal handover. It was much more a function of the fact that we had an integrated team of client and consulting staff – we had three full-time consultants working in different parts of the client organization who, to all intents and purposes, were client staff. ❜

E-business projects made the weakest link in the consulting chain even weaker, and it was ironic that it was the new kids on the block – the specialist e-consulting firms – whose reputation suffered most as a result. One senior buyer of consultancy in a financial institution described how one project went awry:

❛ We brought in an e-specialist firm to help us develop our online business from scratch. In terms of developing our thinking, they were absolutely excellent – generating lots of challenging ideas – and we ended up with what we see as the 'blueprint' for our digital business. As a precursor to implementation, we asked the consultants to cost this blueprint, which they did. But, six months down the line, they turned round and said, 'We got it wrong.' They had underestimated the costs of integrating the website with our legacy system – and not just by a few percentage points: the projected costs were more than twice the original estimate.

The problem here was not that the costs changed, but the way in which the consulting firm handled the issue.

If they had made it clear at the outset that the costs were difficult to estimate and likely to change, our board could have accepted that, albeit reluctantly. It was the fact that they let us believe that the costs were more solid than they actually were, and did not prepare the ground for the revised estimate, that was the problem. They did nothing to set our expectations. Moreover, the consulting firm could not understand why we were upset. They kept telling us that the money was immaterial because we were investing in a business for the future. We recognize this, but they had to understand that our culture was such that money does matter – we have budgets which we are expected to work to, and strict cost control. What we needed was someone who would come over in our direction just a bit, to help manage our transition from our established way of thinking into this new environment. But they would not make that compromise. ❜

The e-business consultancies essentially reduced the separation of *people* in the transition from strategy to implementation (by creating highly effective multi-disciplinary teams), but did nothing to reduce the separation of *process*. This can be contrasted with the incumbent consulting firms who, having been initially slow to react to the e-business consulting opportunity, sought to reduce the separation of *process* but were hampered by vertically divided organizations which made multi-disciplinary work (reducing the separation of *people*) difficult to achieve. Each segment of the market had one of the trump cards: neither had them both.

PROPOSITION DEVELOPMENT

What clients want and need is for consultants to succeed along both of these dimensions, to reduce the degree of separation among people and across processes. They saw the first signs of it during the e-business boom, and, since then, have been reluctant to return to more traditional models of consultancy. At the time, those signs were called 'proposition development'. This was a term used to describe projects that brought together dedicated people from both client and consulting organizations, with a variety of skill sets, often in a different physical locations, who were tasked with delivering complete 'propositions' in a short space of time. The model was hugely attractive to clients, not simply because it promised speedy results, but also because it made the benefits of using consultants more visible. These were not teams of inexperienced MBA graduates toiling behind the scenes, but individuals with in-depth expertise working long hours on the client's site (or a substitute for it). While the dot.coms that gave rise to this way of working have disappeared, clients continue to demand this approach. This is not an area where consultants can put the clock back.

The following case studies illustrate how this approach works in practice. In the first, the Met Office used consultants to make a rapid response to a significant competitive threat. In the second, Cable & Wireless integrated consultants into their team to implement a complex, global e-HR system.

Case study: creating new customer value at the Met Office

The Met Office is one of the world's leading providers of environmental and weather-related services. Who would have expected this government department to have an award-winning website and mobile weather service?

By 2001, the amount of 'free' weather information available on the internet (not all of it accurate) was causing growing concern to the Met Office, as it threatened its ability to raise revenue through charging for weather services. Not surprisingly, the Met Office was keen to develop an electronic capability of its own, to differentiate itself from its competitors, provide new revenue streams, and to meet its public charter to provide free, best-of-breed services to the general UK public (objectives which themselves are clearly conflicting).

Impact Plus, one of the UK's fastest growing consultancies, was asked to help in developing and then implementing an e-business strategy. Sue Rockhill, Impact Plus' project manager describes what happened next.

'We focused the Met Office on its key competency as a global leader in the accuracy of its forecasting. In terms of an e-business strategy, that meant providing personalized and localized weather-related services through a significantly revamped website, and through mobile phones. In addition it was planned that users could tailor the weather information they required in terms of location, timing and frequency.

The proposition was that the mobile weather services should cover the entire UK land and sea areas and be available to any mobile phone on any mobile network, by Short Message Service (SMS) text messages and via Wireless Application Protocol (WAP). But the scale of the task became apparent almost immediately. Part of the offering needed to be ready eight weeks after the strategy sign-off, and the complete proposition needed to be complete a further eight weeks later, the day when the Met Office wanted to launch its new brand. Timescales were tight.

The implementation program was tasked with the development and implementation of: specific customized technical information in a format suitable for delivery via both channels; revenue-generating products and services; and a website with global reach and content, accompanied by an integrated web/mobile internet offering. It was also charged with reviewing the business processes key to sustaining this strategy; developing and maintaining relationships and contacts with e-business partners; and marketing the overall proposition and its associated products and services.

We worked together wherever possible; this collaborative approach was helped by the fact that we had collectively developed a customer value proposition that both met customer requirements and made commercial sense. We also did not have a predetermined approach: the methodology we used was unique to this project and specifically designed to address its major challenges.

As a result of a vendor selection exercise, we selected a wireless infrastructure provider to provide wireless development expertise. By providing a combination of IT software development, wireless and strong project management skills, we were able to ensure that this provider delivered the required web and mobile services to the required standards, timescales and budget. Moreover, because of the short amount of time involved, no "community trial" was possible. Instead, we set up a 'friendly user trial' that ran in parallel to some of the development work, and targeted friends and family of those involved on the project.

As a result of this joint work, the full launch of the Met Office's products took place as planned, 16 weeks after the start of the project.

In the eyes of the Met Office, the key lesson learned on this project relates to the power of teamwork, with us – the consulting team – adding expertise, energy, discipline and determination. ’

Case study: global e-HR at Cable & Wireless

Cable & Wireless is a major global telecommunications business with revenue of over $11 billion and customers in 70 countries. Like most large companies, it recognized the enormous challenges involved in forging a strong strategic partnership between HR and the rest of the business. Martin Hayton, the Group HR Director, had also accepted another challenge: introducing consistent HR processes worldwide, supported by a radically different HR organization. He believed that e-enabling many traditional HR processes would greatly reduce the administrative burden, allowing HR staff to focus on activities where they could become true business partners. Moreover, the e-enablement of HR operations was fully in line with Cable & Wireless' strategy to move all its business operations online and to transform itself into a truly global business.

In hiring consultants to help with this process, Cable & Wireless chose to work with niche providers because they wanted to use their own resources and capabilities as far as possible – something that was recognized as important if the changes involved were to be successfully embedded in the organization. One of the companies they chose was Partners for Change. 'We chose them for the e-HR programme,' says Martin Reddington, the e-HR Programme Director at Cable & Wireless, 'because we liked their facilitative style and the fact that they were committed to transferring their skills and capabilities of their people as part of the overall process. We knew that they would help us to find ways to do as much as possible for ourselves.'

Mark Williamson at Partners for Change gives the consultant's view:

‘We believe that consultants provide best value when used in small numbers to supplement a client's own capabilities, bringing in-depth experience, together with appropriate tools and methods, to bring about success. We identified roles where we could have maximum impact, allowing people from Cable & Wireless to play to their individual strengths and take responsibility for the results. A highly-leveraged way of working meant that only four Partners for Change consultants were needed to provide the required program and change management skills, quickly integrating with the Cable & Wireless core team of 30 people. Our input included helping to: develop the business case; design and obtain buy-in for new business processes; draw up the systems requirements; assess the extent of change involved; and manage local stakeholders and potential champions.

As a cornerstone of our approach, we built a benefits realization plan, matching specific benefits to named members of the HR leadership team, agreeing how the benefits would be achieved, and gaining their commitment to proportional budget reductions in future years. To deliver the benefits as quickly as possible, we recommended structuring the program into two parallel streams – a long-term plan aimed at delivering all the potential benefits, and "early implementation projects" which would demonstrate tangible, measurable benefits within the context of the long-term plan.

All Cable & Wireless employees now have access to a common "employee portal" through which all e-HR functions are made available. In terms of features, global reach and accessibility, this portal is one of the most ambitious and sophisticated in the world.

What worked particularly well in the project? It was clearly crucial that this was a tangible, clearly-defined project, which meant that we could all focus on a common aim. But I think that the fact that we had a completely integrated project team, responsible for all aspects of delivery, made a tremendous difference. We did not think about design in isolation from implementation, or about implementation without considering the change management implications. Working closely with people also means that, as consultants, we could transfer our skills much more effectively; we could introduce best practice and ensure there was a clear, structured approach overall, but without being seen to be heavy-handed. Our support team was targeted where it was most needed, and we did not attempt to fulfil roles more appropriately performed by the client.’

Overall, the payback period of the project was less than two years, and it is expected to provide annual benefits of up to $20 million, with approximately $13 million saved in the first year; this is on target to achieving more than 30 per cent savings of overall HR costs. The core employee self-service system demonstrates the less tangible benefits: in the US, there are 2,000 regular users; 40 per cent of employees in Europe had updated their personal records within a week of the system being launched.

According to one satisfied end-user:

‘I had expected the e-HR programme to be like previous IT initiatives: much promised but little delivered. Using the new system has turned my scepticism into enthusiasm. It is good to know exactly what the company has on file about me, and I find it very helpful to see exactly how my benefits package is made up. I can also see how things fit together in the global organization, and in my role that is vital.’

Characteristics of proposition development

So what are the defining characteristics of this approach?

- People from different backgrounds and different organizations are thrown into the melting pot together. Cultures may clash, tempers may rise, but the end product is something that combines insights from many different perspectives.
- Diversity and conflicting views are overcome by focusing on a shared objective, usually related to having a tangible effect on a client’s customers or employees.
- By focusing on tangible effects, the benefits of the project are more visible and measurable.
- Predefined methodologies are replaced by structured but highly customized approaches to delivery.
- Tight deadlines and physical proximity mean that formalities and bureaucracy are minimized.
- Individuals are empowered to take decisions that, elsewhere, might require authorization by an extended chain of command.
- The emphasis shifts from developing plans to creating dynamic models within which multiple scenarios can be evaluated.

Above all else, this style of working is a counter balance to the structure necessarily imposed by working on a defined project – clear goals, distinct roles, unequivocal responsibilities – all of which we discussed in Chapter 6.

While the disciplines of project management are necessary if anything substantial is to be achieved, some of those same disciplines, enforced to rigidly, may compromise the quality of the output – they may establish a damaging demarcation between clients and consultants, they may encourage people to think only about their own immediate objectives, not about the project as a whole. The proposition development approach is a valuable antidote to this because it establishes an environment in which boundaries – between clients and consultants, between different streams of work, between different skill sets – become blurred and in which people can focus on the end, not the means.

SUMMARY

1 There are two reasons why good ideas fail to move beyond the drawing board (or the consultants’ report):

- Planning and implementation are perceived to be separate processes.
- Different teams of people are used to plan and implement.

2 The need to minimize time to market during the e-business boom of 1998–2000 challenged the way in which many consultancies worked, forcing them to bring people

with different skill sets together (from their own firm and from their client's organization), to work in parallel in realizing a client's goal. Further steps, creating a separate environment in which people, for example, made this 'proposition development process' a highly effective one.

3 While the dot.coms that gave rise to this way of working have largely disappeared, proposition development remains a very successful way of overcoming the gap which often exists between theory and practice, characterized by:

- ☐ Teams of dedicated individuals working together in the same physical location.
- ☐ Informal interaction, rather than a formalized methodology.
- ☐ Clear focus on a tangible outcome.
- ☐ Empowerment of individual team members.

CHAPTER 13

SELECTING AND IMPLEMENTING TECHNOLOGY

Since Arthur Andersen helped to implement the first commercial application of mainframe computers in business after the Second World War, IT has become integral (some would say central) to the consulting industry, to a point where IT-related consultancy accounts for around 50 per cent of total consulting fees.

This shift is testimony to the seemingly unending shortage of specialist IT skills. Consulting firms have always migrated towards areas of scarcity, whether this takes the form of tools for collecting and analyzing data (as was the case in the 1920s and 1930s) or ideas (true at the height of the dot.com bubble). There never seems to have been a point where IT skills of some kind have not been scarce. As new hardware and software products continue to emerge, it is neither feasible nor desirable for all organizations to keep all skills up to date, and consulting firms now play a fundamentally important role in providing a pool of specialist skills which organizations can call on as required.

But there are negative reasons too, for the exponential growth of IT-related consulting. Faced with technology which they did not understand, clients chose to outsource its application in their business. They took one black box (the technology) and handed it over to another black box (the consultant), with little idea of what might be going on behind the scenes. Clients were not so much outsourcing the implementation process, as washing their hands of it – and consultants, weighing up the scale of fees from IT consulting compared to more conventional management consulting, were happy to accept that work. And, of course, it did not work: offloading a problem is never a recipe for resolving it.

It is possible to divide up IT consulting work, both according to the nature of technology involved and the role that consultants play.

THE NATURE OF THE TECHNOLOGY INVOLVED

One of the main ways in which the consulting industry has changed over the last decade has been its growing 'technocratization', a process that has made it much harder (and less meaningful) to distinguish between IT implementation and a whole host of other consulting services – marketing, human resource management, operations – where IT now plays a fundamental role. Thus, it has become difficult for someone to be an HR consultant who is not also familiar with HR systems. The only area as yet comparatively unaffected by this creeping technocratization has been business strategy, perhaps because it is the most customized type of consulting, and, even here, there are an increasing number of consulting firms who now use technology tools (financial models, for example) to aid, if not drive, the strategy formulation process.

For many companies, the combined aftertaste of Enterprise Resource Planning (ERP) and Y2K has been particularly sour, especially when compounded with over-investment in web-based projects that have yet to yield a positive return. The onus is therefore perceived to be on consulting companies to prove the value of IT projects, irrespective of their size, and to demonstrate that their best practice will make a material difference. Clients want to tie ERP and CRM projects more closely into tangible benefits and organizational change. The remit of consultants in this area is therefore changing to include, at the business process, change alongside the systems implementation, and to design programs more attuned to the context in which they take place.

These issues are already being played out, when it comes to the use of consultants in specific areas of IT:

☐ **CRM** – Although the concepts and technology of CRM are barely a decade old, there is already a feeling among clients that it may not live up to its promise. This perceived lack of delivery has its roots in two areas. Firstly, organizations who were keen to replicate the apparent successes of the earliest adopters, did not subject the idea to a rigorous business case. Because CRM worked well for a competitor, it was assumed that it would work equally well for them – a highly questionable assumption (see Chapter 8). Secondly, CRM projects often concentrated on creating a dialogue with customers through trial and error, rather than on a single, operational deliverable, and this left a significant roster of operational issues still to address. While most large corporations have done something on the CRM front, they have not managed to integrate it into their existing systems and processes. The challenge going forward will be to develop more specific applications of the CRM concept – cross-selling is a good example – which suits a client's unique set of circumstances, rather than assuming that one size of CRM fits all.

☐ **Operations** – Performance improvement is a growing area of consulting, fuelled by a growing number of companies who now have international markets and supply chains. At the same time, it is recognized that there are no generic models: much more attention has to be focused on how an approach is relevant to a particular client, how it will improve their supply chain. Moreover, the concept of the extended enterprise, in which multiple organizations are linked together via integrated systems and common processes, is leading companies to reassess their operational IT systems. What do they need to build in terms of trust between suppliers and buyers? How should they share information? How open are their systems? What kind of collaborative responsibility is there on each side for these kinds of things?

☐ **E-business** – From the lack of coverage in the business press, a client might be forgiven for thinking that e-business has disappeared. In fact, there is substantial evidence to show that what was termed 'e-business' a few years ago has now been subsumed into other work – strategy development, channel management, internal efficiency, and so on. Consultants working in this area say that they have not seen a diminution of this kind of work from their larger corporate clients, but rather that their approach has turned away from looking at new business models, towards questions of how big corporations can e-enable ideas and technologies on an end-to-end basis.

☐ **Human Resources** – Business-to-business and business-to-consumer concepts are being superseded by business-to-employee – the application of web-based technologies to facilitate HR-related processes (often on a self-service basis) and enterprise-wide communications. These are not traditional HR systems, but much more sophisticated views of how individuals can be better developed, and how their intellectual capabilities and experience can be applied to the benefit of a business. The change is being driven by an increased emphasis on value-based management, whether that is shareholder or stakeholder value. There is a systems component to this, but also an equally important HR component – the behavioural dimension of organizations, the motivational drivers and value systems of individuals.

Across these different types of technology, two factors are increasingly driving the way in which organizations are using consultants – complexity and integration. Companies seeking to link together multiple front- and back-office systems, sometimes between different companies, need a combination of:

- ☐ Highly specialized input (often from consultants who either work directly for the relevant software manufacturer, or for a broader-based consulting company which has direct links with the manufacturer).
- ☐ Program management (which may, depending on the nature of the project, need a consulting firm with no substantive links between themselves and the software suppliers involved – in order to ensure their objectivity).
- ☐ Business process and organizational change consultancy (provided either by a broader-based or highly specialized consulting firms).

As a result of these demands, the roles that consultants play within organizations varies hugely, from the most advisory (helping a company devise a technology strategy and decide on the appropriate suppliers) to the most hands-on (implementing and operating systems); and from taking a focused, highly specialized role, to one where the consulting firm is responsible for a complex project in its entirety and for managing the input of other consulting firms. The following case studies illustrate this range. The first based on PA Consulting's work with the Swiss railway industry, and the second on work by Cap Gemini Ernst & Young with Nasdaq Europe, and the third on work done by PwC Consulting.

Case study – developing a technology strategy for wireless communications in the Swiss railway industry

Switzerland's Bundesamt für Verkehr (BAV) – the Swiss Government Federal Office of Transport – and Schweizerische Bundesbahn (SBB) asked PA Consulting Group to investigate the possibility of harmonizing wireless communications across the country's 50 railway operating companies. On the strength of PA's work, railway companies in Switzerland are now introducing a unified GSM-R (GSM for Railways) service which can meet the needs of the rail industry.

Phil White was PA's assignment leader:

‘An off-the-shelf approach was not going to work here. The unique aspects of the Swiss rail system – the sheer number of railway companies, the mountainous terrain and complex frontiers – posed entirely new challenges. Moreover, each company had essentially been using its own choice of radio system. Given that the companies often operate over the same lines, there were disadvantages to this fragmentation: if one company's personnel needed to talk to another's, additional terminals usually had to be installed, since the systems were not compatible with each other. International traffic used another different communications system.

Fragmentation of the system was also an obstacle to the introduction of the European Train Control System (ETCS), a standard that makes it possible to transmit signals directly to the train in lieu of the usual track-side signalling. This new international inter-operable automatic train control system is a European initiative, born from the objective to define and introduce a pan-European traffic management and train command/control system. ETCS enables the introduction of automatic safety systems, to ensure that trains never pass red signals even with increased frequency of services. In an international operating environment, it does not make sense for trains to be able to use ETCS on their journey through other countries, but not Switzerland.

In the light of this, BAV had been working with the biggest railway companies, SBB and BLS, to assess the possibility of introducing a common communication and signalling system, and had tentatively identified GSM-R as the most appropriate technology (though there were other candidates). It was important that any technology chosen was not only appropriate to the task but also fitted in with the policies and standards of other European countries.

The client therefore asked PA Consulting for independent advice as to whether and how it should standardize the wireless element of railway communications. At the same time, we were asked to evaluate alternative technologies and recommend the most suitable one; and develop a model for delivering a new system, identifying the costs, benefits and risks at each stage of introduction. The model had to take account of the various stakeholder interests and the special circumstances such as the Swiss terrain. In short, BAV needed PA to help it move from what it already had – the knowledge that a national communication system was desirable – to what it needed – a firm basis for introducing such a system.

To confirm the viability of a standardized system and to determine the best architecture, we carried out interviews with a large sample (around half) of the 50 Swiss railway companies. These interviews gathered information about current and planned activities and their communications implications, and also about the communications solutions currently in place. We then compared the various proposed solutions with the companies' individual and collective requirements. From this work, it became clear that a unified system was a realistic possibility, and that GSM-R was the best of the available systems. GSM-R fitted in with the strategies of other European rail systems, a point confirmed by our research in other countries including Germany, Sweden and the UK. Discussions with infrastructure and terminal vendors confirmed that, while the railway market was small compared with public GSM systems, it was solid enough to render any risks on the supply side manageable. Our research also indicated that a Swiss GSM-R system would have worthwhile revenue-generating potential, and would enable the introduction of subsidiary applications, such as advanced data services to train passengers.

While the case for GSM-R emerged as persuasive, the best approach to implementation was initially less clear. There were four options for the operator of a Swiss GSM-R system: a single large railway company, such as SBB; a third party such as an existing GSM network operator; the government; or a new service provider to be set up by a group of railway companies. Following discussions with the various railway companies in which we compared these models, we recommended the creation of a new service provider by a consortium of railway companies, as the option most likely to satisfy the varying needs of all. This recommendation took account not only of hard factors such as costs and risks, but also of softer ones such as the attitudes and sensitivities of the companies involved. To guarantee that the interests of all stakeholders would be represented, we recommended that the consortium of companies running the GSM-R provider should include representatives from smaller rail companies as well as the largest.

Finally, we had to consider the practicalities of migration: who should be adopting the new system and when? The right answer depended both on the benefits of GSM-R and on the capabilities of each company's existing communications systems. It seemed likely that GSM-R would represent technological overkill for the smallest operators of local mountain railways. In the event, we proposed that a group of larger companies should lead the introduction and adoption of the GSM-R system, with smaller ones following later as appropriate, in some cases only when their existing systems became obsolete.

Having helped choose the technology, the business architecture and the migration path, we modelled the chosen solution in detail. To arrive at a meaningful assessment of the investment that would be required, the model incorporated the costs of infrastructure, terminals and operation. It also assessed the additional cost of providing guaranteed system availability required for ETCS level 2. Finally, it highlighted the risks entailed in roll-out – an important consideration in a complex time-critical operating environment. From this model, the team was able to derive a roll-out plan, broken down into year-on-year steps.

One of the greatest challenges of this assignment was the need to satisfy so many different interested parties. Although the large companies were bound to dominate the decision-making process to some extent, it was important that the smaller stakeholders were also represented, otherwise the eventual solution would not gain acceptance. We took care to involve as many of the railway companies as possible, interviewing their representatives in person, wherever they were based. Through joint meetings with several companies, the team kept the companies informed of the progress of the assignment and of the recommendations as they emerged, soliciting feedback.

The client called us in because they wanted someone to challenge their ideas and thrash out a watertight answer. This was not a case where we just had to respond to a set of pre-defined objectives; rather than a list of options, the client was looking for a practical way forward, evaluated from every angle so as to minimize risk.’

Case study – program management at NASDAQ Europe

In 2001, Nasdaq Europe launched the first stock exchange designed specifically to meet the needs of the European market and to operate on a totally pan-European basis. The event also marked a giant leap towards Nasdaq's ultimate vision of a single, worldwide, 24-hour securities market. At the heart of the exchange is Nasdaq's new European Trading System (ETS).

Nasdaq needed to move quickly, but replicating its American systems was not an option:

- ☐ The regulatory regime, trading conventions, clearance and settlement processes are all different in Europe.

- ☐ There is also a high proportion of cross-border trading between different countries and increased competitive activity from the mergers of existing exchanges.
- ☐ ETS would need to be tailored to European requirements. The detailed design of the business processes and IT systems therefore had to be carried on virtually a 'greenfield site' basis.

The whole program was one of the most ambitious and innovative ever carried out in the European financial world, presenting a unique challenge to the IT professionals, financial experts and senior managers involved: Cap Gemini Ernst & Young was responsible for program management.

When Nasdaq took control, the program had already been underway for some time, following a 1999 Easdaq initiative. This initiative had started with three big advantages: backing from top management; an enthusiastic in-house team of financial IT professionals; and hardware, software and networking components from vendors (such as TIBCO, Reuters and Sun) with established reputations in this very specialized field. But there had been a missing ingredient, and a vital one: program management. There was limited experience of managing large, complex IT projects, of delivering them on time and within budget, and of realizing the planned benefits. It was this ingredient that Cap Gemini Ernst & Young, with a strong track record in bringing significant financial services projects to a successful conclusion, was asked to supply.

Says Phil Godolphin, the vice-president at Cap Gemini Ernst & Young:

‘We quickly realized that the program needed to be relaunched, both internally and with the Members and external parties.’

Joan Minogue, the Cap Gemini Ernst & Young Program and Implementation Manager, describes what happened:

‘This meant putting in place a logical structure for the entire program to ensure that delivery dates were met, and revamping all internal and external communications relating to the project.

We introduced the key concept of separate but coordinated work-streams into the project which we jointly managed with Nasdaq, including: implementation readiness, systems testing, training, and technical support for hardware, software and networking. The Program Office owned and managed the milestone plan – a series of well-defined target achievements or "milestones" for each of the work-streams, which, if completed on schedule, would guarantee the success of the program as a whole. Communications are not an optional extra in major projects of this kind, but vital to the maintenance of momentum. We therefore set up weekly progress reports from all the work-streams, with a monthly high-level report to the board. There were weekly team leader meetings, moving to daily meetings nearer go-live, monthly communication meetings for all program staff, monthly supplier meetings and a monthly progress bulletin for Nasdaq's Members (which were critical to ensuring their ongoing commitment to the project).

Nasdaq Europe and Cap Gemini Ernst & Young faced several key challenges during the project, including the need to ensure that the ETS was fully pan-European and to build massive scalability into the system in order to accommodate planned expansion. We had to address the special challenge of working with several third-party vendors (hardware, software, market data vendor and networking companies), as well as the 40 Members and their IT staff and, of course, Nasdaq's own staff. It was also a high risk project: the conventions of stock exchanges everywhere (not to mention the requirements of the European regulatory authorities) dictate that all players in the marketplace must have equal access at all times, and this means that it is impossible to run any form of pilot. Despite the complexity of the project, everything had to go live simultaneously. Achieving this while minimizing its obvious risks involved building a carefully graded series of five simulations ('dress rehearsals', as they became known) into the program plan. The lessons learned at each simulation were fed back into the systems design. Finally, because the implementation was not being "overlaid" on an existing operational platform, a new organization had to be built, along with new processes and procedures.

Nasdaq's style is collaborative and this was key on a project such as ETS, which involved many parties and interdependencies. It also matched Cap Gemini Ernst & Young's preferred style of working and greatly facilitated open communication throughout the program. Indeed, the success of the exchange was dependent on all components and the wider program team working together as planned. For example, the implementation plan was built with input from all parties, and the overall view shared to give each player insight into the "big picture".

When the day came to go live for real, everything went exactly as predicted, and all 40 Members starting to trade immediately. Ann Neidenbach, Chief Information Officer at Nasdaq Europe told us: "The true success of any project is measured by looking back afterwards to see what could have been done better. When I look back, I see very little that I would have changed." ❱

Case study – developing a single customer view

In 1999–2001 a large UK insurance company ran a program to establish its new UK direct retail financial services business. The business offers a new customer proposition to the marketplace, and has provided a step-change in the way the company markets business to its customers in a multi-channel environment – over the phone, over the web, and via e-mail. The new business provides a highly customer centric service based on improved customer information.

The program to establish this business involved a team of more than 250 people and 20,000 man-days of effort from the company itself and a number of third parties. PwC Consulting was the main implementation partner, assisting with program management, business transformation, and delivery and implementation of a new systems infrastructure. The majority of its consultants on the project were involved in one project. In particular, the establishment of a near real-time single view of the customer.

A single view of customer provides a consolidated view of customer holdings, activities and contact history across product types and therefore enables customer facing staff to understand their customers better and, as a result, enhance the customer experience. This particular solution will also enable multi-channel access (for example, direct access to data by customers over the web), improved customer segmentation, and the ability to design, launch and track multi-channel customer marketing campaigns.

In order to implement the single view of customer, many of the insurance company's existing processes and systems needed re-design. In particular, the systems landscape needed re-engineering to place the operational single view of customer at the centre, linking channels, servicing, sales and marketing systems. This was achieved through the use of enterprise application integration tools that maximized application independence, minimized intrusion on existing applications and provided an extensible model for future business initiatives.

The scale of the systems and business transformation, the need for rapid speed to market and the constraint of re-using existing systems for proposition servicing and sales all meant that a complex and integrated business and technology solution was needed. The project pulled together cross-functional, multi-disciplinary teams to develop a business and systems design, a process that concentrated on redefining the existing systems landscape as a set of collaborating "components", each with a clear statement of role and responsibilities within the overall solution.

The team then refined the design by "testing" the results of the processing, in a paper based exercise, against a series of pre-defined business events. This helped to create joint understanding and ownership of the solution across the project team as a whole. By focusing on business events (for example a phone call from a new customer requiring motor insurance) and the business's response to this (providing a quote), we arrived at a common working language for all team members regardless of their experience or background. The process also enabled the team to examine the "events" from different perspectives – process, systems, and data – in order to ensure that the final product would deliver the end-to-end "customer experience" required.

The detailed technical design, development and systems testing work was distributed amongst a number of technical teams. Each team had a clear statement of processing and data requirements which "their component" had to support within the overall system – a strategy that meant a variety of technical approaches could be applied, each tailored to the skills of the development teams, the nature of their development tools and the scale of change required.

Much of the success of the program and Customer Single View Project in particular, arose from the way in which PwC Consulting and their client worked together, respecting the value provided by different third party perspectives, and learning and improving as the program progressed. From a formal perspective, the project teams were managed jointly by PwC Consulting and client project managers, and the teams themselves involved people from both sides plus other third parties. PwC Consulting's performance was evaluated on a monthly basis against a balanced scorecard as a way of encouraging and rewarding positive behaviour. On a less formal basis, the "one team" approach was reinforced at all levels. All the work was carried out by joint teams and while the consultants were expected to bring the recommendations, there were no "eureka" moments where they turned up bearing a pre-conceived "answer".

Throughout the program, there was also a focus on knowledge transfer: post implementation reviews were conducted for all projects, coaching plans were developed with "buddies" where appropriate; and a dedicated "knowledge harvesting" project was run for the joint benefit of PwC Consulting and the client, capturing best-practice and lessons learnt. Examples of the lessons learnt include:

- ☐ The value of regular and tactical releases to demonstrate value and capture learning
- ☐ The feasibility of taking new releases from concept through to delivery within a three month timescale
- ☐ The appropriateness of using "Rapid Application Development" for specific phases and applications up to a certain project scale, but the need to follow the more traditional IT delivery approach for very large scale systems integration projects from the design phase onwards
- ☐ The critical importance and value of co-locating business and IT project teams

The full benefits of the program to the client will be realized over the next 5 years as the number of customers, the range of products offered to those customers, and the expected profitability of the business increases. Meanwhile PwC Consulting and their client have worked together to create a single view of the customer that enhances customer experience by enabling customer facing staff to understand their customers better.

THE CRITICAL SUCCESS FACTORS IN MANAGING IT CONSULTANCY

As in other areas of consulting, the key to managing IT consultancy successfully is to understand from the outset exactly the role which a consulting firm is asked to play. Are they being brought in to challenge your assumptions, or to implement a plan which you have already developed? Are you expecting them to have business skills (perhaps to help with organizational re-design), technical skills (knowledge of a specialist package), or a combination of both?

Different processes require different skills, but all are dependent on the same critical success factor: transparency. Transparency is evidently what is missing in the 'black box' scenario, but it is often missing too, where the clients are looking to buy in a specific skill. Because they do not have this skill, they often do not know what they are buying and, even when the consultant is sitting in their office working for them, they often do not know how to evaluate their work.

Between them, these three case studies cover seven of the eight primary roles that consulting firms play when it comes to IT (see Figure 13.1). The seventh role – ongoing management – is discussed in more detail in the following chapter on outsourcing.

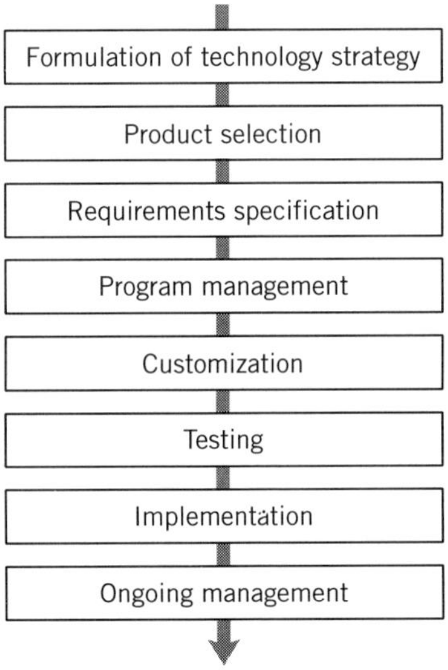

FIGURE 13.1: The eight primary roles of IT consultants

Formulation of technology strategy

The work of PA Consulting with the Swiss railway industry is a good illustration of how consultants can add considerable value at the most preliminary stages of an IT project – the process by which an organization develops an overall vision for its use and exploitation of technology, and chooses between different models (and suppliers) in terms of realizing this vision. There are two specific aspects of this work that client corporations find hard to do for themselves: questioning the scope, complexity and underlying assumptions of the project as a whole, and arbitrating between different interested parties, each of which may be pursuing their own specific agenda. In reality, both of these issues are highly interrelated: IT projects become complex largely because the various factions involved become reluctant to compromise any of their working practices in order to achieve a simpler system. A degree of 'this is how we have always done things, so this is what the system must do' thinking comes into play.

Because consultants are outsiders, they are better positioned to cut through such internecine debates, and can spend time both establishing the rationale for a *feasible* system and building cross-organizational consensus around it. In PA's case, these different parties took the form of the individual railway companies – the contribution which the firm made was as much in terms of developing agreement between the companies as it was in validating BAV's original strategy. The case study illustrates the process working well: when a technology strategy sits on a shelf gathering dust, the problem often stems from a lack of success in gaining people's agreement – their belief that that this is the right strategy. Of course, this is not a problem that besets only IT consulting – Chapter 11 explored the important role that consultants can play more generally, in terms of helping organizations and individuals believe that a given strategy should be pursued.

The critical success factors for this type of consulting are therefore that the consulting firm should have an ability and willingness to question assumptions made – for example, by rationalizing the scope and complexity of a strategy by persuading those involved in using it that they have to change how they do things, that the strategy cannot accommodate all their varied needs. Moreover, the client should give the consulting firm the opportunity and support required to build a consensus around the right strategy among potentially conflicting interest groups. This is a part of the strategy formulation process which is missed, often because the client does not believe it to be particularly important. Words like 'communications' and 'focus group meetings' can seem pretty intangible when they sit side-by-side with more technical terms in a consultancy's proposal – but they are just as critical.

However, formulating a technology strategy differs from business strategy in two respects:

1 Most obviously, the knowledge base of consultants involved in this kind of work includes an understanding both of broader technology trends and how other companies are using them for competitive advantage, and of the specific strengths and weaknesses of how a given technology can be applied to a given client. As this suggests, technology and business knowledge should not be mutually exclusive: technology strategies are best developed by the (comparatively rare) people who have a good knowledge of both areas.

2 Less obviously, but just as important in the more networked environment in which many corporations now operate, is a good knowledge of the strengths and weaknesses of different hardware and software suppliers, and of how these are likely to impact a particular client.

Product selection

Such skills take centre stage when it comes to helping client organizations choose between the multitude of different hardware and software combinations available. This type of consulting work is much less process-based than strategy development, and requires much greater depth of technical knowledge to match the constraints of a client's legacy systems with the apparent opportunities of new packages. But the consulting firm involved should not just excel in terms of its knowledge of the external IT industry: it also has to help the client make the crucial 'make or buy' decision. Should a client buy a pre-existing package and change its processes to meet its needs (the cheapest route), or should it customize the package or even develop its own application (the most flexible route)? Again, this is a decision which a client organization will find hard to take for itself, if only because not everyone in the organization is in a position to be completely objective (for example, the IT department may believe it will serve the needs of its users better and prove its worth if it builds the system itself).

As the PA Consulting case study illustrates, the key issue here is independence. The value that consultants add lies in their ability to evaluate all potential suppliers (internal and external) equally. A consulting company which has very strong links with a particular supplier and stands to earn considerable fees from implementing that supplier's hardware or software, is hardly in a position to give an objective opinion.

Requirements specification

High-level choices need to be backed up by a detailed understanding of what the final system should look like. Not having these is clearly a recipe for chaos. At the same time, it is easily possible to specify a system in too much detail: you can take too long to complete the specifications process; you might also end up with specifications that are so detailed that no one reads them, or that the project's overall objectives become lost among them.

The problem here is less to do with the nature of the problem or technology, and much more to do with intractable differences between the culture of business and the culture of technology. Defining the requirements of a system is a process that is, at least in theory, designed to bridge the traditional gap between the people in the IT department and their users. Neither side has much understanding of what the other does: conventionally, users see their IT colleagues as unresponsive and inflexible, and IT people believe that their systems would run quite happily without the interference of users. During the process of specifying the requirements for a new system, the users are supposed to document their business needs, and the IT people involved are supposed to translate these into technical terms. Considerable debate ensues, because each side speaks a different language and, in an effort to cover all possible issues and risks, the resulting specifications can stretch over several volumes. In theory, consultants can improve both the efficiency and effectiveness of this process by speaking both languages. In practice, they often add a third – managementspeak.

One of the knock-on effects of the pressure to bring an idea to market quickly during the 1998–2000 e-business boom has been to question whether substantial documentation is the best way to specify the requirements of a system. New technologies lend themselves to dynamic prototyping, whereby users and technologists sit down together to map out what part of a system should look like, with the technologists translating what the user says directly into software – with no intervening documentation. The result is not only quicker, but it also brings these two, often warring, factions together far more effectively.

This has repercussions for the use of consultants. In the days of traditional documented specifications, the consultants involved did not have to be knowledgeable about the software into which the requirements would ultimately be translated (indeed, it probably helped not to be too familiar with it). For prototyping, the reverse is true: this type of work can only be done by consultants who know how to implement the hardware/software which has been decided upon.

Program management

Someone has always had to be responsible for the overall control of the IT project from both a budgetary and timing point of view, but four factors are now making this role absolutely critical. IT projects:

- ☐ Are becoming increasingly complex, involving multiple packages and suppliers, and more interdependencies.
- ☐ Need more in-depth, specialist expertise, rather than 'generic' IT skills – which can make cross-team communication highly problematic.
- ☐ Are more likely to be compressed into short periods of time, meaning that more tasks have to take place in parallel, rather than sequentially.
- ☐ Are not just IT projects, but embrace changes to business process, organizational design, etc.

IT program management has therefore evolved into being a skill in its own right. Although many of the issues here are generic ones that apply equally to non-IT projects (see Chapter 6), Cap Gemini Ernst & Young's work with NASDAQ Europe illustrates some of the particular challenges of IT projects: not only was this a complex project in technical terms, but it also involved multiple vendors and cross-border functionality. Its program management therefore embraced conventional project control techniques – developing and monitoring project plans, tracking progress towards the delivery of key milestones – but also an ability to negotiate with the multitude of different parties involved (one of which was the client itself), and to facilitate communication in an environment where the specialist suppliers might easily have not talked to each other.

This is a very different kind of program management from the administrative function typical of many large-scale IT projects, even very recent ones. Clients and consultants were equally likely to view this as a role that could be undertaken by 'project managers' with no specific skills or experience. Working in the project office used to be something that consultants who could not be assigned to any other client project were asked to do – hardly a recipe for added value. But, as the Cap Gemini Ernst & Young case study demonstrates, the role of the project office has evolved into being something much more strategic. Its role is not so much to monitor developments, but to be a driving force behind the project as a whole, ensuring that a wide range of people and organizations can collaborate to achieve a common goal.

As a client trying to maximize the value you obtain from using consultants, you need to focus on this key issue. There are considerable benefits to employing consultants as program managers: not only should the consultants involved have a track record in this field, and proprietary tools and techniques, but they should also be capable of being independent arbitrators when it comes to ensuring that different groups (internal/external; IT people/users) can all work productively together. However, if the consultants are still treating program management as an administrative backwater, then the value they have to add is minimal. Ask yourself: is my program management office staffed by leaders, not bureaucrats, people who are capable of driving cooperation?

Customization, testing and implementation

The balance of customization to pre-packaged software varies from client to client (some are more predisposed to develop their own applications than others) and from project to project (speed may be more important than flexibility). In broad terms, however, the major shift we saw in the 1990s (from companies developing their own code, to buying off-the-shelf packages – although these might still require considerable customization) is being superseded by an environment in which the packages *themselves* are not being customized, so much as the technical environment in which they operate (the links between different product databases, between front- and back-office systems, between old and new, internal and external). The aim, in effect, is to combine the flexibility of customization, but in a controllable environment.

Not surprisingly, the role of consultants has been shifting alongside this, as the case study of PwC Consulting's work demonstrates. With multiple channels and legacy systems to integrate, PwC Consulting needed to develop some means by which the multiple parts of the system could be integrated without falling into the trap of building a structure that would be unable to accommodate future changes in scope and scale. In this environment, the input of consultants is becoming polarized: they may be specialists in one of the component parts of this picture, or they may be specialists in the integration of 'layers' of the system (the middleware). In each case, their role may include redesigning business processes, training and change management where appropriate, as well as application development, testing and data conversion; but it is becoming increasingly difficult for firms to play both roles at once, simply because of the level of specialist knowledge required. At the same time, this integration becomes an even more important issue, if the resulting architecture is to resemble anything other than spaghetti. It is critical to see these two roles – the specialist and the integrator – as being quite distinct. As with other areas of IT-related consulting, consultants have considerable value to add in both roles, but can easily destroy that value if the roles are confused.

SUMMARY

1 IT-related consultants account for around 50 per cent of the consulting market, covering a wide range of business functions (CRM, HR, supply chain, etc.) and multiple roles (from high-level strategy to detailed implementation).

2 Looking back on the considerable amounts of money spent on ERP and Y2K projects during the 1990s, many organizations are now questioning the value of large-scale IT projects. This has direct implications for the consulting firms involved in this type of work, as clients increasingly look for value for money from IT projects and smaller-scale, more tactical initiatives.

3 Looking at examples of best practice in IT projects suggests that, irrespective of technology, the business process involved or the role played by the consulting firm, collaborative working, and finding a balance between structure and flexibility, are the two key issues. Consultants can play a major role in carrying out specialist IT work, creating an environment where collaboration can take place, and in ensuring that flexibility is balanced with structure – but only where these two roles (the specialist and the integrator) are treated as distinct.

CHAPTER 14

OUTSOURCING

Outsourcing provides a means of contracting non-core processes to third parties who have specific expertise in the appropriate field. It means cutting process costs by sharing them across other organizations, and improving service by using organizations that have in-depth expertise in a given field. Although conceived in the 1980s, outsourcing has only recently come of age, as the technology required to allow two or more organizations to access simultaneously the same data and processes has only become available with the widespread use of the internet. Prior to this, outsourcing anything other than comparatively simple administrative tasks was prohibitively complex. But there has now been an explosion in the types of outsourcing deals being done. In 1997, most outsourcing was IT outsourcing whereas a wide array of business processes are now being outsourced, such as human resource management, tax and accounting, legal services. Nor is it just the scope of outsourcing that has broadened; the role of the outsourcing provider has also shifted significantly, from an organization which performs a comparatively menial task for the lowest possible price, to one that offers specialist expertise and strategic input to its clients.

With the growth of outsourcing, the input of consultants has evolved in two directions:

- ☐ Providers of outsourcing services (and this may involve transferring employees from the client's organization to the consulting firm).
- ☐ Advisers on the optimum outsourcing arrangements, in terms of helping to develop the business case, to evaluate and select an appropriate service provider and to smooth the transition process (change management, training, etc.).

This chapter explores these two roles and looks at how clients can maximize the value that consultants bring in each case.

CONSULTANTS AS OUTSOURCERS

Over the last decade, the role of consultants has been shifting away from its traditional advisory one. Responding to chronic client concern about the transition from theory to practice (see Chapter 12), advisors have given way to doers – consultants who are prepared to take on clients' processes and manage them on their behalf. Today, many of the world's largest consulting firms earn a significant proportion of their revenue from this area. Indeed, for these firms, outsourcing is not simply important in terms of its top-line contribution, but in the extent to which it promises large-scale, long-term projects in an industry accustomed to surviving on very short order books. While other sources of consulting revenue may fluctuate according to prevailing market conditions, outsourcing promises some predictability.

Case study: Abbey Life

Abbey Life, a leader in the UK life and pensions market, and now part of the Lloyds TSB group, is no stranger to the need to deliver excellent customer service while increasing efficiency and reducing costs. However, in 2000, the company faced an even greater challenge when it sold its sales operation to Zurich Financial Services/Allied Dunbar assurance, effectively closing its doors to new business.

Neil Tointon, Director of Business Relationships at Abbey Life, describes the situation faced by the company:

‘It was essential to maintain an excellent level of service for our existing customers, but their number would naturally decline over the coming years. We also needed to provide staff with a positive future. In a situation where business is no longer growing, more able employees often look for positions in other organizations.’

At the same time, the company was keen to increase the efficiency of its client and administration legacy systems. Abbey Life was handling more than 1.75 million policies via 18 disparate systems. The age of these systems and their lack of technical uniformity were constraining the company's ability to move quickly to address new market demands, such as euro-compliance. As such, Abbey Life was finding it increasingly difficult to justify future investment in them.

Abbey Life's dilemma prompted one of the most ground-breaking and substantial outsourcing agreements that the UK financial services market had ever seen – a £225 million ($338 million) deal over ten years to outsource all of its life and pensions processing and administration to Unisys. In order to support Abbey Life's requirements, Unisys established a totally new subsidiary, Unisys Insurance Services Limited (UISL) which now employs the vast majority of Abbey Life's staff and actively markets its leading-edge services to other insurance companies in the UK. UISL has already achieved a market-leading position by becoming the largest provider of managed life and pensions administration services in the UK.

As this kind of outsourcing arrangement was unprecedented, it was essential for Abbey Life to choose an organization with the experience and flexibility to make the project a success. Tointon says:

‘With Unisys there was no attempt to impose a pre-conceived solution on Abbey Life. They came to us with a strategy which would adapt to our business, not the other way round. They listened hard and fast so that the final solution used the best of both companies' skills. They also did not flinch from the commercial challenges, and demonstrated plenty of courage and long-term vision in a relatively new business area.’

Derek Dean UISL's IS Director, takes up the story.

‘Abbey Life required an efficient, cost-effective and fully integrated solution that would manage its administration systems for the lifetime of its life assurance customers. When Abbey Life considered all the options, migrating all of its polices to a single system hosted by a third party made the most strategic and financial sense.

UISL provides comprehensive support for the complete portfolio of life, pensions and investment products. In addition to providing a low-cost platform, it has the capability to support a whole range of sales and delivery channels, including the internet, WAP and interactive digital television. It offered Abbey Life optimum flexibility to accommodate new products, services and channels quickly and easily, thereby addressing the company's customer service objectives. The outsourcing agreement transferred all risk from Abbey Life to UISL. A comprehensive suite of service levels was established to ensure that Abbey Life's business priorities were mirrored in the UISL business strategy. It was essential that we provided a real business benefit for Abbey Life, both in terms of growth and people's career development, as well as ensuring a seamless and enhanced service for customers.

Outsourcing on this scale requires a partner with the experience, skills and technology to be capable of minimizing disruption to customer service. In addition, the transfer of staff to the partner organization requires efficient planning to ensure that any sensitive employee transfer issues are handled carefully. These were the main challenges we faced but, by means of effective communication and cooperation, the transfer to UISL went extremely smoothly. Abbey Life's employees now have a clear view of their future and are working in an organization where their careers and personal development prospects are much brighter than before.

We went to great lengths to ensure that Abbey Life staff made a smooth transfer to UISL without any disruption to either business or customers. People who were working with a closed-book life company, with little chance for growth, now work for the largest third-party administrator in the UK life processing business, within a high-growth, dynamic environment.

UISL has brought together two sets of people with complementary ideas and capabilities. Abbey Life is keeping ahead of a competitive industry by streamlining its business and focusing on providing existing customers with services of optimum efficiency and reliability.’

The outsourcing agreement has delivered substantial benefits for Abbey Life, including a saving of 20 per cent over the best in-house solution, greater employee retention, the migration of 18 legacy systems to a single one, and a leading-edge solution that offers multi-channel distribution.

LESSONS FROM THE FIRST GENERATION OF OUTSOURCING

Templeton College in Oxford has carried out some of the most extensive global research into what does and does not work, in the field of outsourcing. The research highlights eight key factors which significantly increase the probability that an outsourcing contract will be successful (defined here in terms of the extent to which it has achieved its anticipated benefits).

☐ **Senior executives and IT managers make the outsourcing decision together.** IT functions and their internal customers have rarely enjoyed a happy relationship and, in the early outsourcing contracts, both sides separately saw outsourcing as an exit route. Non-IT executives would decide that they had had enough of escalating costs and apparent inefficiencies, and put their IT departments out to the lowest-price bidder, almost completely bypassing their IT managers. Equally, IT managers, eager to move to an environment in which their skills were valued, would decide to outsource themselves with little end-user consultation.

☐ **The outsourcing organization has solicited internal and external bids.** In the past, a 'grass is always greener on the other side of the fence' attitude has predominated, with external suppliers seen to be the only potential source of cost savings or enhanced service. Experience has, however, shown that organizations are more likely to reap the rewards they expect from outsource if they solicit bids for the work from the internal department currently responsible for the process, as well as from external suppliers. At the very least, the internal bid provides a definitive benchmark against which the external bids can be assessed. More positively, they can indicate areas of specialist expertise internally (for example, about applications that require a considerable understanding of the business to be able to support), which an external bidder might lack.

☐ **Proactive contract management after signing.** One of the most common reactions to signing an outsourcing agreement was to breathe a sigh of relief. 'We have outsourced the problem, now we can get on with other things' was a typical sentiment. But there is plenty of evidence to suggest that serious problems arise where clients do not stay actively involved in the arrangements.

☐ **Outsourcing chosen for the right reasons.** First generation outsourcing was often a measure of desperation; having struggled to improve the cost efficiency and delivery capability of their IT departments over many years, corporate executives simply chose to wash their hands of the problem. Much has since been learned about the need to explore all possible options, as well as outsourcing, in order to understand their relative strengths and weaknesses, and to avoid seeing outsourcing as a panacea for management conflicts. You need to be certain of the positive value which outsourcing brings and, if necessary, look at alternative sources of value (improved service, shifting from fixed to variable costs, and so on).

☐ **There are multiple, rather than single suppliers.** The earliest outsourcing contracts were almost all between one client and one supplier. This resulted in an 'all your eggs in one basket' approach for both sides: clients were too dependent on a single supplier; suppliers took on specialist work that they were not well equipped to do. Appreciating that this strategy was unsatisfactory for both sides, outsourcing deals have become more complex, involving a host of suppliers, each of whom is a specialist in a particular area.

☐ **Gut feel is replaced with hard data.** One of the key problems facing any outsourcing client or supplier is that misinformation often abounds, especially in an environment where many people move from one company to another and are consequently concerned about their future welfare. Users, too, may be worried that the move to outsource a particular function will result in a lower level of support in crucial areas. To counter this tendency to misinformation, it is important to collate as much hard data as possible. Specifically, this means validating user and employee satisfaction levels both before and after outsourcing, so that subsequent discussions can be based on facts, rather than anecdotal complaints.

☐ **Transparency wins.** When companies first started negotiating with outsourcing suppliers, they adopted a secretive approach in order to achieve the best possible deal from the supplier. This confrontation style has largely given way to a more collaborative style of working, in which both sides share information and try to establish common commercial goals.

☐ **More speed, less haste.** Another characteristic of these early negotiations was that they were rushed, as companies tried to complete complex deals to prespecified deadlines. It was a process which inevitably favoured the outsourcing supplier, as clients cut corners, carrying out only cursory assessments of the potential suppliers, and using the latter's standard terms and conditions rather than drawing up their own. Moreover, critical issues were often left until after the contract had been signed, at which stage the outsourcing client had little left with which to negotiate. The lesson here is a simple one: open-ended negotiations provide more leverage for the client.

UNDERSTANDING COMPETING VALUES

Taking these lessons on board is only part of the solution.

While a growing outsourcing market has brought with it greater understanding of the critical success factors that need to be considered in making outsourcing work, and of the major pitfalls to be avoided, the process of setting up a successful outsourcing deal remains a complex one. As Mark Granovetter[1], a US academic points out, 'Outsourcing is driven by economic actions, but embedded in social relations'. Having a foolproof process for delivering **economic** value serves little purpose if you do not also have a process for delivering **social** value.

The difference between the types of value is a perceptual one, but hugely important none the less. Suppose you are an HR Director. You decide to outsource your HR function because it is widely perceived to be costly, inefficient and bureaucratic to the rest of your organization. By handing over the routine, everyday tasks to one of the new specialist HR services providers, you are planning to cut costs and improve efficiency (the service provider would automate and streamline your HR processes), and free up the time of the small, residual HR department to take on more strategic, value-adding tasks (succession planning, personal development, and so on). The negotiations go smoothly: you have completed the hand-over, and are now sitting at your desk waiting for the comments to come flooding in from your colleagues, congratulating you on the improved service, the greater efficiency, etc. But it does not happen; instead, the same niggling complaints continue. So what has gone wrong? In fact nothing may have gone wrong, it is just that you are in a position where you cannot win.

If you ask people in an organization whether a particular business is effective or not, their response is determined by how they define effectiveness in the first place. Unfortunately for the client considering improving the effectiveness of a business function by outsourcing it, there can be almost as many definitions of effectiveness as there are employees in an organization. It is not easy to build consensus across a whole organization about the effectiveness of one of its component parts, because everyone sees that component part differently. As two US academics, Robert Quinn and John Rohrbaugh commented[2]: 'Organizational effectiveness is not a concept . . . it is a socially-constructed notion – a value-based judgement.' This has a direct impact on any decision to outsource it.

Quinn and Rohrbaugh developed a model designed to help organizations identify key differences in the way that organizational effectiveness is defined. Essentially, they asked people to define what an effective business unit would look like along three axes: flexibility/control, means/ends, and organization/individual. These axes can be modified and expanded to take account of the business unit being considered. Thus, an assessment of an IT department could be carried out along the following dimensions:

- ☐ **Structure:** should the business unit be centralized (responsible for carrying out the wishes of the corporate centre, with authority to force other business units to comply with its

[1] Mark Granovetter, 'Economic Action and Social Structure: the Problem of Embeddedness.' *American Journal of Sociology*, (1985)

[2] Robert E Quinn and John Rohrbaugh, 'A Spatial Model of Effectiveness Criteria: Towards a Competing Values Approach to Organizational Analysis', *Management Science*, (1983)

approach), or decentralized (helping local business units to achieve their own strategies, and therefore answerable to them)?

☐ **Expertise:** what kind of knowledge base is most important for the business unit? Is it more important for the individuals within that business unit to have specialist knowledge (to be experts in some field) or to have a good understanding of the business itself?

☐ **Contribution:** what is most important for the business unit, in relation to the other business units in the organization? To keep its costs down, or to create value and/or generate revenue?

☐ **Perspective:** where should the attention of the business unit be? On external issues (customers, markets), or internal ones (efficiency, internal service delivery)?

☐ **Planning horizon:** should the business unit's thinking be short-term or long-term?

☐ **Focus:** should the business unit concentrate on strategic issues, or should it be looking for tactical gains?

Treating each of these dimensions as a continuum (centralized–decentralized; technical knowledge–business knowledge; efficiency–value creation; external–internal; long-term–short-term; strategic–tactical) allows you to plot the variations in people's perceptions. Let us return to our example of the HR Director. Supposing you had preceded your decision to outsource by comparing how other parts of your organization view your department, you might have produced charts like those in Figures 14.1 and 14.2. These charts compare the views of two departments: an internally-focused finance department (Figure 14.1) and a externally-focused customer services department (Figure 14.2). Each department has chosen to define the organizational effectiveness of the HR department (the shaded area on each chart) in its own image. Thus, the finance department believes that the HR department should be centralized, cost-conscious and add value through its technical know-how (exactly like the

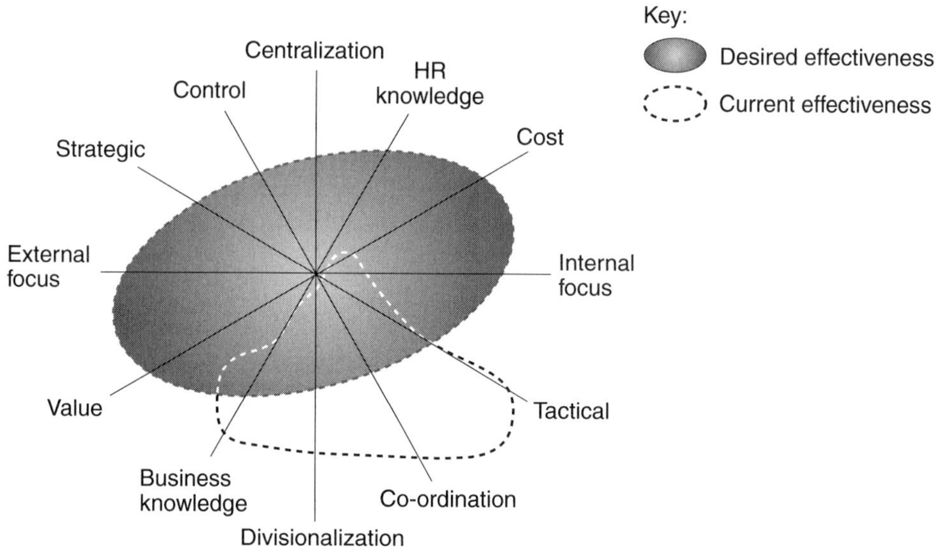

FIGURE 14.1: The organizational effectiveness of an HR department, as seen by a finance department

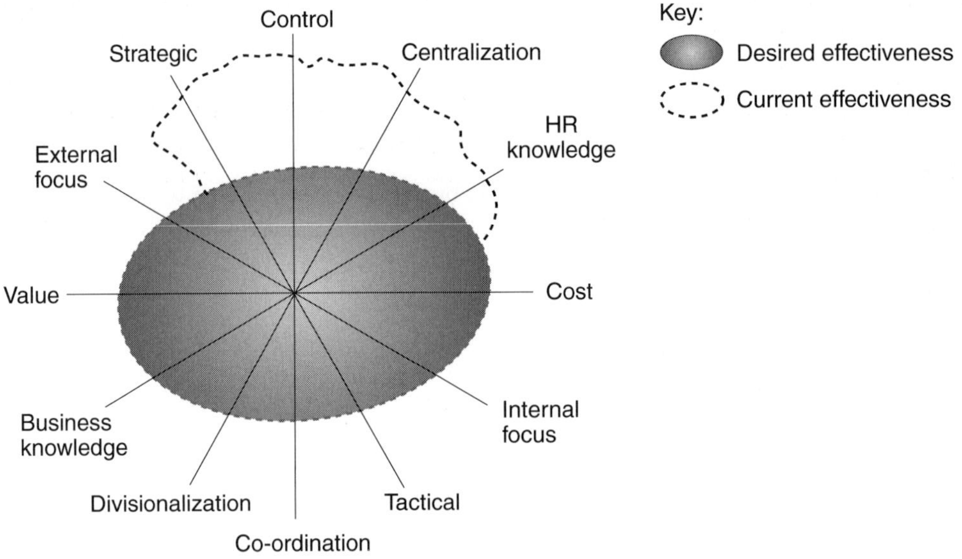

FIGURE 14.2: The organizational effectiveness of an HR department, as seen by a customer services department

finance department). By contrast, the customer services department believes that the HR department should be tactical, committed to creating value and possessing a high level of knowledge about the business (exactly like the customer services department). The irony is that, if you now compared how your HR department is rated by these other departments, you might find that each one has the opposite view – the finance people think that the HR department is too tactical and follows the lead of the other business units too much, but the customer services department regards the HR department as too centralized and control-orientated. In other words, the HR department cannot win.

When it comes to outsourcing, you need to understand from the outset the extent to which people's perceptions not only vary, but may be in diametrical opposition with each other. Where there is a great variance in perceptions, it will be extremely difficult to persuade everyone that the process of outsourcing a particular function – once completed – has been a success, simply because everyone in the organization that outsources has a different definition of what success should be.

CONSULTANT AS ADVISOR

Competing values theory illustrates why so many clients use consulting firms in the second role mentioned at the beginning of this chapter – that of independent advisers and arbitrators during the outsourcing process.

- ☐ By virtue of the fact that they are outsiders, consultants can play a bipartisan role, negotiating settlements between the different factions in a client's organization. This is very hard for either the client department that is to be outsourced or its internal customers to do, as neither side is disinterested in the outcome.

☐ Consultants can therefore play a valuable role in establishing, agreeing and communicating the metrics that will be used to measure the performance of the outsourcing provider (service levels, etc.).

☐ Moreover, the disinterestedness of consultants can also be of use when it comes to evaluating and selecting a preferred bidder, and during the process of negotiating a contract. Hiring consultants who have extensive experience of outsourcing should help you:

1 Design a realistic transition process and understand the change management issues involved.

2 Develop an appropriate evaluation process – one suited to your needs as a client and the characteristics of the project (discussed in Chapter 2) – which facilitates consultation between the different groups of people within your organization, and incorporates key lessons from other projects with which the consulting firm has been involved.

3 Identify a short-list of potential outsourcing providers.

4 Advise on legal issues during contract negotiation.

Typically, this role includes:

☐ Developing the business case based on the likely benefits and costs of outsourcing as opposed to keeping the function in-house.

☐ Identifying the business requirements and monitoring the outsourcing agreement, once in place, to ensure that these are met.

☐ Defining how the benefits post-outsourcing will be measured, and quantifying the impact of the inevitable risks.

☐ Ensuring that all the appropriate parts of the organization are involved in the process of selecting the outsourcing provider and implementing the agreement; that the necessary sponsorship for the project exists at a senior level; and that all the relevant stakeholders are consulted.

☐ Managing the impact at all levels – on people and processes, as well as the organization as a whole.

☐ Managing the technical migration of the legacy systems to the new supplier.

☐ Reviewing the actual benefits.

Case study: Sabre – brokering the outsourcing deal

Internal perceptions about what constitutes organizational effectiveness are not the only problem when it comes to outsourcing any business function. Another key lesson from outsourcing agreements made over the last 15 years is that there is a correlation between organizations which have real expertise in buying in services of this type, and the extent to which the anticipated benefits of an outsourcing deal will be realized in practice. Essentially, if you are good at purchasing, you are very likely to make a good outsourcing 'purchase'.

But what should you do if this is not one of your organization's core competencies? Although it may sound like overkill to hire a consultant to hire other consultants, that is exactly what you *should* do, as the experience of Sabre illustrates.

Sabre Holdings Corporation is the global leader in information technology for the travel and transportation industries. Its *Sabre®* computer reservations system processes approximately 40 per cent of all travel reservations globally, and is used by 47,000 travel agencies over four continents. Sabre also specialized as a supplier of total IT outsourcing services to companies in the travel and transportation industries, supporting major airlines such as American Airlines, US Airways and Gulf Air, plus other transportation companies in the rail and rental car markets.

In 2000, the company's core business was based on the distribution of travel marketing technology and solutions, directed at providing travel information to travel agencies, corporate planners and travellers, as well as a reservation system and technology systems to airlines; by contrast, its IT outsourcing proposition was showing only limited growth. A decision was therefore taken, not to seek additional IT outsourcing contracts, but to focus instead on developing and marketing its travel reservations software. Sabre would sell its outsourcing business, outsource its own technology platform and create a long-term partnership with the buyer.

A team from PA Consulting Group was brought in to provide the insight and skills needed to plan and execute the fundamental changes required. Key responsibilities of the PA team included managing the tendering and evaluation process, advising on the negotiation strategy and facilitating the negotiation sessions, developing and negotiating the outsourcing contract, and providing support and coordination for transition planning.

PA's project manager, Jonathan Cooper-Bagnall gives the details:

‘We were involved from the outset. Our first major task was to assist in one of the most critical activities – effective planning. Only by careful planning and rework of its activities would Sabre meet its aggressive goal in the required timescale. This included the contractual aspects and also the other activities that would need to be undertaken, such as the development of a service management organization, business process reengineering and a focus on the future transition.

We developed a statement of requirements for the required outsourcing services and asked four companies to respond. We then managed and fast-tracked an evaluation process in order to clarify the benefits of the returned bids and provide focus for the next stage of the project. Jointly with Sabre, we developed a dual negotiation approach, which meant that discussions with two potential bidders were conducted in tandem – something that resulted in a higher purchase price and a reduction in the cost of the outsourcing service purchase by a factor of several millions of dollars. Throughout the negotiation and evaluation phases, we supplemented Sabre's in-house team, helping to develop the contract, specifying service levels and service credit criteria, and developing and refining charging structures.

As an outsourcer, Sabre had consolidated its customers' IT environments and centralized resources to a single, shared environment. Even with its new direction, Sabre still required services from this consolidated shared environment. This situation was made more complex still by the fact that some of the systems to be outsourced would still be dependent on Sabre personnel's experience of the core reservation system. It was important for the outsource partner to have access to Sabre resources, to allow continued development of systems which would now be in the outsourcer's control.

We brought experience in best-practice contract development, enterprise systems and the airline industry to help Sabre draw up a services agreement which fully satisfied the development requirements, application delivery and support – and the operational services that were needed to support Sabre's new business direction.

The fact that we worked closely with Sabre throughout this complex transaction was crucial to the project's overall success. We complemented the Sabre team by bringing to the project the necessary skills and experience to meet the very ambitious project objectives, and to plan and deliver the fundamental changes required.

In March 2001, a tripartite agreement was signed between Sabre and EDS (Electronic Data Systems Inc). Part of this agreement was the signing of a $2.2 billion, ten-year outsourcing contract with EDS. Under the deal, EDS acquired Sabre's airline infrastructure outsourcing business and internal IT infrastructure assets for $670 million. Sabre also retained net working capital of $108 million, bringing the total value of the agreement to Sabre to $778 million. EDS and Sabre would jointly market IT solutions and services to the travel and transportation industry, with approximately 4,200 Sabre employees transferring to EDS.

Through the sale and the purchase back of outsourcing services, Sabre and EDS have entered into an industry-shaping partnership that will deliver innovative solutions in a fast-changing market.'

SUMMARY

1 In the rapidly growing outsourcing market, consulting firms provide outsourcing services and help clients to set up effective outsourcing arrangements. Because of the importance of objectivity in the latter capacity, these two roles are largely becoming mutually exclusive.

2 The mixed results of outsourcing during the 1980s and 1990s offers several important lessons in terms of how these contacts should be established and managed:

- ☐ Senior executives, and those executives in the department to be outsourced, need to make joint decisions.
- ☐ Internal as well as external bids should be solicited.
- ☐ Outsourcing should be done for the right reasons, not simply as a kneejerk reaction to saving money.
- ☐ As the business processes to be outsourced become more varied, a single organization is unlikely to be able to offer effective outsourcing services in all areas – multiple agreements will need to be negotiated with different specialist providers.
- ☐ Misinformation and rumour needs to be replaced by hard data.
- ☐ Both the outsourcing organization and the outsourcing provider should be open and transparent – partnership working is more likely to be successful than an adversarial relationship.
- ☐ Negotiations should not be rushed.

3 However, it is very difficult for an organization to carry out all parts of the outsourcing process by itself, not least because different parts of the organization are likely to have different views about the anticipated benefits. Consultants can play a crucial role in bringing an objective view both to the internal issues and the process of selecting, evaluating and negotiating with an outsourcing supplier.

CHAPTER 15

CONSULTING AND ORGANIZATIONAL LEARNING

There has been a significant shift in the consulting industry over the last 20 years, away from its traditional ground of advisory work, and into actual management. Outsourcing (discussed in the previous chapter) is the most extreme manifestation of this trend, with clients handing over the management of important (if not strategically so) processes to suppliers capable of carrying them out, either more effectively, or more efficiently, or both. However, the problem with outsourcing is that it does little to increase an organization's ability to solve a problem (such as make a given process more efficient), but asks someone else to solve it for them. There are many occasions where such an approach can be completely justified – no organization needs to be expert in everything it does – but there are other instances where organizations would do better to acquire that knowledge themselves.

The obsession with time to market during the heyday of the 1998–2000 e-business boom is a good example of this. In its earliest form, people assumed that time to market was an absolute concept – they even talked of 90 days as being the window of opportunity for any given venture: take longer than 90 days to develop your idea, and your competitor would launch it first. But, as the euphoria of 1999 dissipated, it became clear that time to market was much more important as a relative idea; the key lay, not so much in beating a given deadline (90 days), but in organizations beating the mental and cultural timescales and deadlines they often, implicitly, adopt. Thus, what mattered was for an organization to do something it thought it could not do (launch a product in three months instead of the usual six). It was this that created the strong sense of the miraculous suddenly being possible, which characterized this period (an issue which was also touched on in Chapter 11). For companies looking to experience this 'miracle', hiring a team of consultants to perform the miracle on their behalf clearly did not work – the miracle was only miraculous because it involved a lumbering bureaucracy sloughing off the inertia of decades.

While fashion currently favours outsourcing (a response to economic uncertainty and downturn), we should not ignore the fact that, once economic confidence returns, organizations will be looking to expand into the new areas of opportunity. Instead of wanting to off-load a problem to someone else, they will want to learn how to exploit it themselves.

So can consultants play a role in helping organizations to learn? It sounds like a contradiction in terms – the equivalent of *telling* someone to be empowered. This chapter considers this issue, beginning with two case studies where consulting firms have helped organizations learn, rather than do something for them.

ASSISTING ORGANIZATIONAL LEARNING

Case study: gaining eXperience at BT

In 2000, BT was in the process of launching a series of complex new propositions, but take-up was slower than expected. Research showed that this lack of success could be attributed to three causes:

1 Sales advisors lacked the confidence and capability to discuss the new propositions with customers.

2 The prevailing classroom-based training approach, as well as being slow and expensive, was only capable of building a level of awareness of new propositions, not an ability to sell them.

3 Inconsistent approaches to selling new propositions were having a negative effect both sales revenue and customer satisfaction ratings.

Having worked successfully with BT in the past, Accenture was asked to help. The eXperience Programme was launched, in which Accenture worked side-by-side with BT to build an e-learning platform that would deliver immediate sales capability and proposition knowledge to 4,500 sales advisors and managers in BT's telemarketing sales channel. The objective was to double conversion rates and to reduce the time taken to hit sales targets from between 4–6 weeks to a single day.

Paul Stokes, a leading designer in the eXperience programme and a consultant at Accenture describes how the application was put together:

'The eXperience Programme made use of advanced learning design, delivered by cutting-edge technology. It consists of a proprietary learning approach and technology developed by Accenture that has demonstrable advantages in terms of the speed, scale, and depth of the learning it delivers. The resulting application is a web-based simulation that puts the customer at the heart of the learner's experience, by emulating the user's actual interaction with customers in simulated telephone conversations. Key to the success of this approach is the fact that the learner is able to practise "real life" customer interactions in a safe environment where they can learn from their mistakes and successes.

Having run a very successful pilot of the application with a limited number of users, we were told that the details of the BT Choices proposition had been leaked to the press 13 days early. Our client was therefore faced with a major quandary: launch early and risk not having the sales advisors up-to-speed and lose sales; or launch on schedule and risk being beaten by competitors. The solution was to release our application five days ahead of schedule, and train up practically all the customer advisors in one of BT's customer service centres in time to handle the first customer enquiries and sales.

This would not have been possible if the client and ourselves had not worked together to develop and validate the content of the application. Two people from BT joined our team to create the learning application, and we were heavily dependent upon the support and input of those the application would impact. An implementation organization, created within BT Retail for the eXperience Programme, was leveraged to facilitate both the development of the application and its rollout. This organization also provided vital feedback and delivery mechanisms. Conversations with simulated customers were delivered to 4,500 sales personnel over a four week roll-out period, providing the sales advisors with the knowledge, skills and capability to sell the new proposition from day one (half the time it would have taken using a conventional classroom-based learning approach). Moreover, compared to a control group using the traditional classroom approach:

- ☐ Sales revenues and conversion rates had doubled.
- ☐ Customer satisfaction rose by nearly 30 per cent.
- ☐ Training time went down by 50 per cent.
- ☐ By building confidence and capability to sell, advisors were able to sell in one-twentieth of the time.

The learning approach taken by eXperience is delivering a higher quality of learning than traditional techniques, as well as providing a platform that can be used repeatedly. The rapid development and deployment of these simulated conversations, along with the business results achieved, clearly demonstrate that is possible to impact performance dramatically in order to deliver real business results, consistent proposition knowledge and a more customer-centric culture at BT.’

Case study: global leadership for Novo Nordisk

The pharmaceutical sector is an increasingly harsh environment in which to operate. Patents come under attack, customers demand better products at lower prices, competitors merge to pool resources, and talented staff have a high price on their head.

Novo Nordisk has operated successfully since the early twentieth century, and is the world leader in diabetes care. It also produces and markets products for coagulation disorders, growth disorders and hormone replacement therapy. In 2000, with an increasingly diverse product range serving multiple market sectors, Novo Nordisk's senior management decided to demerge the business into two separate entities, Novo Nordisk and Novo Zymes, allowing greater operational freedom and increased market focus.

Novo Nordisk, which has its headquarters in Denmark, employs 14,000 people in 68 countries. As a new business, albeit with a long history, the executive team wanted to seize the opportunity following the demerger in order to engage the wider management team to help them deliver the new strategic focus, leverage the multi-cultural nature of the company and develop their leadership talent pool.

With such a diverse managerial team in terms of geography, culture and experience, a major factor in growing the business would be determined by how well these future leaders could be developed and encouraged to become advocates of the new strategic focus.

To address these issues, Novo Nordisk worked with Hay Group to develop a global leadership program. Hay Group has a reputation for delivering solutions in the field of people performance, and was able to draw upon a model that it has researched and developed which measures the impact of leadership upon organizations. From its research centre in Boston, and from hundreds of projects worldwide, Hay Group was able to collate and analyze the data in its London office to trace explicit links between the actions and nature of leadership and the required results of an organization.

But it was not only Hay Group's experience that Novo Nordisk wanted to draw upon. Zoe Gruhn, who led the project for Hay Group explains:

‘In choosing a partner, Novo Nordisk were looking for an organization that shared its philosophy on how to develop individuals. They wanted a process-driven team to ensure a high degree of flexibility in producing the program, and a team which could deliver creative solutions and was fun to work with.

We initially worked with Novo Nordisk to develop the "Strategic Business Leadership Program" which was designed to provide senior managers with a good understanding of Novo Nordisk's vision and strategy and how to execute it, build business and strategic management competencies and promote networking. The program required managers to focus on both their soft and hard skills, and was based around a simulation package, "StratX", which was supported through group discussions and individual coaching.

While the program proved effective, it was felt that the results could be even more profound if hard and soft skills were addressed separately through tailored programs. This led to our second project, "The Leadership Foundation Program".

In designing this program, we worked closely with Novo Nordisk's Internal Leadership Development Consultant to get under the skin of the organization and design a program that would not only be conceptually robust, but also be accepted and valued by its intended audience. Board-level consultation was undertaken to ensure that the program aims were closely aligned with business strategy.

The program was targeted at vice-presidents and senior managers, a group who are often the focus of management training initiatives and who usually treat an invitation to anything resembling a "management training program" with the same enthusiasm as a trip to the dentist! To overcome this cynicism, we developed a two-pronged strategy: we worked with the client to develop an internal marketing campaign to raise awareness, and we created a flexible design which allowed participants to choose from a selection of modules, and thereby tailor the program to their own specific development needs.

A major objective of the program was to lead the participants through a journey of personal and professional discovery. Prior to the start of the program, each delegate was asked to complete an array of diagnostic tools (including 360-degree feedback based on Novo Nordisk's leadership competencies and direct reports about the climate they create in their work units – "what it feels like to work around here"). The results of these diagnostics served as a benchmark against which the individuals' development, both during and after the program, could be measured.

Once the program reached the residential stage, it offered participants:

- ☐ A comprehensive personal development and implementation plan.
- ☐ A shared understanding of how to lead others effectively in a constantly changing environment.

- ☐ A set of practical tools to help individuals become more effective in the business environment in which they operate.
- ☐ Practice in developing the critical competencies that underpin emotional intelligence and effective leadership.

Although the leadership development program offers many immediate benefits for participants (85 per cent of whom rated it as "highly effective"), we are aware that its long-term success requires a permanent change in behaviour. We therefore devised a support strategy aimed at maintaining the improvements made during the program itself. These included:

- ☐ A post-program meeting between the participant and their manager to agree a personal development plan.
- ☐ An area on the company's intranet site where participants can access additional materials and share experiences with other program alumni.
- ☐ The opportunity to undertake satellite programs to fill any specific competency gaps identified during the program.

It is still too early to say what effect the leadership development program will have on the company's performance over the next decade and beyond, but early signs are good. The company expects a 15 per cent operational gain this year and, unlike other pharmaceutical companies, is not trimming its investment plans. Over the last 12 months, the company's share price has remained unchanged, an impressive performance given that most leading indices have experienced double-digit percentage falls in this timeframe. ❜

LEARNING THE LESSONS ABOUT LEARNING

A common factor in both cases described above is how they marry new ideas about learning with the tried-and-tested (computer-based training which enables participants to focus on the 'experience' of dealing with customers; grounding the learning from classroom-based lectures in the context of personal development plans and the impact that individuals have on their environment). Indeed, a key point is that many of our conventional assumptions about learning do not work well when translated to a business context. And yet clients still hire consultants to deliver workshops designed to bring people up to date with current trends, and provide an opportunity to debate their applicability or otherwise to their daily lives.

By contrast, in an article in the *Sloan Management Review*[1], academic Claus Otto Scharmer has argued that:

> ❛ Given the pace of organizational development, the traditional approaches to learning are no longer useful to describe and promote new learning, since the experience base of an organization can no longer simply be extended to the changes and innovations that are taking place in the "new economy". ❜

Instead, Scharmer makes the case for something he calls 'presencing':

> ❛ Organizations and their leaders can develop their capability by engaging in a different kind of learning cycle, one that allows them to learn from the future as it emerges, rather than from reflecting on past experiences . . . The term refers to the capacity for sensing, embodying, and enacting emerging futures. ❜

[1] C Scharmer, 'Presencing: Learning from the Future as it Emerges', paper presented at the conference on Knowledge and Innovation, at the Helsinki School of Economics, Finland, (2000).

Although writing at the height of e-business euphoria, his comments remain directly relevant to a rapidly-changing business environment. There is a distinction here between styles of learning which tend to sustain the *status quo* and those that actively encourage change (contrasted in Table 15.1)[1].

STATUS QUO LEARNING	CHANGE-ORIENTATED LEARNING
Single loop – intended to reinforce existing ideas and perceptions	Double-loop – designed to change perceptions
Non-reflective – little attention is paid to reflecting on the ideas learnt in a practical context	Highly reflective – the lessons learnt are applied
Instrumental – the lessons are simply regarded as new tools and techniques	Transformational – the learning process is designed to free people from a self-imposed, restrictive view of the world
Presents only one viewpoint	Presents multiple viewpoints which create new opportunities for learning

TABLE 15.1: Differences between two types of learning

Maximizing the contribution that consultants can make to organizational learning involves recognizing the differences between these two modes.

Consultants tend to be used to delivering what is in effect *status quo*, not change-orientated learning. Why? Partly habit: most clients and consultants tend to think of the learning process in conventional terms and are largely unfamiliar with new research on cognitive theory; partly economics: *status quo* learning is cheaper than change-orientated learning because (from the consulting firm's point of view) it involves reusable components (research on trends, tools and techniques), and (from the client's point of view) it is a discrete activity (taking people out of their day jobs for a week at the most); also, partly fear of the unknown. By contrast, change-orientated learning is new, potentially expensive, open-ended (when does a 'transformational' process finish, if ever?), and high-risk.

For all of these reasons, it will require clients and consultants working together to resolve this issue: where an easy way out continues to exist, some consultants will be prepared to offer it, and some clients will be prepared to buy it. Clients need to be more circumspect and challenge whether the 'learning process' they are buying is going to translate into changes in attitude or behaviour. They need to accept that people learn in different ways and over different timescales, and not go straight for the clear-cut solution that offers plenty of content but very little process, even if this is far easier to manage. And consultants should – collectively – resist the temptation of offering clients an easy way out, of giving the impression that organizational learning can be an off-the-shelf package in the same way that an IT application is.

[1] I am indebted to Gary Hannaway at Kingston Business School for his help in researching this topic.

SUMMARY

1 Although the current trend is for organizations to outsource more areas of their business (see Chapter 14), consultants do not always have to be 'doers', taking over processes and managing them on their behalf. Paradoxically, consultants can make a valuable contribution both in training and developing people within client organizations, and in helping those organizations.

2 Much of this contribution can be made through 'change-orientated' learning processes, which differ from conventional '*status quo*' learning in that they challenge people to question their assumptions and thus make them open to change.

3 However, this type of learning is often regarded with suspicion by clients and consultants alike, as it is viewed to be untested, expensive and delivering only uncertain benefits over ill-defined timeframes.

PART 3

OUTCOMES

CHAPTER 16

MEASURING THE VALUE OF CONSULTANCY

Almost every brochure of every consulting firm mentions the word 'value'. Yet, the irony is that the consulting industry's most over-used word is also its least well-defined.

'Delivering value', 'working in value-added partnerships' – what do phrases such as these actually mean? And if they do not mean anything, why use them? The simple answer is that 'value' goes to the heart of what consultants *should* bring and what clients *think* they are buying. It is remarkably easy to trawl through the business press and find cynical comments about consultants who are perceived to be scarcely better than corporate ambulance chasers. Take Lewis Penault's *Consulting Demons* as an example:

> ‘Simply put, consulting is at its most organized, intimidating best when it is working to maximize its take from the client. Its key vulnerabilities, on the other hand, are rooted in using some of the most impressive people in the world to do too many questionable things too fast.’ [1]

The vast majority of criticisms levelled by the likes of Penault come down to one issue: the fact that neither consultants nor clients have readily available mechanism for measuring value. If both sides were able to put a value on the intervention by the consulting firm (whatever form it took), then clients would have a better tool for monitoring and controlling consulting projects, and consultants would have a more transparent and therefore acceptable basis on which to price projects.

So why don't we 'value' the input of consultants? Why does the Interbrand equivalent for the consulting industry not exist? If we can measure something as intangible and complex as the value of a brand, surely we can measure the value that consultants bring.

THE OBSTACLES TO MEASURING VALUE

The reason why there is no standard methodology for doing this is, in fact, twofold: it stems not only from genuine problems in valuation, but also from the fact that both

[1] Lewis Perault, *Consulting Demons: Inside the Unscrupulous World of Global Corporate Consulting* (John Wiley & Sons, 2000)

clients and consultants have been willing to expend much effort trying to overcome those problems.

As two Chicago journalists, James O'Shea and Charles Madigan asked, in relation to the $500 million spent by AT&T between 1989 and 1994:

> ‘What is the value of advice? . . . Trying to measure its value in dollar terms is a frustrating, almost hopeless enterprise. Advice is worth whatever an advice buyer is willing to pay for it.’ [1]

Subjectivity is the first obstacle: the ‘value’ added by consultants who help a company to streamline its business by cutting certain activities may be seen to be huge by senior managers whose number one priority is to ensure a sustainable, profitable business, but viewed as myopic by those people who lose their jobs. The context is also important. A consulting project may be appropriate for one organization, but not for another – an inherently ‘good’ project may look bad when applied in the wrong circumstances. Similarly, a desperate company, faced with the threat of imminent bankruptcy, may put a premium on a solution which a competitor with a much more secure trading position would regard as worthless.

Moreover, even if the variations in context could be discounted and a figure for ‘value’ identified, it would still be difficult to understand the extent to which the consultants involved had contributed to that value being created. For example, a client might hire a consulting firm to increase the effectiveness of its sales force, perhaps through a combination of implementing new systems, change management and training. When sales increase after the project is completed, the consulting firm might congratulate itself on a job well-done, and so might the client, on hiring a consulting firm that has made a positive difference to its business. But would they be right to be so pleased with themselves? How would they know that the increase in sales was directly attributable to the input of the consultants (the new system, the sensitivity with which change management issues were dealt with, the training) or to other factors (new products, new people being recruited)? In the same vein, when a consulting company claims that the performance of its clients has exceeded those of clients helped by competitor consulting firms, is this differential the result of the first consulting firm's input? It might be a testimony to the fact that the first consulting firm is better than its competitors at picking successful companies with which to work.

Unlike a laboratory, it is very hard to create controlled circumstances in business which allow the direct results of consultancy to be accurately assessed. This is neither a new nor an unrecognized problem. During the heyday of scientific management in the 1920s, Joan Woodward tried to do just that by separating two groups of typists, using one group as testing ground for process improvements, and the other as a control group. To her surprise, the efficiency of both groups improved, forcing her to conclude that the fact that the people in the control group had been pulled out of the mass of typists and made to feel special, made the group perform better.

Even in the clearest-cut projects, the number of variables involved make it almost impossible to separate out the impact which consultants may have had. So what hope is there for complex strategy assignments in rapidly changing business environments?

The problem here is not simply one of complexity and difficulty: there has also been a distinct lack of commitment to find a way of overcoming issues like those raised above.

[1] James O'Shea and Charles Madigan, *Dangerous Company: The Consulting Powerhouses and the Businesses They Save and Ruin* (Nicholas Brealey, 1997)

From the client perspective, it is tempting to blame consulting firms who, for their own nefarious purposes, have shied away from such transparency. Consulting firms cite plenty of good reasons for their stance, but they are also reasonably concerned that any standard methodology for quantifying the value they add would, inevitably, be unable to handle differences between different types of consultants and different types of client. The last few years have demonstrated how unreliable supposedly reliable (and highly standardized) accounting data is, in providing an accurate picture of every type of corporation. Profit and loss statements and balance sheets may have provided an good way of comparing manufacturing companies, but they are much less reliable when it comes to businesses where intellectual capital and other intangible assets are important. In the light of this, how realistic is it to arrive at a set of common standards capable of embracing the very wide range of 'consulting' now undertaken? And even if such a standard could be arrived at, surely it would represent the lowest common denominator of all projects and would therefore be meaningless when it came to valuing a specific one?

However, alongside these justifiable concerns is an undoubted element of fear: fear that the value of particular projects will be exposed as being negligible; fear that the overall value added by consultants may be called into question. An overly-standardized valuation methodology may do the consulting industry a disservice by underrepresenting the value generated by consultants, but a more precise methodology (if it existed) could make public some mistakes which consulting firms would rather conceal.

But clients – perhaps thinking cynically along these lines – are not immune to blame. If the consulting industry has dragged its feet in the issue of valuation, then it is only because clients have allowed it to do so. Where, in all the negative coverage of consultants in the press, has been a systematic call by clients for the situation to change? If consultants stand to be exposed by greater transparency of valuation, then so do clients – exposed for using consultants where they should not, for paying over the odds for projects done more cheaply by their competitors, for making poor decisions. No one who hires consultants particularly wants his or her colleagues to examine that decision with a fine toothcomb. Instead, the consensus seems to be: consultants are useful (otherwise clients would not use them, as much as they do), but clients do not want to find out just how useful consultants actually are because they do not want their decisions subject to too much scrutiny, and because they want to carry on using consultants (negative sniping at the industry notwithstanding).

The problems of measuring the value that consultants do (and do not) add is, quite genuinely, an intractable one. But the situation has not been helped by the reluctance of both clients and consultants to grapple with the issues involved. So what can, realistically, be done?

OPTIONS FOR MEASURING VALUE

Realistically, clients have to accept that this is not a one-size-fits-all problem: there will not be a single solution which standardizes the output of consultancy to the point where all consulting projects can be compared, which does not also blur the different ways in which value is genuinely created. This means that the first step has to be to sub-divide projects, so that comparisons can be made more meaningfully. Taking the issues listed above, it is possible to identify two primary problems:

1. Uncertainty of inputs – complex situations with a large number of variables, or where the role of the consulting firm may be very indirect (facilitating change, as opposed to doing something on a client's behalf).

2 Uncertainty of outputs – where different people may have different definitions of value, or where the value itself is hard to quantify (skills transfer, as opposed to lower costs).

Putting these two dimensions together suggests four types of problem (Figure 16.1).

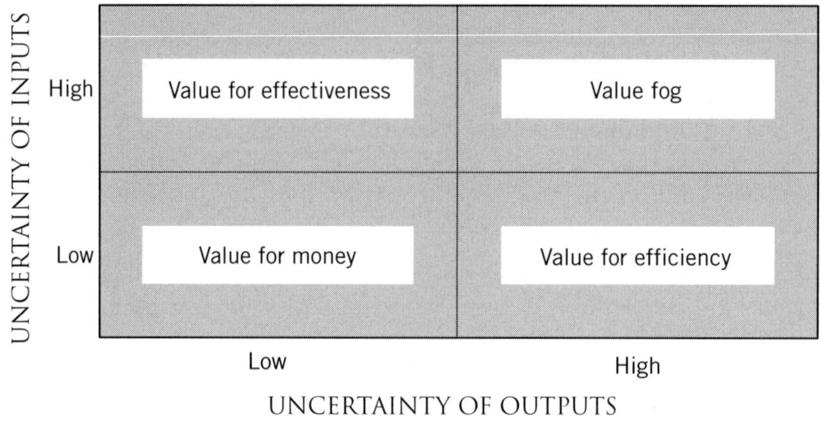

FIGURE 16.1: The four options for measuring value

Value fog

The worst possible situation for both clients and consultants to be in is *value fog*. Here, there are high levels of uncertainty, both on the input and output sides: the consultants are being employed to work in a facilitative way in an area where the success of their work will be hard to measure, and even harder to credit to the consultants. Little can be done here, other than recognize the fog for what it is.

Bringing in consultants is an act of faith, and needs to be viewed as such. It is therefore unfeasible of a client to expect to be able to quantify the value it obtains from its consultants, let alone enshrine this in a payment-by-results contract. It is equally important that the consultants do not pretend otherwise as well. It is tempting for consultants to offer clients the magic solution which they want, but which can rarely be delivered – and so it is tempting, in value fog situations, to pretend that the way forward is clearer than it actually is, to invent vicarious ways of measuring value.

But while there are some situations where value fog may be unavoidable, there are others where that 'fogginess' can be reduced, by making either the inputs or outputs to a consulting project less uncertain.

Value from effectiveness

This occurs where the inputs to a project are highly uncertain, but where the output can be measured. What this means in practice is that, while it is possible to identify a clear goal for the consulting project, it is hard to draw a clear set of causal relationships between that goal being achieved and what the consultants actually do. Clients have to trust that the consultants who they have hired have contributed to achieving the desired goal, but neither side can prove this is the case.

For clients in this situation, the key is to establish those clear goals from the outset, and make them the combined objective of everyone involved in the project, whether consultants or internal people. It is fair to use success metrics which tie into this goal, even though it is not entirely clear how success will be delivered. Everyone involved needs an incentive to do whatever it takes (which may not be what you anticipated at the start of the project) to meet the objectives – what is most valuable is the effectiveness of what they do, not how they did it.

Value from efficiency

The opposite of this takes place where the output of a project remains uncertain (it is not possible to ascribe a clear set of goals with which everyone in an organization agrees), but where the work carried out by a consulting firm can be measured. An example here would be a complex change management project. The overall objective of the project might be hard to define (how can you measure whether an organization has changed?), but consulting firms involved in the project might be playing quite clearly defined roles – designing and delivering an internal communications strategy for example. In such situations, the discussion of what constitutes value needs to be focused around the work undertaken by the consulting firm. How much work can be done for the client's budget? How can the consulting firm demonstrate that it is carrying out its work more efficiently than another firm would have done, or than the client could have done by using its own staff?

Value for money

Of course, in an ideal world, the levels of uncertainty on both sides would be low – it would be possible to measure both the inputs and the outputs for a given consulting project and make a direct, causal link between the two. Although in practice only a minority of projects fall into this group (for the reasons explained above), some do – and it is important that both clients and consultants agree which they are and provide clear, agreed metrics. Such metrics need to capture, on the one hand, the efficiency of the inputs and, on the other, the effectiveness of the outputs, as it is the combination of the two that constitutes that otherwise elusive concept of *value for money.*

Taking these four categories of consulting projects, the overall consulting work being bought by any one client, or undertaken by any one consulting firm, at any one time, can be seen as a portfolio. It is likely that both clients' and consultants' portfolios will contain some projects in each of the four categories, although we might also expect particular clients and particular firms to have a bias to one quadrant. One client might prefer to measure consulting firms in terms of their efficiency, while another might assess effectiveness. One consulting firm might specialize in providing an efficient service, while another might focus on delivery of results. Everyone will have their 'value fog' projects, where both the inputs and outputs prove hard to pin down. Having some kind of balance between the four quadrants is probably crucial: having some ability to measure effectiveness and/or efficiency in some projects should help to negate the cynicism which may flow from having projects in the 'value fog' area.

SUMMARY

1 Lack of transparency in valuing the contribution that consultants make is one of the most fundamental challenges in the client–consultant relationship, and is the source of much negative press coverage about consultants.

2 There are two reasons for this lack of transparency. Firstly, the role that consultants play is hard to quantify because it can be highly subjective, applies differently in different organizations, is often indirect and intangible, and is hard to separate out from all the other variables affecting business performance. Secondly, neither clients nor consultants have been willing to invest in overcoming these admittedly difficult issues.

3 No single way of valuing projects is ever likely to be meaningful. However, it is possible to categorize consulting projects in terms of their level of uncertainty of inputs and outputs. Four categories of project emerge from this:

- ☐ **Value fog** projects – where each party needs to acknowledge the difficulties involved.
- ☐ **Value for effectiveness** projects – where the consulting firm (and other people involved in the project) should be measured according to the delivery of a common goal.
- ☐ **Value for efficiency** projects – where the consultants involved should be measured in relation to their efficiency.
- ☐ **Value for money** projects – where the levels of uncertainty, both for inputs and outputs, are sufficiently low that it is possible to measure both efficiency and effectiveness.

CHAPTER 17

INCREASING THE VALUE ADDED BY CONSULTANTS IN THE FUTURE

The previous chapter looked at the issues surrounding how clients evaluate the work completed by consulting firms, and the factors that make it hard to do so. Like the book as a whole, it primarily focused on consultancy as it exists at present, or is likely to exist in the immediate future. But what of the longer term? Without indulging in too much spurious crystal ball-gazing, what are the major trends affecting the consulting industry, and how will these have an impact on the value which consulting firms can generate?

THE STRATEGIC CHALLENGES FOR CONSULTANTS

Ultimately, consultants create value for clients when the right consulting firm is hired to do the right work in the right way. When they do not create value, it is because one or more of these elements is, in some way, out of synch: the firm does not have the skills to do the work; what the client wanted is not what it needed; the consulting firm's processes are too cumbersome (and therefore too costly). This book has been designed to help clients (and consultants) minimize the chances of such issues occurring, but more radical change needs to take place (on both sides) if what I have elsewhere called the 'consulting conundrum' is to be resolved[1].

The consulting conundrum refers to the fact that there are many aspects of the conventional client–consultant relationship where the aims of each side are not aligned, and even some where they are in conflict. But this is not a conspiracy, either of clients to squeeze as much blood from the consulting stone as they can, or from consulting firms to deceive clients into paying them too much; it is a result of entirely rationale economic behaviour. In a sense, it is possible to see the consulting industry as a giant machine, packed with large and small cogs which are all turning in different directions. Twenty years ago, this machine ran smoothly: because it did not run very quickly, the fact that the teeth in some of those cogs did not quite

[1] Fiona Czerniawska, *Value-Based Consulting* (Palgrave, 2002)

mesh was not immediately perceptible. Clients were perhaps slightly in awe of consultants; the margins of consulting firms were perhaps sufficiently large as to absorb the odd mistake; both sides had room to manoeuvre. But the consulting machine has been speeding up since then – driven by:

- ☐ Clients who have become more demanding in their requirements and more sophisticated in their management and evaluation of consultants.
- ☐ A business environment in which new management ideas appear more often, are disseminated more quickly, and go out of fashion sooner.
- ☐ A more competitive consulting industry in which comfortable margins are rapidly becoming a distant memory.

Sparks are inevitably beginning to fly: those cogs which did not quite mesh are now causing the machine to stutter and shudder. They have not yet caused it to stop, but how much faster can it actually run? If some parts of the machine are not repaired, then long-standing problems – chronic, low-level client dissatisfaction, wide-spread cynicism about the collective consulting industry – may escalate into major issues.

Fixing the machine will take more than a bit of oil and a few replacement parts: some parts need redesigning or scrapping, if the machine as a whole is to add genuine value to clients.

THE RIGHT FIRM

Choosing the right firm will never be easy. There are too many variables, too many people involved for even the most sophisticated corporate purchasers of consultancy to be confident that they can find the best firm for the job all of the time. But, that being said, there are – clients certainly believe – things that could be done to increase the probability that they can identify the most appropriate firm.

Be clear about their strengths and weaknesses

Clients constantly complain that they find it hard to understand what the services of a given consulting firm actually consist of. Even the most cursory glance at the websites of the vast majority of consulting firms supports this concern; the descriptions of their services are often high level and generic, and it is hard to distinguish one from another. Moreover, consulting firms are often reluctant to admit that they cannot do something. However, it is also true that consultants are aware of this issue and claim to be trying to resolve it – hence the number of 'thought leadership' and 'white' papers being generated by the industry.

So why has more progress not been made? Why have clients been complaining about the same issue for the last ten years without success? Because the definition and public articulation of a consulting firm's intellectual capital is one of those cogs in the machine which is not running smoothly – the aims of consultants and clients are not quite aligned. What clients want is precision: without this, it becomes hard, if not impossible, to match the strengths (and weaknesses) of a consulting firm against the strengths (and weaknesses) of a client; clients buy consulting which they do not need, and marginalize their own people. But there is a big downside to precision from a consulting firm's point of view. The more precise a consulting firm is about its services, the less flexibility it has. A firm which says 'we do x' will do well financially while there is a market for 'x', but as soon as clients start wanting 'y', then the firm is redundant. Much better to say 'we do x and y' from the outset (or even better, 'we do a to z'), so that the firm can respond to market changes without having to reinvent their brand or reestablish their credibility with clients. In other words, consultants implicitly equate a broad definition of services with higher, longer-lived profitability; it is not in their self-interest to be precise.

Squaring this particular circle in the future requires effort from both clients and consultants. Clients need to maintain and increase their demand for precision. What exactly do consulting firms mean when they talk about a given service? Exactly what are the skills brought by the consulting firm, and how do these match or overlap with the skills the client already has? Consultants have to recognize that they will create more long-term value by being precise – they will acquire a reputation for not wasting clients' money, which will stand them in much better stead than all their marketing brochures combined.

Avoid junk consultancy

The lack of precision with which consulting firms describe their own services is often matched by an equal lack of precision in the way in which clients articulate their requirements.

Consulting firms generally want to stay in touch with clients' needs; doing so allows them to respond to the market and maintain their fee income. But, in the absence of any reliable or timely information about what clients want, consulting firms react by trying to cover all bases; if there is a faint possibility that a corporation may be interested in a particular issue, then it is worth sending them a brochure on it, producing an article in the newspaper, running a series of adverts in high-profile business magazines. The result is the consulting equivalent of junk mail, and clients react as badly to this as they do to all those other imperatives with which they are daily bombarded.

The difference between junk consultancy and successful marketing is not in the medium or the message, but in its recipient. Match the idea to the client that genuinely needs it, and people stop thinking, 'here is yet another consulting brochure about something the firm is trying to sell to me'; they start to think, 'these people have understood my problem, and they really know what they are talking about.' Solving this issue therefore depends on consultants having better intelligence about client concerns.

THE RIGHT PROJECT

Accessing specialist knowledge

At the beginning of this book, we noted that one of the fundamental reasons why clients hire consultants is in order to access in-depth knowledge, either in a particular industry, or in a particular issue, or both. Indeed, when you ask clients about the value which they obtain from using consultants, specialist knowledge is almost always at or near the top of their list. Equally, when you ask them about what they find least valuable, they typically quote instances where consultants have tried to offer them generic, high level advice.

But increased specialization poses a considerable challenge, particularly to medium and largescale consulting firms, because it is an anathema to the organizational flexibility on which most such firms depend. Highly specialized consultants are much harder to retrain with different skills, if demand for the skills they possess suddenly dissipates; this has become clearer with the recent rounds of redundancies from consulting firms in which, for the first time, consultants (as opposed to support staff) are losing their jobs.

The change required here is primarily an internal one – consulting firms need to rethink their organizational models to move away from structures in which consultants are 'put' or 'belong' in specific business units, and towards a more fluid environment in which individual consultants have more opportunity to follow where their clients are leading. The role of the firm has to change to accommodate this, from telling people what to do next, to providing the tools to enable them to gain in-depth knowledge of an emerging field as quickly as possible.

Integrating skills

A new model of consultancy emerged in the e-business boom, in which consultants with different skills sets – typically strategy, creative/marketing and technology – worked together. The clients who experienced this new way of working were immensely positive about it; instead of a linear process in which a strategy consultancy helped formulate the idea, the marketing consultancy helped to sell it, and the IT consultancy helped realize it, they had a combined process in which all three tasks were iterative and interconnected – something that was not only quicker but also produced a better end product (because all three groups had to talk to each other).

Although established consulting firms now tend to downplay the impact that the e-business consultancies have had on the industry (most of them have, after all, gone bankrupt), they privately acknowledge that integrated working is here to stay, because of the value which clients perceive in it. At the same time, integrated working was not an easy model to sustain on a commercial basis (and the demise of the e-business consultancies is, in part, a testimony to this) – it required more people to be hired, who were utilized less intensively.

If we look at the minority of consulting firms which are managing to make this new model work, they have one thing in common – a strong company culture which acts as a glue to bring people together who have very different areas of expertise. It is a lesson that all consulting firms need to learn.

Sustainable innovation

As we saw in Chapter 8, consultancy is the application of intellectual capital from one company to another; clients have gaps in their intellectual capital and they hire consultants to fill them.

This means that one of the most critical issues facing the industry is where new management ideas come from, and the role that consultancies play in developing and disseminating them. Although consultants often like to present themselves as free-thinkers, the consulting industry has proved considerably more adept at codifying business ideas developed elsewhere (by clients or academics) than at developing ideas itself. However, consulting firms are not the only organizations whose revenue is derived from the standardization of ideas: business software companies can only develop their products because the approach to a particular process or problem has become standardized. Thus, it is now possible to buy software that 'reengineers' processes. To survive, therefore, consulting firms have had to ensure that the speed at which new ideas enter the economy is faster than that at which ideas are standardized and commoditized – and this is one of the reasons for the explosion in business literature and education over the last 20 years. At the same time, consulting firms have become more and more efficient at disseminating (and therefore standardizing) these ideas, so that the whole cycle is speeding up. Because standardized services are easier to manage, consultants are cannibalizing their own services – and improving at it.

Something needs to happen to break out of this increasingly vicious circle, if the whole market for management ideas does not disappear in a maelstrom of short-lived fads. In fact, probably two things need to happen: consulting firms need to put more effort into identifying, developing and testing new management ideas before they unleash them on an unsuspecting market. At the moment, consultants are too quick to scan the business press to pick up on ideas that are only vaguely saleable, often because they are afraid of missing out on 'the next big thing'.

But it is not just consulting firms which have been at fault here: one of the key drivers of this vicious circle is that clients themselves are continually and increasingly looking for instant solutions – 'magic bullets'. Consultants only offer potential panaceas because clients want to believe they exist. Clients, too, need to be more circumspect in adopting new ideas; like consultants, they should not all rush for the same 'big' idea, but work out which of the many smaller ideas are genuinely relevant to them.

Both client and consultant need to be less reliant on structured methodologies. Such approaches may increase the tangibility of consulting work and they may appear to guarantee the desired outcome, but, if implemented too rigidly with too little customization, they significantly diminish the value that is created because they do not take a client's unique circumstances into account.

Data, information and knowledge

Chapter 9 looked at the exchange of intellectual capital between clients and consultants, and argued that, while data and information can both be transferred from consultants to clients effectively and efficiently, knowledge (which is most valuable from the client's perspective) is something that is much harder to transfer to clients because it is much less tangible and explicit. In fact, the challenge facing the consulting industry here is not dissimilar to that faced in relation to innovation: as clients demand proof that something has been transferred from consultant to client, consulting firms are increasingly converting their knowledge into data and information (because these are the most readily transferable forms of intellectual capital, although they are also those least valuable to clients).

Opting for data and information is the easy option for both sides. Effective knowledge transfer will require effort from the client side – what will we *do* with this knowledge? how can we capture it? who else might be able to use it? – and greater realism from consultants.

Making a difference

It is not enough anymore for a consulting company to come in, make a handful of recommendations, and leave the client to decide what to do and how to do it. Too many consulting projects are unfinished, and too many reports written by consultants have remained unread. Quite reasonably, clients want consultants to have some impact on their organizations, otherwise why bring them in, let alone pay for them?

In attempting to respond to this issue, the consulting industry has swung almost to the other extreme – offering to take problems off clients' hands. This might solve an immediate concern, but it does little to change the organization. Maria Montessori, the doyen of pre-school education, once observed that every time a parent does something for a child, they deprive the child of a chance to learn. The same applies to this way of using consultants: every time a consulting firm takes the problem away, an opportunity has been lost for the client organization to learn how to solve it (and other, similar problems arising in the future).

An equilibrium has to be found between the two ends of this spectrum, in which consultants are involved in solving problems, but they do so side-by-side with the client itself. This will require the courage and commitment of both sides. The consulting firm needs to respect the input which a client may have and make good use of it and all other available resources; it also needs to understand the constraints to which a client is inevitably subject. But clients have to play a role as well, and be less ready to offload something perceived to be too difficult. Another good precept of child development is that children who are rewarded for doing a process correctly (for working through a mathematical problem, for instance, but not necessarily getting the right answer) become far more adventurous and willing to try new things, than children who are rewarded simply on the basis that they got the right answer (which tends to make them pick easier things to do). Similarly, organizations do not typically remunerate people because they have increased the collective ability of the organization, but because they have reached the 'right' conclusion (the latter is much easier to measure). This too needs to change.

THE RIGHT WAY

Walking the talk

Consultants, like doctors, have historically been bad at taking their own advice: 'doctor, heal thyself' could easily be translated into 'consultant, advise yourself'. Until now, this has not been a problem; clients assumed that consultants were, indeed, consultants (and not managers), and the margins on consulting work were sufficiently large to cushion the impact of internal inefficiency. But all of that changed with e-business. When companies like Razorfish and Scient burst on the market in the mid-1990s, part of their message was that incumbent firms could not consult effectively in this field because they were – like their clients – products of the 'old' economy: the only credible e-business consultancies were those that shared the working styles and attitudes of the new. Suddenly, clients were entitled to expect consultants to practice what they preached.

Those days may now seem like a distant memory, but that perception lingers, certainly in clients' minds. 'Why should we implement a system that you do not use yourselves?' they ask. 'Why should we use relationship marketing techniques that you recommend, when you are still doing mass-advertising?'

Nowhere is this link clearer than in IT consulting. Almost half of all consulting fees may be derived from IT-related work, but the majority of consulting firms have been remarkably backward in their internal use of technology. Various excuses have been given – 'we put client work first', 'consulting firms are different; the technology that works for our clients would not work for us' – but all of them are beginning to sound a little hollow to clients' ears. By contrast, if you talk to some of the more innovative firms, you tend to find that they are indeed using their own software themselves.

Clients are, quite rightly, forcing consulting firms to walk the talk far more in the future. If both sides are supposed to work in partnership and have value to add, then they should be swallowing the same medicine.

Organizational design and value-chain integration

A consultant advising a consulting firm on organizational design might be tempted to say, 'do not start from here'. A consulting firm needs structure if it is to be managed effectively, and that requirement grows in proportion to its size – the bigger the firm, the more structure it requires. But clients are much more concerned about flexibility, in knowing that a consulting firm can reconfigure its resources to meet the needs of a particular project. Similarly, while clients want to have access to world-class skills, consulting firms require a flexible structure to cope with the vicissitudes of the market on a sustainable basis. What is needed is something between the two, the kind of firm which can balance flexibility with the commercial necessity of exerting control, and can reconcile shifts in client demand without continually swinging between feast and famine.

It is likely that these pressures will drive consulting firms to look at the balance between their 'fixed' and 'variable' resources, with increasingly numbers of people being hired on short-term contracts or secondment, and with specialist firms sub-contracting their own staff to the larger firms (the 'orchestrator' firms described in Chapter 7). Some years ago, it was predicted that the number of people employed on a long-term basis by corporations would shrink, and far more people would have what he termed 'portfolio careers' in which they moved from company to company, developing their specialist skills, reinventing themselves where necessary, but never being part of the corporate centre. It is a model which is becoming increasingly attractive to consulting firms trying to bridge the gap between what their clients want and what the firm can afford to provide. Why have specialists on your books, when you can have a 'virtual' organization designed to bring people in when they are needed?

This recognition will, in turn, drive greater collaboration between consulting firms. For clients, collaboration offers a genuine opportunity to bring together the best people for a job, irrespective of the firm in which they actually work. For consultancies, it provides a chance to be honest about their strengths and weaknesses (knowing that another firm will be able to supply the client's needs), and to offset the loss in revenue that that entails, with lower costs (no more generic advertising!).

Indeed, one single factor which is likely to improve the value that consultants generate for clients, both now and in the future, is collaboration. In an industry long dominated by internecine competition (with many broad-based consulting firms competing along many fronts), collaboration offers a far better *modus operandi*.

AND FINALLY . . .

Maximizing the benefits that consultants can bring is never going to be a one-sided process; it is absolutely true that there are many areas where consultants can be criticized (and this book has tried to highlight the major ones), but it is equally true that clients' behaviour sometimes makes the situation worse. Intelligent clients know this. They know that they cannot expect miracle cures from a consulting firm, and that business issues are always complex and often intractable. They know that consultants cannot guarantee a solution, and that, if they do, then the solution is probably not worth having. They know they have to work together – to collaborate – with consultants, in a relationship in which each side trusts the other, shows respect for the contribution the other can make, and focuses on **value** for money (not costs or fees).

This book has highlighted those areas where greater collaboration between clients and consultants will yield the greatest dividends:

- ☐ When you decide to hire a consulting firm, be absolutely clear why you are doing so. Precisely what resources, skills, knowledge or processes will the consulting firm add that you could not have found internally?

- ☐ When you come to select a specific firm to work with you, what are the attributes most important to you and to the project in hand? What evidence can you see in the behaviour of the consultants and the information they give you prior to signing the contract that will help you make the right decision.
- ☐ When you come to decide how you are going to work with them, what are the key aspects of an effective relationship?
- ☐ How should you behave as a client? For you to be able to trust a consultant, that consultant has to be able to trust you.

Intelligent consultancy needs intelligent consultants *and* intelligent clients.

FURTHER READING

Barcus, S.W. and Wilkinson, J.W., *Handbook of Management Consulting Services*, McGraw-Hill, 1995

Clark, Timothy, *Managing Consultants*, Open University Press, 1995

Curnow, Barry and Jonathan Reuvid, *The International Guide to Management Consultancy*, Kogan Page, 2001

Clark, Timothy and Robin Fincham (editors), *Critical Consulting: New Perspective on the Advice Industry*, Blackwell, 2002

Czerniawska, Fiona, *Management Consultancy: What Next?*, Palgrave, 2001

Czerniawska, Fiona, *Value-Based Consulting*, Palgrave, 2002

Maister, David H., *Managing the Professional Services Firm*, Free Press, 1995

O'Shea, James and Charles Madigan, *Dangerous Company*, Nicholas Brealey, 1997

Scott, Mark, *The Intellect Industry*, John Wiley & Sons, 1998

APPENDIX

MANAGEMENT CONSULTANCIES ASSOCIATION STATEMENT OF BEST PRACTICE

PURPOSE OF THE STATEMENT

The Management Consultancies Association (MCA), Institute of Management Consultancy (IMC) and the Procurement Group of HM Treasury have developed a statement of best practice. It emphasises the working relationships that the client and consultant will seek to achieve in the development and execution of a consultancy contract and establishes a way of working. The statement is not a binding contract, and has no legal status in law. This statement will be reviewed on a regular basis to ensure that the maximum benefit is derived for both parties, and that the spirit of its messages do not weaken with time.

BENEFITS OF THE STATEMENT

Used constructively this statement will benefit both client and consultant by:

1 Maximising the appropriateness of the advice the client receives.

2 Ensuring an appropriate allocation of responsibilities to the party best able to manage them.

3 Working in a supportive and constructive relationship.

4 Having an agreed timetable highlighting key milestones and decision points.

5 Knowing both parties are committed to value for money.

6 Having a structure for resolving concerns or disputes rapidly and at the lowest practical level.

7 Being clear about what is expected of the client and the consultant.

8 Enabling the incorporation of knowledge transfer, where this is appropriate and adds value.

THE PROCUREMENT

Government / Consultants

1.G GENERAL PRINCIPLES

1.1G Be truthful and constructive to, and easily contactable by, consultants and other stakeholders.

1.2G Don't be defensive. The consultants are there to assist your organization.

1.3G Do not be afraid of providing too much information. Consultants would much prefer this to a lack of detail.

1.4G In general, ensure that risk lies with the entity with the greatest ability to manage that risk.

1.C GENERAL PRINCIPLES

1.1C Be truthful and constructive to, and easily contactable by, clients and other stakeholders.

1.2C Respond to the client's initial request and avoid second guessing the problem at an early stage.

1.3C Always listen to the client's opinions first before explaining your own.

1.4C In general, ensure that risk lies with the entity with the greatest ability to manage that risk.

2.G PROJECT DEFINITION

2.1G Select the form of contractual relationship which will facilitate achievement of project objectives. Consider innovative types of agreements, such as frameworks, as alternatives to traditional contracts.

2.2G Identify potential 'life of project' benefits as well as initial investment required.

2.3G Following discussions with representative consultants, develop a list of qualities needed from the consultants.

2.C PROJECT DEFINITION

2.1C Explain to the clients the information that is needed.

2.2C Help the client clarify their needs.

3.G PRE QUALIFICATION & TENDER

3.1G Ask for brief, sensible and relevant information at a preliminary statement of interest stage.

3.2G Restrict the tender list to the minimum that will ensure effective competition recognizing the wide range of consultancies in existence and the nature and scope of their work.

3.3G Always provide an adequate length of time to allow consultants to prepare their proposals, appropriate to the size and complexity of the project.

3.4G Take time to brief all consultants properly on a one to one basis, where appropriate.

3.5G The briefing for the consultants should contain information about the project and the people involved, and should outline broad criteria used at the selection of bidder and evaluation of tender stages.

3.6G Build in the expected outputs from the project and any budgetary constraints which the business case has highlighted.

3.C PRE QUALIFICATION & TENDER

3.1C Respond as fully as possible to the Request for Information.

3.2C Provide constructive suggestions. Explain the pros and cons of various approaches explaining in broad terms the range of approaches available.

3.3C Consultants should always be realistic about the amount of experience they can bring to an assignment and be prepared to validate any claims made.

3.4C Some idea of the necessary time frame to complete the work should be given and key milestones defined along with deliverables at the milestone.

3.5C Ensure the firm has the available and appropriate manpower to perform the work it is tendering for.

3.6C Acknowledge within the bid that additional specialist staff may be necessary and specify whether these would be provided at no extra cost.

3.7G Permit presentations from short-listed consultants of their capabilities and their tender proposals.

3.8G Be prepared to consider professional liability cap, from the consultants, according to the nature of the work.

3.9G Keep bidders informed if there is slippage to decision timetables.

3.10G Give adequate debriefings.

3.7C Where tendering prices vary across Government departments for what might appear similar work, be prepared to give an explanation.

3.8C Be prepared to consider adjusting professional liability cap according to the nature of the work.

3.9C Highlight in the tender whether similar work has been done and demonstrate added value from experience.

4.G AWARD AND CONTRACT TERMS

4.1G Always use equitable Conditions of Contract and those which are appropriate to the type of work being done and the risks being run by both parties.

4.2G The standard conditions of contract should only be amended where strictly necessary.

4.3G Use defined and objective terms. Avoid subjective measures of performance, such as satisfaction.

4.4G Address Intellectual Property Rights (IPR) issues, both pre-existing and those that emerge during the course of the project, recognizing that, in many cases, consultants will wish to retain IPR of generic tools and techniques, while the client will wish to retain IPR which specifically relates to their project.

4.5G Core terms and conditions require unlimited liability. However, recognize that this may need to be looked at on a case by case basis.

4.6G Negotiations should be carried out by staff with the experience and authority to negotiate any agreed contract amendments and clarifications.

4.C AWARD AND CONTRACT TERMS

4.1C Accept that although liability can be limited, higher than normal limits may be required. Be prepared to provide adequate evidence of insurance cover.

4.2C Be prepared to provide client's negotiating team with the background information concerning the project in hand, so they can make informed decisions.

4.3C Define reasonable and demonstrable performance measures and acceptance criteria.

4.4C Be prepared to grant the client title in works that it has fully funded and a limited usage right in your pre-existing Intellectual Property Rights.

4.5C Identify key consultants who will be involved in the assignment and agree, if necessary, the scope of any changes to those consultants during the assignment.

5.G PROJECT

5.1G On appointment, confirm with a written statement the key elements of the way the project will be carried out, to include a plan, deliverables and expectations. This should also contain a risk register defining who is responsible for which risks.

5.2G Throughout the project maintain close liaison with the consultancy team and its director.

5.3G Flag up problems with the project early so that remedial action can be implemented.

5.4G Obtain from the consultants routine progress reports on the project as well as interim results.

5.5G Hold regular reviews on the progress and delivery of the contract and project. Action points arising from review meetings should be agreed in writing.

5.C PROJECT

5.1.C On appointment, create a written statement of the key elements of the way the project will be carried out, to include a plan, deliverables and expectations. This should also contain a risk register defining who is responsible for which risks.

5.2.C Define in conjunction with the client what information is required from them and when it is required for.

5.3.C Do not pilot methodologies without prior agreement from the client.

5.4.C Give bad news truthfully but sensitively.

5.5.C Only assign alternative consultants after client approval and be prepared to explain any impact on supervisory arrangements and fee levels.

5.6G Where necessary and agreed, provide staff, facilities and information promptly.

5.7G Ensure prompt payment of invoices, in accordance with the terms and conditions of contract.

5.6.C Where necessary and agreed, provide staff, facilities and information promptly.

5.7. If using an innovative approach tell the client, and seek prior approval explaining the circumstances behind the decision.

5.8.C Ensure a well established protocol is in place for altering the make up of a team. Ensure it has been signed off by the client.

5.9.C Keep confidential information confidential. It may be unlikely that all client staff are as well briefed as the consultant.

5.10.C Don't hide problems from the client as they will always come to the surface. Inform the client regularly about all aspects of the progress and delivery of the project.

5.11.C Submit prompt invoices that correctly reflect the contract terms.

6.G POST PROJECT

6.1.G At the end of the project both parties should undertake a joint project review to see what they might gain from the experience. This should be within 6 months and no longer than 12 months.

6.C POST PROJECT

6.1.C At the end of the project both parties should undertake a joint project review to see what they might gain from the experience. This should be within 6 months and no longer than 12 months.